The Empresses of Constantinople by Joseph McCabe

The Illustrated Edition

Joseph Martin McCabe was born on the 12th November 1867 in Macclesfield, Cheshire to a family of Irish Catholic background.

At 15 he entered the Franciscan order and spent a year of preliminary study at Gorton Monastery and then a novitiate year in Killarney before Forest Gate in London for the remainder of his priestly education. In 1890 he was ordained as Father Antony.

McCabe was an outstanding scholar of philosophy, and was sent for a year (1893–1894) to study at the Catholic University of Louvain where he learnt Hebrew and, less successfully, Syriac.

In October 1895 he was put in charge of the newly founded Franciscan college in Buckingham. He had however become plagued with doubts about his faith and was to leave both that post and the priesthood in February 1896.

McCabe wrote a pamphlet on his experiences, 'From Rome to Rationalism', published in 1897, which he then expanded into a book as 'Twelve Years in a Monastery' (1897). By now he was decidedly anti-Catholic and sought to undermine religious faith in general. From 1898 he became secretary of the Leicester Secular Society, and was a founding board member in 1899 of the Rationalist Press Association of Great Britain. During his lifetime he wrote in the order of 250 books and pamphlets on science, religion, politics, history.

In amongst this huge canon are two of his many books on the Roman Empire detailing the lives of the various mistresses and queens in the Western (Rome) and Eastern (Constantinople) Empires.

McCabe was also respected as a speaker and delivered, it is believed, several thousand lectures. A staunch advocate of women's rights he worked with both Mrs. Pankhurst and Mrs. Wolstenholme-Elmy on speeches advocating the right for British women to vote.

As the years aged him he became ever more militant in freethought (an epistemological viewpoint that on positions regarding truth they should be formed only on the basis of logic, reason, and empiricism, rather than authority, tradition, revelation, or dogma).

In his essays 'The Myth of the Resurrection' (1925) and 'Did Jesus Ever Live?' (1926) McCabe slammed Christianity as a direct representation of older Pagan beliefs. Slain saviors and their resurrection myths were celebrated across the ancient world before Christianity began. He saw numerous errors, conflicts, contradictions in the Gospel accounts of the Resurrection and thought them unreliable as they had been fabricated over the years by many different writers. McCabe came to the conclusion that Jesus was an Essenian holy man who was turned into a God over the years by hearsay and oral tradition.

In the late 1940's, McCabe accused the Encyclopædia Britannica of bias towards the Catholic Church and levelled the same a few years later at the Columbia Encyclopedia. He was labelled a "Catholic basher" by his Christian critics. McCabe retorted that "Catholics are no worse, and no better, than others."

In 1920 he publicly debated the writer and believer Arthur Conan Doyle on the claims of Spiritualism in London. McCabe had exposed the tricks of fraud mediums and wrote that Spiritualism has no scientific basis.

Joseph Martin McCabe died on 10th January 1955 at the age of 87.

Index of Contents

PREFACE

In concluding an earlier volume on the mistresses of the western Roman Empire I observed that, as the gallery of fair and frail ladies closed, we stood at the door of "the long, quaint gallery of the Byzantine Empresses." It seemed natural and desirable to pass on to this more interesting and less familiar series of the mistresses of the eastern Roman Empire, and the present volume will therefore tell the story of the Empresses, or Queens, as they preferred to be called, who occupied the throne set up by Constantine in New Rome, or ancient Byzantium, until the victorious Turk thrust it disdainfully aside to make way for his more spacious harem.

The eastern or Byzantine Empire has long been regarded in Europe as a world of far less interest than that which centred on the banks of the Tiber: a world of monotonous piety and little adventure or spirit, almost Chinese in its placid and unchanging adherence to traditional and very conventional forms. One is tempted to attribute this error, not merely to the longer concealment of Byzantine antiquities from our fathers and the superior attractiveness of Italy, but, in some measure, to the disproportion of Gibbon's work. By the time the great historian has advanced only one or two centuries in the life of the

East he finds that the superb generosity of his plan has committed him to an unachievable task, and he begins to compress whole chapters of the most vivid and adventurous history into a few disdainful pages; and as Finlay, the proper historian of the Greek civilization, not only lacks the charm which draws each generation with fresh wonder to the volumes of Gibbon, but shares and expresses the same disdain for his subject, his work has not tended to redeem the Byzantine Empire from neglect. Of late years there has been some quickening of interest in the eastern Empire. Professor Bury in this country,[1] M. Diehl in France, Schlumberger in Germany, and other historians, have done much to draw attention to the extraordinary interest and the very lively character of Byzantine life.

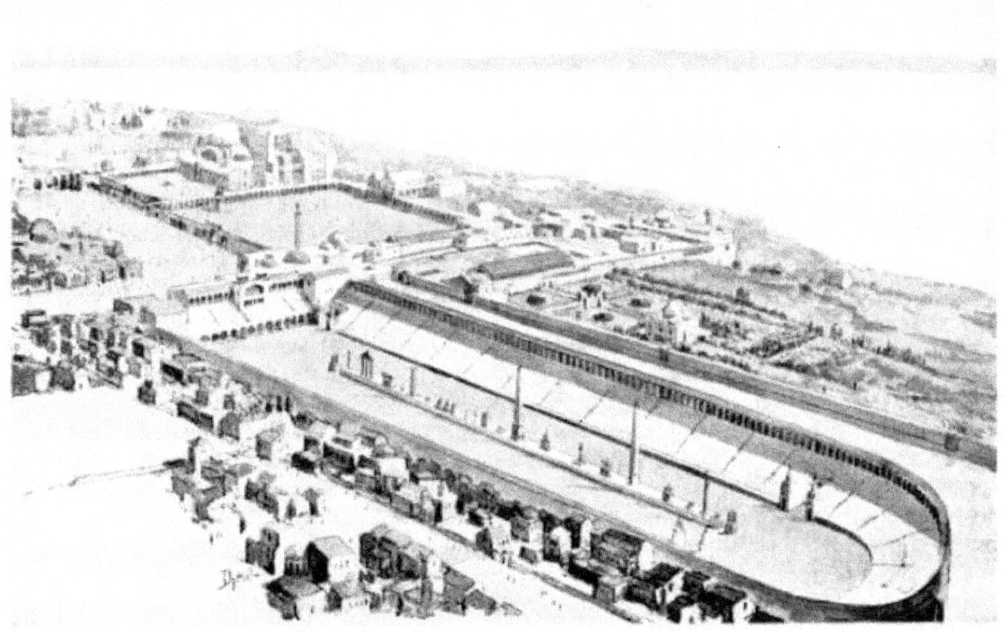

ANCIENT CONSTANTINOPLE, SHOWING THE HIPPODROME, THE IMPERIAL PALACE, AND THE MOSQUE OF S. SOPHIA

FROM THE RECONSTRUCTION BY DJELAL ESSAD AFTER THE PLAN BY LABARTE

When we confine our attention, as we do in this volume, to the Court life and the personality of the imperial women, the interest rises to the pitch of romance, and is often sustained at that height for many chapters. Few Courts in the world have, in their thousand years of history, witnessed so much adventure, intrigue, comedy and tragedy, as that of the Byzantine Empresses. From all quarters of the Empire, in the most varied ways, all sorts of women, from princesses to village girls, tavern girls or circus girls, make their way to the bronze-roofed palace and wear for a season the prodigious jewels and the glittering robes of an Empress of Constantinople; and, as there is no law or method of succession to the throne, the rise and fall of Emperors and Empresses gives a dramatic movement to the story. The notion that the eastern Empresses are enwrapped in a rigid piety and formalism, as they are in their stiff tunics of gold-cloth, is a ludicrous mistake. Their piety is usually external and superficial, and often they make not the least pretence of it; while, even when it is obviously sincere, it is associated with a skill in casuistry which allows a free play of their ambitions, their passions, and even their criminal impulses. Indeed, it is only fair to say at the outset that if a reader passes from the gallery of the "pagan" Empresses into that of the Empresses of Constantinople in the hope of encountering more restful, more virtuous and more domestic types of womanhood, he will be grievously disappointed. We may not find a Messalina among them, but irregularity of life is more evenly distributed than among the Roman Empresses, ambition and intrigue are far more cultivated, and there is a strain of barbaric cruelty running through the greater part of the story which it would have been more pleasant, had it been consistent with truthfulness, to omit. But the biographer should not be a moralist. My simple purpose is to depict, as far as it is possible, the very varied types of womanhood which come into "the fierce light that beats about a throne" in that strange world where Greek and Roman and Syrian blood blend to produce a new character.

The difficulties of the task have been considerable, and may be urged in extenuation of some of the apparent defects of the story. Apart from sketches of the lives of five or six of the Byzantine Empresses, especially those in M. Diehl's fine "Figures Byzantines," the study is entirely new, and the material has had to be laboriously collected from the endless pages of the Greek chroniclers. These chroniclers are largely monks, and in nearly all cases they are little disposed to speak of the imperial women until they either misbehave themselves or come to wield a mastery over men. Their references to the Empresses are usually brief and scattered sentences which have to be gleaned with care, and in hardly any single case do even contemporary writers condescend to give us a portrait of an Empress. Seeing that, in addition, we have not (as in the case of Rome) any statues or portrait-busts of the Empresses, and the few representations of them which have survived (in miniatures, ivories, etc.) are lifeless and conventionalized pictures, it is not possible to bring them before the eye in as satisfactory a way as one could wish. In this, as in the preceding volume, I have utterly refused to follow the genial example of Roergas de Serviez, and allow imagination to come to the aid of fact. But I have carefully gathered and included all that is known about the eastern Empresses, and, lest it be thought that the less-known Empresses might alter the balance of vice or virtue, I have inserted even the scanty references to these.

It remains only to explain the starting-point of the volume. In my "Empresses of Rome," which includes all Empresses down to the fall of Rome, I necessarily included the early Empresses of the eastern series, when east and west were branches of one dominion. It is therefore not necessary to repeat the story of the beautiful and languid Eudoxia, the daughter of a Frankish chief whom a palace intrigue raised to the purple, and who is one of the butts of St Chrysostom's fiery sermons; nor of Eudocia, the Athenian girl who set out to find her father's money and obtained a kingdom, who wrote poems in her native tongue and at last passed from the Court under a cloud of suspicion; nor of Pulcheria, the virgin-sister of Theodosius and rival of Eudocia, who ruled the Empire for her brother and, after his death, took to herself a nominal husband and, with Marcian, was governing the Eastern world at the time of the fall of Rome. I have adequately described her in the preceding volume, and the present story opens at her death in the year 453.

CHAPTER I

VERINA AND HER DAUGHTERS

The Empress's apartments in the sacred palace remained empty for four years after the virtuous Pulcheria had been laid in her marble sarcophagus. The Emperor Marcian was aged and feeble, and, as Pulcheria had guarded even in marriage the sanctity of her vow of chastity, there was none who might plausibly be regarded as heir to the throne. It was such a situation as Constantinople loved; and the thousands of soldiers, eunuchs, nobles and ladies who dwelt in the vast palace, and the tens of thousands of idlers who lounged under the arcades of the great square or chattered on the benches of the Hippodrome, had a large field for speculation.

Their fate, they knew, was in the hands of one man, the commander of the imperial guards, Asper. He was an Arian (or Unitarian), and could not hope to occupy the throne which would soon be at his disposal. The citizens of Constantinople were at least as wanton and passionate as those of Rome had been, but they were fiercely devoted to the sound doctrine of the Trinity, and they would have flung themselves against the bronze gates and marble walls of the palace if an Arian had ventured to don the purple. So Senators and Senators' wives indulged their conflicting hopes and paid their servile reverence to the dying monarch and the vigorous barbarian commander.

Marcian died in the year 457, not without a superfluous rumour of poison, and expectation rose to the height of fever when the worn frame was entombed with all the rich ceremony of the Eastern Court. Then there came the first of the long series of surprises and dramatic successions which were to enliven Byzantine history for many a century. Asper announced that his steward Leo, a tribune, or subordinate officer, of the troops, was to receive the imperial crown. A barbaric soldier and his wife were to occupy the golden throne, and all the nobility of Constantinople hastened to kiss their purple slippers.

Leo the Isaurian is one of those quite unromantic figures which the restless waves of Roman life often washed into the world of romance: one of the many raw highlanders who had set out from Asia Minor to make their fortune in the glittering metropolis of the East. A few years of useful military service had won for him the rank of tribune and the confidence of the commander, and Asper thought that he could rely on the docility and gratitude of the big simple-featured soldier. Wholly illiterate, with no larger experience than the control of Asper's servants, a man of rough, hairy face, powerful frame and blunt ways, he suddenly found himself transferred to a throne that gleamed, as few thrones did, with "the sands of Indus and the adamant of Golconda."

His wife, the Empress Verina, shares alike the earlier obscurity and the sudden elevation to the extraordinary splendour of the Byzantine Court. We know nothing of her nationality or extraction; and, as the only relatives who gather about her when her hand dispenses the gold and the favours of a great empire are just as obscure as herself, we may be sure that her origin was humble enough. A soldier like Leo would select his mate in a lowly world, and we shall see later that Verina permitted no scruple to restrain either her passion or her ambition. But there was personality in the new Empress: an able and vigorous intelligence, a masterful ambition, a virile tenacity of purpose, and an equally virile disdain of scruples and of priests in the pursuit of her ambition. She must have been much younger than her husband, who was nearly sixty years old. She not only survived him for more than a decade, but she filled that decade with the most spirited adventures, and she admitted, or attracted, a lover after the death of her husband in his seventy-fourth year.

It is one of the most singular features of Verina's story that she remains almost as obscure and insignificant during the seventeen years in which she reigned with her husband as she had been before her elevation, yet in her later years reveals a character of remarkable vigour and great interest. We have, therefore, little concern with the reign of Leo, and will rather make ourselves acquainted with the imperial world in which the Byzantine Empresses will move.

New Rome, or Constantinople, had been founded by Constantine on the site of the more ancient city of Byzantium, and is so faithfully replaced by the modern city that its situation needs little description. It spread over the triangular point of Europe which runs to a tongue between the Golden Horn and the Sea of Marmora, and was protected by a double wall from invasion on the land side; in fact, it was in time enclosed entirely within thirteen miles of stout wall.

The lower portion of this triangular area, a vast domain of more than half-a-million square yards, sloping gradually to the silver shores of the Sea of Marmora, was reserved for the imperial palaces and gardens. Running parallel with the imperial palace, to the north, was the Hippodrome, into which the story of the Empresses will repeatedly take us. Like the Great Circus at Rome, on the model of which it was built, it was the most commanding and venerated institution of the frivolous people. Its spacious long-drawn arena was flanked by tiers of seats which could accommodate tens of thousands of people—some authorities say a hundred thousand people. A lofty imperial gallery, the kathisma, surveyed the races and the spectators from the north-eastern end, and a great purple awning gave protection from the burning sun. Beyond the Hippodrome and the palace was the chief square of the city, the Augusteum, which corresponded to the old Forum at Rome or the Agora at Athens. Under the shelter of the double colonnade which surrounded it the idlers of Constantinople held their endless fiery discussions of the last chariot race, the last heresy, or the last revolution: the studious bargained for books: the amorous made traffic in love. It was the heart of the city. On the south side of it was the great gate of the palace: on the north side the church, or cathedral, of St Sophia: the Senate House faced it on the east: and from its western side ran the main street of Constantinople, the Mese (or Middle Street), lined with colonnades, which passed more or less continuously along the central ridge of the triangular area which the city occupied. A city was, in those days, and for many a century afterwards, a palace and a cathedral: we can only say of the million citizens that they were packed into the spaces not occupied by Church or State, especially in the region between the Mese and the Golden Horn, where fire and pestilence periodically fed on their crowded tenements.

With the palace we need a closer acquaintance. Verina would be familiar with the massive iron gate on the south side of the square through which, as the Emperor rode in, one might catch a glimpse of the great bronze door of the palace. Through this gate the obscure woman of the people was now borne on her litter, to be crowned mistress of the world. The front part of the palace was burned by the people in 532, but we may assume that it had the general plan of the later structure which experts have reconstructed for us.[2] The door led into a spacious hall—known as the Chalke on account of its bronze roof—which was richly adorned with statues, marbles and mosaics. Constantine had despoiled the world to enrich his palace and city, and this entrance hall had a great store of treasures. Crossing the hall one entered the apartments of the troops who guarded the palace and whose spacious quarters formed an immense and formidable approach to the imperial palace. More than three thousand selected troops, divided into three classes, formed this imperial bodyguard, and we shall more than once find their halls swimming with blood as some frantic mob or adventurous usurper seeks to penetrate to the palace. The palace grounds were, of course, surrounded by lofty and unscaleable walls.

Verina would pass first through the lines of the Scholarians, whose golden shields and lances, and gold helmets surmounted with red aigrettes, would form a glittering corridor. Ascending the marble steps at the far end of their hall, the purple curtains being drawn aside, she would pass between the Excubitors, a regiment of powerful warriors with two-edged axes, and the Candidates, or white-robed troops, gleaming with gold; the second and third lines of defence. At the end of these palatial barracks three ivory-plated doors, hung with curtains of purple silk, opened into the Consistorium, a large hall lined with marble and mosaic, in the floor of which were set porphyry slabs to indicate the successive spots where even kings must thrice prostrate themselves before approaching to kiss the feet of—Leo the Isaurian. A throne, covered with purple and heavily laden with gold and jewels, was raised under a golden dome at the upper end of the room.

Three pairs of steps and three bronze doors—for this wondrously elevated peasant and his obscure wife must not pass through the same door as ordinary mortals—then led to an unroofed terrace, lined with columns and precious statues, on one side of which was the chapel of the Saviour, and on the other the ancient gold-roofed banquet-room. Then at length Verina would find herself, probably for the first time, before the door of the palace proper, or the main palace, Daphne. Passing between the crowds of stewards, secretaries, domestic officers and great ladies, with masses of subordinate servants behind, all bent in profound reverence, she would enter by the bronze doors into the Augusteus, or vestibule of the palace: a hall crowded with choice bronze and marble statues and mosaics. Fresh legions of servants— the population of the palace must have been more than five thousand even at this early date—and groups of pale eunuchs now crowded to do homage, and the fortunate woman surrendered herself to her tire-women, to don the gold-cloth tunic, the purple mantle and the heavy jewellery of an empress.

The coronation would probably take place in the church of St Stephen, within the palace, and it seems that Verina and Leo then crossed the gardens and terraces to receive the homage of the Senators and nobles in the outlying palace of Magnaura. We know it at a later date as a vast hall lined with coloured marbles from the most famous quarries of the world, its floors strewn thick with roses, its wonders lit by fourteen massive silver lamps which hung from heavy chains of silvered bronze between its marble columns. But the wonderful golden sparrows which piped their mechanical notes on golden trees, and the golden lions which lashed their tails and roared before the throne, and the organs of silver and gold, belong to a later date in Byzantine history. From Magnaura the royal procession returned to Daphne, and mounted the spiral stair which led to the royal lodge, with a small palace in its rear, overlooking the Hippodrome. There the men of Constantinople rang out their Greek cry of "Many years!" to the rustic tribune and his wife who had so suddenly been lifted to this giddy height, and were, no doubt, rewarded with chariot races. The coronation day would end, as was usual, with a banquet in the Triclinon, a dining-hall in the space between the apartments of the guards and the palace proper. Its lofty roof was of gold, and on its nineteen purple-draped tables only golden vessels were set; some of them—at least, at a later date—were so heavy that they had to be lifted from their purple chariots to the table by machinery. And after such a banquet as only the palace could command, amidst some two hundred of the highest nobles of the greatest empire in the world, Verina would retire to her ivory or silver couch to brood over this prodigious turn of the wheel of her fortune. We shall find numbers of equally romantic elevations, and just as many tragic falls from splendour to obscurity, in the long story of the Byzantine Empresses.

Unfortunately, the coronation does not yet bring Verina plainly before us, and we must pass the seventeen years of her husband's reign almost in silence. To explain this obscurity it is not enough to say that it was the custom of the Byzantine Court to keep its women in seclusion. As long as the stream of imperial life flowed evenly they were, generally, content to idle the sunny hours behind the thick hedge of eunuchs and maids, in some sequestered palace or other in the vast gardens, where many fountains and the soft breath of the sea and leafy groves cooled the air. They did not even feel the exclusion of women from the tense sensations of the Hippodrome, for one could witness the thrilling races from the windows in the upper gallery of the church of St Stephen. But we shall see speedily enough that this ceremonious seclusion no more intimidated the imperial women, when they were imperial, from playing their part in public life than the pomp and display of the palace intimidated the people of Constantinople from talking to their monarch, when occasion arose, as if he were a village chief. Verina remained quiet and obscure because life flowed evenly and she had no cause to interfere with its course. The promptness with which she sought, or accepted, consolation after the death of her husband does not suggest that she was very deeply devoted to Leo. He was, however, a shrewd and strong man, though rough and uncultivated, and he seems to have left little room for his wife's interference.

The Empress's quarters in the palace, or assemblage of palaces, are very imperfectly known to us. Daphne itself, the original palace, to which later Emperors would raise stupendous rivals, cannot have had very numerous apartments. It would assuredly not be possible to hide a bishop there for years, as the Empress Theodora afterwards hid a bishop in her apartments; to say nothing of the subterraneous dungeons which Theodora is said to have filled with her prisoners. But there were several detached palaces in the grounds, and no doubt the Empress had the use of one of these, standing in its own gardens and groves, and protected by its army of eunuchs. Verina had had one daughter, Ariadne, before her elevation to the throne. A few years afterwards she again gave promise of motherhood, and adjourned for delivery, as custom demanded, to the Porphyra Palace by the sea, a small square mansion whose walls were lined with red, white-spotted porphyry. But it was another girl, Leontia, that she brought into the world, and who lay beside her under the sheets of gold-cloth to receive the homage of the notabilities.[3]

Many years of this placid existence pass before we catch another glimpse of Verina. The legendary life of St Daniel Stylites, the emulator or successor of the famous Simeon of the Pillar, says that the prayers of the holy dweller on a column procured for the Empress a boy in 462, but the effectiveness of his prayers seems to have been limited, as no such child has found its way into serious history. Leo was now ageing, and the question of the succession must have been keenly discussed. It is at this point that Verina, who seemed doomed to pass again into obscurity, begins to reveal her personality. Asper and his son still seemed to dominate Constantinople, but their power was being silently undermined. Leo was filling the palace and the army with his own compatriots, and a conflict impended between the Isaurians and Goths, between Leo and Asper.

Amongst these Isaurians a young man named Trascallisseus—or something approaching it, for the Greeks make sad work of the Asiatic names—won the favour of Leo, and approached nearer to the throne. The orthodox chroniclers are severe on Trascallisseus, and depict him as "a veritable Pan"— dark, ugly, hairy, ungainly, heavy-footed and ignorant. The Isaurians were not a handsome race, nor had they the least ambition to adopt the culture of the Greeks, yet the portrait is probably overdrawn. Trascallisseus seems to have been a robust, sullen, illiterate, intriguing young man, with no apparent grace of body or character, but Leo was minded to marry him to Ariadne, and thus mark him for the throne.

Verina apparently desired the succession of her brother Basiliscus, and, as a vast fleet of more than a thousand vessels was about to be sent to wrest Roman Africa from the Vandals, she obtained the command of it for him. Verina could watch from the palace gardens the sailing of the great armada which was to win the purple for her brother. And in a few weeks a fugitive vessel returned with the terrible news that the expedition had failed, the navy had been burned, and the great army of a hundred thousand men sunk or scattered by Genseric. Basiliscus had fled shamefully at the first shock, and had retired to hide his disgrace in private life at Heraclea in Thrace.

It was the turn of Trascallisseus. His name was changed to Zeno, and he was married to Ariadne and promoted to the highest honours.[4] Verina had now to resign herself to a hope that she would share the power with Zeno and her daughter, but the struggle of Isaurians and Goths had first to be settled, and the settlement interests us. In less than two years the struggle ended with a victory of the Isaurians—a victory that has inscribed the name of the Emperor in the chronicles as "Leo the Butcher." We do not know the course of the quarrel, but one day in the year 471 the marble and bronze palace rang with the clash of swords. Asper and his elder son were cut to pieces by the eunuchs within the palace. No doubt Verina and her family had their boats moored at the foot of the garden, as we shall find others doing, but the terrible axes of the Excubitors and the long swords of the Candidates held back the tide of Goths and covered the marble floors with their corpses. The Isaurians were masters of the Roman Empire.

Leo died three years afterwards. It is said that he wished to crown Zeno before he died, but that the people were bitterly opposed to it. He had, therefore, in order to secure the succession, associated his infant (or boyish) grandson Leo with his imperial power, and had died shortly afterwards. The mother and grandmother now came to an agreement with Zeno, and, when the father came to do humble homage to his imperial child, the boy, prompted by Ariadne and Verina, put the crown on the father's head, and the Court applauded the succession of the Emperor Zeno. The sickly child died nine months afterwards (November 474), leaving Zeno in sole possession of the throne.

Here begin the adventures of Verina, and at length her virile character is revealed to us. Her second daughter Leontia was married to a son of the Western Emperor Anthemius—it was the period of ephemeral Emperors that preceded the extinction of the Western Empire—and a niece of hers was wedded to the Western Emperor Julius Nepos; though the latter connexion soon proved its tragic futility, the Emperor fleeing from Ravenna and falling by the hand of a bishop a few months after coronation. While promoting this apparent scheme for the reunion of the Roman Empire, Verina began to assert her personality more vigorously at Constantinople. She still lived in the palace, and seems gradually to have won its officers: as venal and corrupt a body as ever adorned a court. The works of contemporary Greek historians survive only in tantalizing fragments, or summaries, or they would undoubtedly furnish a remarkable picture of Byzantine life in the next ten years, when three Empresses occupied the stage. We can but piece together with caution the fragments we find in the chronicles, and endeavour to deduce the character of the Empresses from their actions.

Verina now had a notorious lover named Patricius, and was eager to set him on the throne instead of Zeno. Her daughter Ariadne, a commonplace, docile woman, clung to her husband, and the palace divided into two hostile parties and awaited the result. It is piquant to remember that Constantinople was at the time an intensely religious city. Its patriarch overshadowed those of Alexandria and Rome; its populace divided its interest almost equally between chariot-racing, vice and the suppression of heresy; and to its great church of St Sophia, or to the numerous chapels within the area of the palace, were conducted with splendour the important relics which were constantly being "found" in Palestine. But the frivolous citizens ignored the practical enjoinments of their religion until the periodical fire, or plague, or earthquake threw them into a spasm of repentance, and the population of the palace seemed to hold themselves entirely dispensed from such common laws. Verina, at least, knew neither weakness nor scruple in the pursuit of her ambition.

In November 475 Zeno fled across the water to Chalcedon. Ships were kept for such emergencies at the foot of the gardens, so that an imperial family might be well on the way to the Asiatic shore before an enemy could break through the hedge of guards. Zeno, protesting that his life was threatened by

Verina's servants, fled precipitately, since he left Ariadne under the power of her mother. It seems that Verina virtually imprisoned her daughter, but Ariadne escaped and joined her husband. From the coast they travelled, in a common cart, to the wild fastnesses of Isauria, from which another turn of the wheel will presently recall them to the glittering palace.

Zeno had been morose and unpopular, and it had not been difficult for Verina to detach the Senators and troops from him. They had, however, no mind to accept the virtual rule of Verina herself by putting her paramour on the throne, and, to her great mortification, they summoned her discredited brother Basiliscus from his exile in Thrace, and clothed him with the purple. The change brings on the scene a third Empress, Zenonis, who was made "Augusta" by her husband as soon as he was crowned.

We have hardly time to make much acquaintance with Zenonis during the brief splendour of her husband's reign, but her momentary appearance is not without romance. Passionately devoted to the more philosophical religious sect, which maintained that there was but one nature in Christ, she pressed her husband to espouse its cause and restore its persecuted members. Constantinople was soon aflame with religious controversy. Zenonis secured the return from exile, and appointment as patriarch of Alexandria, of Timotheus Ælurus. Timotheus gathered "all the scum of Alexandria"—the orthodox historian says—that could be found in Constantinople, and conducted them in procession to the church of St Sophia. But how Timotheus fell off his ass, to the delight of Constantinople, and how Peter the Fuller was summoned to fill the see of Antioch, and how Basiliscus wrung money out of the wealthy orthodox churches, must be read in the pages of ecclesiastical history. Zenonis was impelling her husband to his doom.

A much less serious defect in Zenonis, from the Constantinopolitan point of view, was that she united with her zeal for the Monophysite faith a genial disregard of its moral implications. A nephew of her husband named Harmatius rapidly became one of the most luxurious fops of the city. His lavishly spent wealth, his lovely hair and pink cheeks and handsome person, and his reputation for gallantry, made him the idol of the frequenters of the Hippodrome. Basiliscus made him prefect of the city, and he delighted its lower populace by moving amongst them in the shining armour of Achilles. Duty frequently called him to Court, and his charms conquered the susceptible Empress. For some time they sighed and crossed fiery glances as they met in the open chambers or corridors, but at length the eunuch Daniel and the midwife Maria were bribed to facilitate their desire. Such, at least, was the belief of Constantinople, and the power of Basiliscus was further shaken.

His next fatal mishap was to quarrel with Verina. He had her lover Patricius assassinated, and the enraged Empress began at once to pay further gold to buy back the allegiance of Senators and officers to Zeno. The zeal of Basiliscus for his heresy had now completely alienated the people and embittered the clergy. He had ventured to send officers into the churches to proscribe the great Council of Chalcedon, which had condemned the heresy, and the city was profoundly agitated. Vast crowds of men, women and children shouted their orthodox hymns in the streets and filled the black-draped churches. When Basiliscus angrily left the city for a distant palace, the saintly Daniel descended from his pillar, followed him, and spoke to him in very plain language.

In these circumstances Verina was encouraged to further her plan, and the news soon reached Constantinople that Zeno had left the mountains of Isauria and was in command of an army. Two generals, Illus and Trocundus, were sent against him, and were bought by him. The very meagre chronicles now indicate a desperate struggle between Basiliscus and his sister. The Emperor began to trace the plot and execute the plotters, and Verina fled for her life to the sanctuary of St Sophia. We shall see often enough how frail a protection the law of sanctuary afforded against the anger of an Emperor, but Harmatius, who seems to have despised his lover's husband, helped her to escape, and she seems either to have crossed to Asia or concealed herself. Harmatius himself was now sent against the rebels. Swearing the most solemn oath of fidelity to Basiliscus that the clergy could devise, he straightway sold his services to Zeno for the promise of a cÆsarship for his son and the perpetual command of the armies for himself.

The career of the romantic Zenonis then came to a rapid and tragic close. As the troops of Zeno marched into the city Basiliscus and his Empress fled to the church of St Sophia, and endeavoured, by promises of undoing their heretical work, to induce the clergy to make Zeno respect the sanctuary. After a time an imperial officer came to the trembling wretches by the altar, and stripped them of all their imperial ensigns, to be taken to Zeno and Ariadne. Zeno scrupled to drag them from the altar, and they were at last induced to come forth on the solemn assurance that their lives would be spared. It was now their turn to sail for Asia. They were sent to an obscure village in Cappadocia, and imprisoned in a tower. One tradition reports that they were killed on the journey, but the more persistent and convincing report is that the door of the tower was sealed with masonry, and the brother of Verina and his Empress were doomed to a slow and horrible death by starvation. It was the second revolution in three years, and Verina had been an active element in both.

Exile had not improved the temper of Zeno, and the restoration of his rule was at once stained with murder. He reflected gloomily on the prestige of the handsome Harmatius, and easily persuaded himself that he who had been faithless to one master might be faithless to another. Soon afterwards the luxurious officer was cut to pieces as he ascended the spiral stair from the palace to the Hippodrome; his son was stripped of the robes and ensigns of Cæsar and was sent to take a minor order of the Church at Blachernæ. But for the intervention of the more humane Ariadne the youth would, like his father, have exchanged his high dignity for death.

Constantinople seems to have regarded the murder with indifference, but an avenger arose in the provinces and the two Empresses had soon grave cause for anxiety. For a time Constantinople trembled under the menace of the formidable barbarians, but they at length returned to Italy without having penetrated into the city. A more serious danger fell upon the palace in the following year, however, when the younger daughter of Verina joined for a moment in the conflict of ambitions. Leontia, it will be remembered, had married Marcian, son of the Western Emperor Anthemius. On the ground that she had been "born in the Porphyry," while her elder sister Ariadne had been born before the crowning of Leo, her husband demanded that the Empire should be assigned to him, and marched on Constantinople at the head of an army. He broke through the defences of the city, and some of the chroniclers actually assure us that he surprised the guard of the palace in their midday siesta. It is at least certain that Zeno and the Empresses fled in alarm, and a vigorous action would have put Verina's younger daughter on the throne. Marcian seems, however, to have postponed the occupation of the palace until the following day, and the commander Illus, secretly transporting fresh troops from Asia, restored the balance in favour of Zeno and Verina. Marcian was visited with the more refined punishment of the Byzantine world—he was forced to enter the priesthood—and Leontia retired into obscurity.

But the romance of Verina and her daughters had already entered upon a fresh chapter. Verina had welcomed her returning son-in-law at the palace, and her earlier expulsion of him and Ariadne was overlooked in view of the important share she had had in securing their return. We can, however, well understand that Zeno regarded her with suspicion and distrust, and would welcome the first opportunity to remove her from the palace. The argument which he had applied so remorselessly to

Harmatius plainly extended to his imperial mother-in-law. The writers of the time represent him as not taking a prominent part in the events that followed, but it is difficult to doubt that his secret commands directed the whole intrigue.

In the year 478 a soldier attempted to assassinate the commander Illus, and he confessed—under torture or bribery—that he had been instructed by Verina's steward Epinicius. The steward was given into the custody of Illus by the Emperor, and was sent under guard to a castle in Isauria. Illus followed, and easily induced the steward to impeach his mistress. Illus then returned to the city, and arranged with Zeno a plot for the capture of Verina. It is clear that the Empress-Mother had great power in Constantinople, and that they dare not openly touch her. Illus was to go to Isauria, and pretend that he feared danger from Zeno. The Emperor was then to ask Verina to take to Illus with her own hand a letter of indemnity, and, when she reached Isauria, she was to be imprisoned there. We should find it difficult to believe that so naive a plot could entrap the virile and experienced Empress were we not expressly assured of it by the highest authorities. In a few weeks Verina was enraged to find herself imprisoned in a Papirian fortress, one of the strongly fortified castles of remote Isauria. One authority observes that they first compelled her to take the vows of a nun, but we may decline to believe that they troubled to place so frail and so superfluous a chain on such a woman.

From the lonely hills of Isauria Verina at length found a means of communicating with Ariadne and securing her interest. Zeno, to whom Ariadne appealed, referred her to Illus, and, when that general was summoned to the Empress's apartments, and implored with tears to release her mother, he bluntly asked: "Do you want to be rid of your husband and wed another?" Ariadne returned stormily to her husband, and declared that either Illus or she must leave the palace. "If you can do anything, I'm with you," said the distracted Emperor, who was overshadowed by the vigorous commander. Presently, as Illus was mounting the spiral stair to the Hippodrome, a soldier in the pay of Ariadne's chamberlain fell upon him. Illus was saved, except for the loss of an ear, by his guards, but he prudently decided that Constantinople was injurious to his health and requested the Emperor for a change of air. He was appointed commander of the eastern troops, took with him the patrician Leontius and a distinguished company, and reached Antioch only to declare himself in rebellion and Leontius Emperor.

In the extraordinary confusion of events which the meagre chronicles transmit to us Verina had obtained her wish in an unexpected manner. A messenger came to her in her solitary prison to say that she was to crown Leontius at the city of Tarsus and join forces with him and Illus against Zeno. Verina was not the woman to hesitate. She crowned Leontius, a cultivated Syrian noble and excellent soldier, at Tarsus, and issued a characteristic letter to the officials and commanders of the Empire:

"Verina Augusta, greeting to our prefects and Christian peoples. You know that the Empire is ours, and that after the death of our husband Leo we, trusting to improve the condition of the commonwealth, raised to the throne Trascallisseus, who was afterwards called Zeno; now, however, since we perceive that he is deteriorating, and on account of his insatiable avarice, we have thought it needful to give you a Christian Emperor, adorned with piety and justice, that he may save the commonwealth and administer war with moderation and prudence. We have therefore bestowed the imperial crown on Leontius, most pious of Romans, who will guard us all with care and prudence."

The throne of Leontius was set up at Antioch, and the aged Empress turned with her confederates to face Zeno's troops. It was to be the last act of the stirring drama of her life. Zeno acted with unaccustomed vigour, and in a few days Verina and her companions were flying to Isauria. They shut themselves in the Papirian fortress and prepared to sustain a long siege. In the middle of the siege

Verina died, and was spared the humiliation of the final defeat. Four years afterwards the heads of Illus and Leontius were exhibited on poles at Constantinople, but the body of Verina was decently interred there by her daughter.

The loss of contemporary historians prevents us from obtaining the closer acquaintance with Verina which her romantic story leads us to desire. Of her personal appearance and nationality we know nothing. One is tempted to conceive her as a Syrian woman of the type of Zenobia or Julia Domna: a virile and masterful personality, ambitious and unscrupulous, subtle and astute rather than cultivated, paying no more than a merely external and superficial regard to the teaching of the new religion of the Roman world. It remains to say a few words about the Empress Ariadne before we consider the next great Empress of the Byzantine world.

In the few peaceful years which followed the death of Verina life at the palace became sombre and painful. Zeno was morose, suspicious and unpopular, and increased the gloom by the usual device of executing, or murdering, suspects. Their only son came to a lamentable end. The officials in charge of his education felt that it would be more profitable to themselves to teach him vice and luxury rather than the manly arts which his parents required, and he was profoundly corrupted. His ostentatious vanity invited ridicule, and his indulgence in unnatural vice and intemperance ruined his constitution. He fell an early victim to dysentery, and his father plunged into deeper bitterness amid the splendours and pleasures of his palace. Ariadne must have awaited the end with impatience, and it is not improbable that she already chose a partner to share her throne. Popular rumour afterwards said that she buried Zeno alive. It was said that he used to fall into a kind of trance after his gluttonous meals, and that Ariadne in disgust bade the servants seal him in a tomb; the legend even represents him as recovering and crying in vain to be relieved, and one version pretends that, when the tomb was eventually opened, he was found to have eaten his boots and belt. The truth seems to be that he was subject to epileptic fits, one of which ended his life in April 491.

Ariadne at once nominated for the Empire a peasant of northern Greece who had a very subordinate position in the military service of the palace. A tall, handsome man—though one of his eyes was grey and the other almost black—of strong, quiet character, he seems to have been chosen by Ariadne as her future husband before Zeno died. He was unmarried, though past middle age. One of Ariadne's eunuchs secured the consent of the Senators to the strange nomination, and Anastasius obtained the applause of the people by remitting their debts to the treasury. The only opposition came from the patriarch, or archbishop, who had in earlier years been compelled to prevent Anastasius from setting up an unofficial pulpit in the streets of the city and teaching his favourite heresy. Anastasius genially forswore his heresy for so high a price, was at once crowned Emperor, and married Ariadne on the fortieth day after the burial of Zeno. Docile and clinging as Ariadne had been in her earlier years, she fully reveals herself as the daughter of Verina in her middle life. But the twenty-five years of life which remained for her are years of obscurity, as far as the Empress is concerned, and we will not linger over them. Storm after storm broke over the palace, where she lived, but she seems to have taken no part in public events. The Isaurians marched on the city to demand the throne for the brother of Zeno, and a long struggle ended in the complete destruction of the power of the Isaurians. Then Anastasius returned to his Monophysite heresy, and the streets of the city and towns of the Empire rang with defiance and anathema. On one occasion, in 512, the mob burned the monasteries which Anastasius favoured, and so angrily assailed the palace that the ships were made ready at the quays to conduct Ariadne and her husband to Asia. Anastasius had been guilty of the additional indiscretion of attempting to reform the morals of Constantinople and forbidding contests with wild beasts in the arena.[5] Ariadne lived until the year 515 or 516, when she must have been about seventy years old. So completely was she overshadowed by her second husband that the only reference we find to her in the chronicles is that on one occasion she begged Anastasius to make a certain appointment, and he refused.

CHAPTER II

THE EARLY LIFE OF THEODORA

The next Empress to occupy the superb apartments in the palace, with their couches of ivory and silver and their regiments of fawning eunuchs and silk-clad ladies, was assuredly one of the most remarkable figures that ever sat on a throne. The Empress Euphemia hardly ever issues into the pages of history from the becoming seclusion of the women's quarters in the palace, but the few details which we have concerning her suggest the most incongruous figure that imagination could place in such a world, and a brief account of her romantic elevation is a necessary introduction to the equally remarkable and better-known story of the famous Empress Theodora. The Roman Empire seemed to be deterred by some faint recollection of its early democratic spirit from admitting the hereditary principle; but the absence of this arrangement for securing the succession, together with the complete lack of any really democratic arrangement, often threw it into a chaotic confusion when a ruler died, and made its internal history a thrilling succession of romances and tragedies, with an occasional page of comedy. In this case it is comedy.

Anastasius, after playing his successive parts as peasant, lay preacher, soldier and ruler of the world, had passed away, amid the derision and rejoicing of his people, in the year 518. His nephews had feeble pretensions to succeed him, but the most powerful man in the city, the Prefect Amantius, decided that the purple should pass to his friend Theocritus. He therefore sought the commander, or Count, of the Excubitors—the more formidable guards of the palace—and placed in his hands a large sum of money for distribution among the troops. Justin, the said commander, was an Illyrian peasant who had won promotion in the wars. He was in his later sixties, though still a powerful man, with handsome rosy face and curly white hair; but under this disarming exterior he concealed an ambition and astuteness which the prefect failed to suspect. He distributed the money in his own interest, and passed unopposed from the modest quarters of the guard to the more luxurious chambers of the palace.

Euphemia was the wife of Justin, and it may safely be said that no woman ever experienced a more romantic elevation. In his military days Justin had bought a barbaric slave named Lupicina, and raised her to the rank of his concubine; though no doubt he married her in the course of time. She retained the uncouth and illiterate manners of her class, and Constantinople must have smiled to see her in the richly embroidered robes of purple silk, with cascades of diamonds and pearls falling from her gorgeous diadem. The acclamation of the crowd changed her name to Euphemia, and she retired to the congenial privacy of her palace. Justin brought his equally illiterate mother Bigleniza to the palace from her rustic home, and the two women no doubt contracted a fitting friendship in their wonderful new home. Of public action on their part there is no question, and the events of the next few years do not concern us. I will say only that, after securing his throne by cutting off the head of Amantius and crushing Theocritus under heavy stones in his dungeon, for venturing to resent the trick he had played them, Justin ruled with moderation, if not prudence, for nine years. Euphemia died three or four years before him, living just long enough to see, and emphatically resent, her successor, the notorious Theodora.

In approaching the story of Theodora it is necessary to premise a few words on the authority which has provided most of the sensational statements about her, and to pay respectful attention to the efforts of some recent historical writers to discredit those statements. The general outline of her story has been made familiar by Gibbon, who has genially dilated on the elevation of one of the lewdest actresses and most notorious prostitutes of Constantinople to the position, not merely of mistress of the greatest empire of the time, but also of patroness of an important branch of the Church and the daily companion of saintly monks and bishops. Since Theodora is very commonly described by the chroniclers as at least equal in power to her husband, the great Justinian, and since the next most powerful woman in the Byzantine Empire at the time is assigned a similar origin to that of Theodora, the world has long reflected with amazement on this spectacle of the Roman Empire at the feet of two imperfectly converted prostitutes. Such a situation could not pass unchallenged before the more critical tribunal of modern history, and there are scholars who have rejected entirely the romantic story of the youth of Theodora.[6] The majority of historians, including the two chief living authorities, Professor Bury and M. Diehl, regard the story as true in substance though unreliable in detail.

The more romantic statements concerning Theodora are taken from a work that purports to have been written by the greatest contemporary historical writer, Procopius, but there are writers (such as Ranke and Bury) who regard the work as, at the most, a later compilation of notes left by Procopius, and in any case it is so envenomed in temper, and occasionally so reckless in statement, that it should be regarded with suspicion. The problem cannot be discussed at length here, but it is necessary to justify the large use I am about to make of the work (the "Anecdotes") which bears the name of Procopius.

If it were true, as is sometimes said, that we had no authority for the impeachment of the character of Theodora beyond the "Anecdotes," we should have to hesitate very seriously, but this is by no means true. Procopius ("On the Persian War") represents her as playing a most unscrupulous part in the ruin of John of Cappadocia. Liberatus (a contemporary cleric) and Anastasius exhibit the Empress to us corrupting the papacy itself and deposing a venerable pontiff by the most cruel and flagrantly dishonest charges. Zonaras and other writers accuse her, not merely of avarice, as Mr Mallett says, but of the most heartless and unblushing corruption in feeding her avarice. There is every reason to regard Theodora, after her elevation to the throne, as a woman devoid of moral scruple. But we now have ample confirmation also of the story of her origin. The statement of an eleventh-century writer, Aimoinus, that Justinian took his wife from a brothel, shows, in spite of its wild inaccuracies, that some such tradition was found in European literature quite apart from the "Anecdotes." But the publication in the nineteenth century of the writings of John, Bishop of Ephesus, has furnished a decisive proof. This Monophysite bishop and cultivated writer, who lived for years beside the palace of Theodora, and whose sect received the most imperial and incalculable benefits from her, speaks of her as "Theodora of the brothel"; and he uses the phrase in such a way as to intimate plainly that this was the name by which she was known in Constantinople before her elevation to the throne.[7] Indeed, the fact that the author of the "Anecdotes" does not assail the chastity of Theodora after her marriage increases our confidence in his account of her earlier life; as he did not intend to publish his work—it was not published until 1623—it would have been just as easy to invent or collect legends about her after as before her marriage. On the other hand, the temper of the writer is so bitter and malignant that we must reserve our judgment in regard to the details of his strange narrative. He has gathered together every defaming rumour about Theodora and Justinian that circulated in Constantinople, even admitting nonsense obviously unworthy of a serious writer, and we cannot sift the true from the legendary. The source of his animosity cannot be determined. From the tone of his remarks on religion I gather that he was one of the many surviving pagans who were forced into outward conformity with the new religion, and, after giving formal praise in his historical works to Justinian and Theodora for the splendour of their reign, he relieved his soul, in this secret collection of notes, of the deep disgust he felt at the contrast between their characters and their professions and between the glamour and the misery of their empire. It must be remembered that the thoroughly Christian and very weighty authority, Evagrius, is just as severe on Justinian; there was in Justinian, he says, "something surpassing the cruelty of beasts," and any prostitute could despoil a wealthy man by a false charge (say, of unnatural vice—a trick of Theodora's) "provided she let Justinian share her vile gain." It is the common teaching of the authorities that the Empress was worse than the Emperor.

In point of fact, there is nothing implausible or improbable in the details of Procopius's story of Theodora's early life, and the judicious reader will merely make allowance for the rhetorical strength of its superlatives. Her father Acacius had been a keeper of the bears which were baited in the Hippodrome in the reign of Anastasius. The Hippodrome at Constantinople united the functions which at Rome had been divided between the circus, the theatre and the amphitheatre. Its chief attraction was the chariot-racing which provided the central and most thrilling sensation of Roman life.[8] Between the races, however, there were contests with wild beasts in the arena, and there were the numerous nondescript performances which occupied the theatre at Rome—mimes (actors by gesture), clowns, acrobats, conjurers, etc. Acacius was bear-keeper to the "greens," and, when he died, his widow promptly secured another partner and claimed the office for him. But the superintendent Asterius had sold the office to another man, and the shrewd widow appealed to the sympathy of the crowd by parading in the Hippodrome, the heads and hands of her three daughters crowned with the emblems of virginity. The "greens" jeered—possibly at the sight of the eldest daughter, Comitona, a loose girl of seventeen, dressed as a Vestal Virgin—but the "blues" received them with sympathy; a distinction which the pale and slender little Theodora would never forget.

The mother, who is said to have come from Cyprus, either before or after the birth of Theodora, then pressed the fortunes of her daughters in the theatrical world. Comitona was already a mime (or actress without words) and, as was usual, a prostitute. The young Theodora presently began to attend her elder sister, and is said to have begun her career of infamy as she waited among the slaves and lackeys on the fringe of the Hippodrome. When she in turn became an actress, her pretty pale face, lithe figure and unrestrained gaiety and dissoluteness made her a great favourite. She stripped to the narrowest limit of decency which the very liberal law permitted, performed the most nearly obscene ribaldries which the Roman theatre allowed, and was pre-eminent for the abandonment of her gestures and movements; and in the hours of the night, when the wealthier patrons of the Hippodrome entertained themselves in perfumed chambers with the actresses and courtesans, Theodora was in the greatest favour.

It is absurd to say that this is to impute to Theodora "a moral turpitude unparalleled in any age." It was the common turpitude of that age, of our age, and of every intervening age. The theatre, indeed, no longer admits the very broad licence which was admitted at Constantinople, but the performances which are ascribed by Procopius to Theodora are innocent in comparison with certain performances which may be witnessed, in semi-publicity, in very many cities of Europe to-day. Of Theodora's private behaviour—that she practised both forms of unnatural, as well as natural, vice—one need only say that it is, and always has been, common to her class. An actress at that time meant a woman of loose conduct. The imperial decrees and the Church fully recognised this, and it is significant that one of the theatres—if not the one theatre—of Constantinople was called "The Harlots," and is so named in an imperial document. Procopius is merely imputing to Theodora the common practices of loose women of her time and our own. And when, in later pages, we come to realise the fiery and unrestrained temper of the beautiful Greek, we can well believe that she was at that time one of the worst of her class.

Not less plausible is the next chapter in the life of Theodora. A wealthy official, Hecebolus, induced her to accompany him to the African province which he was to administer, and her very brief career at Constantinople came to a close. M. Diehl conjectures that this occurred in 517, in her eighteenth year, and that she remained a few years with Hecebolus. However that may be, she was, about the year 521, ejected from the governor's house, and she passed to Alexandria, and thence to Antioch and the other cities of Syria and Asia Minor. It is most probable that this was the time when, either at Alexandria or Antioch, she became a convert to the Monophysite faith. The question of the true character of Christ had racked and rent the Eastern world, amidst all its ribaldry and vice, for two hundred years, and the burning issue at this time was whether the nature of Christ should be described as single or twofold; the Monophysites held that there was but one nature in Christ, and were bitterly opposed to the "Synodists," or supporters of the orthodox Council of Chalcedon. It may seem incongruous to drag in so solemn an issue on so defiled a page of biography, but it is essential for the understanding of Theodora's career.

According to Procopius, Theodora still practised her evil profession in the cities of Asia. For the next few years, however, there is much obscurity about her movements, and the biographer cannot proceed with great confidence. One eleventh-century writer represents that Justinian and the commander Belisarius chose their wives in a loose house in Constantinople; another equally remote and unreliable chronicler says that Justinian found Theodora living a modest life, supporting herself by spinning wool, in a small house under the portico—a very strange residence for a virtuous woman. I prefer still to follow the very plausible story (in substance) of the "Anecdotes." At Antioch Theodora went in great distress to visit Macedonia, an actress who had influence with Justinian. It is hardly strained to conjecture that this was the real occasion of her introduction to Justinian; that she went on to Constantinople with a recommendation to him and was at once taken into his house. Beyond question she was his mistress for some years before he married her.

Justin had brought from Upper Macedonia, and educated in the schools of Constantinople, the favourite nephew who was to become the Emperor Justinian. At the time when Theodora came back to Constantinople, about the year 522, he approached his fortieth year: a handsome, wealthy and free-living bachelor, of fresh and florid complexion and the curly hair of a Greek. His reputation was somewhat sinister: his influence unbounded. In entertaining the populace on his elevation to the consulship in the previous year he had spent about £160,000, and had turned twenty lions and thirty leopards together into the arena. He was plainly marked for the throne. The pretty pale face and bright eyes and graceful figure of Theodora captivated him, and her experienced art enabled her to profit by the infatuation. Justinian lived in the palace of Hormisdas on the shore of the Sea of Marmora, and Constantinople would take little scandal at his connexion with Theodora. Four or five years' absence would have enfeebled the memory of her earlier career, and the zeal for the true religion—the Monophysite heresy, which she paraded from the moment of her connexion with Justinian—would ensure the genial indulgence of the frivolous population. Justinian had her made a "patrician" (or noble), lodged her in his beautiful palace, and showered his favours upon her. It is at this point that Bishop John begins to describe his co-religionists appealing to the protection of "Theodora of the brothel" from all parts of the Empire.

There were two obstacles to marriage. Justin was feeble and senile, and little able or disposed to resist his nephew's whims, but Euphemia strongly opposed the marriage until her death in 523 or 524. The more serious impediment was the standing law of the Roman Empire, that a noble could not wed a woman of ill-fame (an actress, tavern-girl or courtesan). Justinian afterwards removed this restriction, but it must have been in some way overruled by Justin, and many authorities believe that the first law in the Justinian Code on the point was really promulgated by Justin. A daughter seems to have been born before the marriage, possibly before the connexion with Justinian, as John of Ephesus confirms the statement of Procopius that Theodora had a marriageable grandson before she died (in 548).

The next step for the enterprising young Greek was the attainment of the throne. Justin was pressed, as he aged, to associate his nephew in the government, and, although he nervously refused for some time, he at length (April 527) conferred the supreme dignity of Augustus on his nephew and of Augusta on Theodora. She now entered upon the full splendour of imperial life, and no parvenue ever bore it with more exaggerated dignity than the ex-actress, as we shall see. There must have been many who smiled when Theodora first witnessed the old sights of the Hippodrome from the imperial chapel of St Stephen, or sat for the homage of the Senators in the long gold-embroidered mantle, with the screen of heavy jewels falling in chains from her diadem upon her neck and breast, as we find her depicted in a mosaic at Ravenna; but her formidable power and her unscrupulous use of it would soon extinguish the last echo of her opprobrious nickname.

The early years of Theodora's power were spent in enlarging the prestige of her position and in recompensing her friends. The existent palaces could not meet the requirements of the woman who, a few years before, had begged money of an Antioch courtesan. Justin had to annex his palace of Hormisdas to the imperial domain and build fresh palaces. The favourite residence of Theodora was the cool and superb palace of Hieria across the water, and in spite of the lack of accommodation for her enormous suite and the terrors of a whale, popularly named Porphirio, which infested the waters of Constantinople at the time, she frequently crossed to it.

At home, in the sacred palace, she led a life strangely opposed to that of the temperate, accessible and hard-working Justinian. Rising at an early hour she devoted a considerable time to the bath and toilet, by which she trusted to sustain her charm, in spite of delicate health. After breaking her fast, she again retired to rest before she would consent to receive courtiers and suitors. In view of her paramount influence with the Emperor many sought her patronage, or dreaded to incur her terrible resentment, by seeming indifferent to it. Numbers of nobles waited, sometimes for days, in the hot ante-room to her apartments, standing on tiptoe to catch the eye of the pampered eunuchs who passed to and fro. After a long delay they might be admitted to kiss the golden sandals of Theodora, and listen to her august wishes. No man was permitted to speak except in reply to a question. In the course of time, as we shall see, the highest nobles eagerly submitted to this humiliating treatment, in order to preserve their wealth from the extortioner. Dinner and supper, at which, though Theodora ate little, the most opulent banquets had to be served, occupied the further hours of the day, together with Theodora's abundant devotions and converse with holy men.

Her friends were generously admitted to share her advantages. The "Anecdotes" tell a story of an illegitimate son of hers who discovered his birth, came to the Empress for recognition or money, and was at once despatched to another world. That seems to be one of the calumnious fables which the writer too eagerly admitted into his indictment. The "Anecdotes" themselves rather show that Theodora did not make every effort to conceal the past, however strongly she might resent discussion of it. Her sister Comitona was certainly married in the first year of her reign to a wealthy and powerful noble. It is not so certain, but probable enough, that she cherished her earlier theatrical friends, Chrysomallo and Indara, and found wealthy husbands for their daughters. The woman whose name we shall find most closely connected with hers, Antonina, the wife of the great general Belisarius, is said to have been her tirewoman before she married Belisarius. This would account for Theodora's coolness until Antonina won her by securing her revenge on John of Cappadocia, when Theodora is said not merely to have overlooked, but promoted, the vices of her friend. There is, at least, no room for doubt about the character of Antonina.

But while Theodora admitted these mute reminders of her earlier life, she turned with extraordinary severity upon her earlier colleagues as a body and undertook the purification of the city. The decrees of Justinian for regulating the morals of Constantinople—decrees which go so far as to define the penalties for people who made assignations in churches, and on the strength of which bishops were castrated and exhibited in public for unnatural vice—are generally ascribed to her influence. She had the imperial net dragged through the loose houses of Constantinople, and five hundred of the occupants were imprisoned in an ancient palace on the Asiatic shore: a form of enforced piety which, the carping Procopius says, drove many of them to suicide. Many writers think this zeal for purity inconsistent with the story of her earlier life. It has rather the appearance of a feverish affectation of repentance, and must be balanced by the many proofs we have of Theodora's really corrupt and unscrupulous character. One may recall that Domitian drastically punished the vices of others. Procopius would have us believe that Theodora compelled unmarried women to marry, and that when two delicate widows fled to the Church to escape her pressure, she had them dragged from the altar and married to men of infamous life. Yet, he says, vice was rampant in Constantinople, and protected by the Empress, when money was paid into her greedy coffers. Such details we cannot control, and must reproduce with reserve; we know only from other sources that she extorted money by corrupt means.

And the most singular and piquant feature of Theodora's life at this period was her zealous patronage of the Monophysites. Long before her coronation, from the time when she became the mistress of Justinian, the joyous news of her elevation flew throughout the Empire among the persecuted heretics. They had had their hours of triumph under Basiliscus and Anastasius, but with the accession of Justin the orthodox had returned to power, and the twofold nature of the gentle Christ had been urged with bloody arguments. From the monasteries and towns of the provinces pilgrims now began to arrive at the Hormisdas palace in great numbers, and through Justinian she obtained relief and money for them. When she entered the imperial palace the procession increased, and, while the nobles of Constantinople were detained for hours before being permitted to kiss her feet, ragged monks and unlettered deacons strode into the imperial apartments without a moment's delay.

So zealous, indeed, was Theodora for their edifying conversation that she kept them as long as possible about her. St Simeon of Persia came to plead the cause of his persecuted brethren, and was induced to live for a year in the luxurious palace. Arsenius of Palestine, one of the chief firebrands of his province, was cherished by her; though Procopius affirms that he at length lost her favour and was crucified. Orthodox monks were even permitted with impunity to rebuke the terrible Empress. A holy hermit came one day to chide Theodora for her heresy. Ragged and dirty, with garment so patched that hardly three inches of cloth of one colour appeared in it, he admonished her in fiery language. Theodora was so charmed with his piety that she sought to add him to her domestic collection of sanctities. When persuasion failed, she resorted to corruption; we read the story, not in the "Anecdotes," but in John. She had a large sum of gold concealed in linen and imposed on him, but the fiery monk hurled it across the palace, crying: "Thy money perish with thee." St Sabas, also, the unlettered and unadorned abbot of an orthodox monastery at Jerusalem, came to ask her patronage. His piety excused his heresy in her eyes, and she kept him for days at the palace, and humbly asked his prayers that she might have a son. The grim monk refused, and, when companions asked how he could scorn the request of so generous a patroness, he replied: "We do not want any fruit from that womb, lest it be suckled on the heretical doctrines of Severus."

So great at length became the number of pious pilgrims from the provinces, and so eager was Theodora to retain them near her person, that the Hormisdas palace, which Justinian had richly decorated for her and enclosed within the area of the imperial palace, was converted into a monastery. Then were witnessed the quaintest scenes that ever enlivened the passion-throbbing palace of the Eastern Emperors. Five hundred monks, of all ages and nationalities, of every degree of sanctity and raggedness, were crowded in or about its marbled walls. Every form that monastic fervour had assumed in the fiery provinces of Syria or Egypt was exemplified in it. The orderly community sang its endless psalms and macerated its flesh in the rooms where Justinian had dallied with his mistress: little huts were scattered about the grounds for those who were called to the life of the hermit: and even columns were set up here and there for those who would imitate the more novel and arduous piety of St Simeon Stylites, and pass, at the open summit of the column, a kind of existence which the polite pen must refrain from describing. All the beggars of Constantinople gathered for the crumbs of this remarkable colony, and crowds of citizens pressed to witness this singular oasis of virtue in the most corrupt city of the world. Theodora rarely let a day pass without crossing the gardens to receive the blessing and enjoy the pious conversation of such of the saints as would deign to converse with a woman.

How she went on to put a courtly heretic upon the archiepiscopal throne of Constantinople, and, by an extraordinary piece of intrigue and corruption, depose a pope and replace him by one who pretended to favour her designs, we shall see presently. We must now set forth the imperial career of Theodora in chronological order, and learn what kind of character this remarkable woman maintained amid the chants and prayers of her deeply venerated monks.

CHAPTER III

THE EMPRESS THEODORA

We have seen how Theodora rewarded the friends, and must now see how she punished the enemies, of her earlier career. It will be remembered that her father had been a servant of the "greens" of the Hippodrome, but that this party had greeted her mother with derision when she appealed for sympathy with her three children, while the "blues" received them compassionately. Twenty years afterwards the young circus-girl had become the most powerful woman in the world, and the blues began to tyrannize with impunity over their rivals. In the earliest years of the reign of Theodora and Justinian we find them swollen with conceit and encouraged in the perpetration of every kind of disorder. The livelier "sparks" of that faction advertised their formidable character by adopting the trousers and sandals of the fierce Huns and trimming their hair after the fashion of those terrible invaders; they wore long moustaches and beards, shaved the front part of the head, and cultivated long hair at the back.

A few outrages soon taught them that the laws would not be enforced against them, and before long the city of Constantinople became, during the night, a land of terror. The citizen who dared to pass along the streets with a gold clasp to his belt or his cloak or money in his purse was robbed, and women could not move after nightfall. The continued silence of the authorities encouraged the blues, and drew all the dissolute elements of the city into their ranks. They now began to force the doors of the houses, plunder the coffers, rape the wives and daughters, and carry off the more handsome slaves and boys. At the least resistance their deadly poniards were drawn, and murder became frequent. When the authorities intervened, none but the greens were punished. The evil rapidly spread from night to day, and from the metropolis to other cities. It would be futile in this case to quarrel with the details given in the "Anecdotes." The great riot into which the greens were stung by this reign of terror is an historical fact; and nothing but the vindictive memory of Theodora can explain how Justinian, the great legislator, permitted so appalling a disorder.

Theodora meantime enjoyed the conversation of her monks and hermits, and even Justinian seems to have been unconscious that he was slipping the leash of beasts whom he might be powerless to control. At length, on 14th January 532, the greens stirred. The Emperor appeared in his kathisma at the Hippodrome, and an appeal was made to him for justice. His officer replied disdainfully, and a long and curious conversation took place.[9] The Emperor still refused to grant the impartial administration of justice or to punish the murderers, and the greens left the Hippodrome. They gathered in strength in the streets, and, although Justinian prudently sent to learn and partly to remove their grievances, they remained in arms. Belisarius was now sent against them with a troop of Goths, and the rioting and burning began. Unfortunately for the Court an accident then happened which had the singular effect of uniting the two factions against the troops. Seven criminals were to be executed, and Procopius cannot conceal the fact—in spite of his insistence that the blues were never punished—that some of the seven were blues and some greens. After five of the seven had been despatched, the rope broke, and the crowd demanded the acquittal of the remaining two. The authorities refused, and, as one criminal was a blue and the other a green, the factions turned in common anger upon the prefect and the troops.

The terrible riot that followed during four days must be read in history. The first part of the palace, the great church of St Sophia, and many other churches, mansions and public buildings were destroyed. Priests who rushed into the fray holding aloft the disarming emblems of their faith were cut down. On the fourth day, a Sunday, Justinian entered the Hippodrome with a Bible in his hand, and took a solemn oath to spare the offenders if they would disarm. "Ass, thou art perjuring thyself," was the infuriated answer; and he retired to contemplate with Theodora the impending ruin of their reign. On the following day the crowd forced Hypatius, nephew of the Emperor Anastasius, to accept such purple robes as they could obtain, marched with him in triumph to the Hippodrome, and exulted in the downfall of Justinian and Theodora, who were believed to have fled to Asia.

The "great" Justinian makes a lamentable appearance throughout the whole riot, which he had guiltily occasioned, but Theodora and the abler ministers were not minded to yield. As they gathered in the hall of the palace, to which the cries in the Hippodrome must almost have penetrated, the chief eunuch Narses came to report that by a judicious distribution of money he had distracted the factions and weakened the cause of Hypatius. It is probably this news that turned the scale in the wavering counsels of Justinian and his ministers, but it was Theodora who pressed it home. The speech which Procopius assigns to her is worth reproducing, though we cannot regard it as more than a rhetorical paraphrase of the words she used:

"In my opinion this is no time to admit the maxim that a woman must not act as a man among men; nor, if she fires the courage of the halting, are we to consider whether she does right or no. When matters come to a crisis, we must agree as to the best course to take. My opinion is that, although we may save ourselves by flight, it is not to our interest. Every man that sees the light must die, but the man who has once been raised to the height of empire cannot suffer himself to go into exile and survive his dignity. God forbid that I should ever be seen stripped of this purple, or live a single day on which I am not to be saluted as Mistress. If thou desirest to go, Emperor, nothing prevents thee. There is the sea; there are the steps to the boats. But have a care that when thou leavest here, thou dost not exchange this sweet light for an ignoble death. For my part I like the old saying: empire is a fine winding-sheet."

Some such sentiments, we may believe, were urged by Theodora, and affected the decision. The populace was penned in the Hippodrome, and Justinian's officers and troops stealthily surrounded it. Rushing in at the various entrances, they fell with such fury upon the people that the sun went down on the corpses of between thirty and forty thousand citizens heaped in its arena or on the terraced seats.

The health of Theodora suffered from the strain of this terrible week, and she went to take the waters at the Pythian baths in Bithynia: a crowd of nobles and four thousand soldiers and eunuchs forming her retinue. Meantime Justinian set about the congenial task of re-erecting the Chalke (or front part of the palace), the church of St Sophia and the other ruined buildings, on a more splendid scale than before. We shall see later by what means he and his Empress obtained the prodigious sums of money they needed for their enormous expenditure. We will also postpone for a moment the early relations of Theodora to the general Belisarius and his romantic spouse, and consider the next important episode in which her character is seen.

In spite of the orthodoxy and religious zeal of Justinian, his wife had such influence over him and apart from him that in the year 535 she secured the see of Constantinople for the Monophysite Anthimus, to the unbounded delight of her sect and amidst the furious maledictions of the orthodox throughout the Empire. Rome was at that time regarded only as a sister Church of great authority and antiquity, but its venerable Bishop Agapetus was summoned to the Eastern metropolis and he succeeded in ousting Theodora's favourite. Agapetus, however, died soon afterwards at Constantinople, and Theodora now conceived the bold design of putting a Monophysite pope upon the throne at Rome itself. For the remarkable events which follow I am not using the "Anecdotes" at all. The story is told in substance by a contemporary ecclesiastical writer, Liberatus the Deacon, of Carthage, and the chronicler Victor, and is repeated, with large and legendary additions, by Anastasius, the Roman librarian, of the ninth century.

In the suite of Agapetus at Constantinople was an ambitious and courtly deacon named Vigilius, who contrived to let his accommodating temper become known to the Empress. He was taken to her apartments, and he promised, if the Roman see and a large sum of money were bestowed on him, to reinstate Anthimus and the other Monophysite bishops. In the meantime the Gothic ruler of Italy had appointed a certain Silverius to the Roman see. Theodora tested him with a request that he would restore Anthimus, but he refused; murmuring, it is said, as he wrote the letter: "This will cost me my life," as it did. The Byzantine general Belisarius had meantime taken and occupied Rome, and a few words must be said to introduce him, and his wife Antonina, into the story of Theodora.

I have previously mentioned an eleventh-century legend concerning Belisarius and Justinian and their wives. It was said that the two men had one day entered a house of ill-fame, found there two captive and fascinating Amazons named Antonia [Theodora] and Antonina, and married them. The myth seems to have crystallized about a belief that Antonina had risen from the same depths as Theodora, as the "Anecdotes" say, and the fact that Antonina was a woman of abandoned character and a leading lady in the service of the Empress seems to confirm this. In any case, she is openly assailed by Procopius (her husband's secretary) in his historical works as "capable of anything," and is described in the Lexicon of Suidas as "an infamous adulteress." She had married Belisarius, and accompanied him in 533 on his brilliant campaign for the recovery of Africa from the Vandals. With them went a handsome and foppish Thracian youth named Theodosius. He was fresh from the baptismal font, in which the patriarch had washed away his Monophysite heresy, and it was believed that the presence of so sacred a youth would bring luck to the fleet. Before they reached Carthage Antonina enjoyed the secret love of the youth, but a servant betrayed them, and Theodosius fled to Ephesus, where we must leave him for a time. It is said that Antonina had the servant's tongue cut out.

**THE EMPRESS THEODORA AND HER ATTENDANTS
MOSAIC OF THE 6TH CENTURY IN S. VITALE, RAVENNA**

Belisarius passed from the subjugation of North Africa to a victorious war in Italy, and he and Antonina were staying at a palace on the Pincian Hill at Rome when the deacon Vigilius—now, no doubt, a priest—came with the commands of Theodora. "Trump up a charge against Silverius, and send him to Constantinople," the order ran, according to the Roman librarian, and as the more authoritative Liberatus affirms that the charge was false, and was supported by mendacious witnesses and forged letters, there is no possibility of freeing Theodora from this grave imputation. The Pope was summoned to the palace, where Antonina lay on a couch with Belisarius at her feet. Antonina at once charged him with treasonable correspondence with the Goths. We may or may not believe the picturesque version of Anastasius: that the servants at once stripped the Pope of his robes, dressed him as a monk, and interred him in a distant monastery. It is certain, at least, that Silverius was, at Theodora's command, deposed on a false charge and thrust out of sight. Vigilius became Pope, and the fate of Silverius is unknown to history.

I cannot entirely omit a later sequel to this sacrilegious and unscrupulous deed, though it rests only on the feebler authority of Anastasius. For a few years Theodora demanded in vain that Vigilius should fulfil his promise. He had, he said, come to see the heinousness of such a promise, and could not discharge it.

In 544, therefore, Theodora sent an officer to Rome with a command which Anastasius gives in these words: "If you find him in the church of St Peter spare him, but if in the Lateran or the palace, or in any other church, put him on ship at once, and bring him to us. If you fail, I will, by Him that liveth for ever, have your skin torn from your body." It is known, at least, that Vigilius was shipped away from Rome at the end of 544; but that he was at once taken to Constantinople, and that Theodora had him dragged through the streets like a bear, is untrue. He reached Constantinople after her death. We cannot therefore follow the deposition of Vigilius as confidently as we follow the sordid story of his elevation, but we can have little doubt that Theodora punished him.

Another authentic episode of the time reveals the same unscrupulous disdain of principles in the patroness of the Monophysite sect. The story is told by Procopius, not in the "Anecdotes," but in his open and authoritative work "On the Persian War," in spite of his usual extreme care to suppress offensive details. The Prefect of Constantinople, John of Cappadocia, had incurred the bitter hostility of the Empress. The very unattractive portrait which Procopius supplies, and Gibbon reproduces, of John prevents us from thinking that in this case an innocent man was persecuted. While he freely promoted all the schemes of Justinian and his notorious steward to wring money out of the citizens—"by fair means and foul," as Zonaras says—he levied his private tithe on all their gains, and was popularly believed to indulge in secret the most sensual tastes and the even worse abominations of some pagan cult. He seems to have been the one man to regard Theodora with open disdain, and she retorted with venomous hate. Although guards surrounded his bedroom, he started every hour from his feverish slumbers to look for the expected assassin.

His value to Justinian enabled him to keep his position until the year 540, when Belisarius and Antonina returned from Italy to Constantinople.[10] Antonina remained in the city while her husband went against the Persians. She feverishly summoned her Thracian lover from the monastery in which he hypocritically lingered at Ephesus, but the wrath of Belisarius held him aloof. Whether or no Antonina then deliberately sought the intervention of the Empress, we cannot say, but she proceeded to merit it. She learned of Theodora's hatred of John, and conceived a plot for his destruction.

John had an ingenuous and amiable daughter who seems to have been not unacquainted with the political situation. Twice had the brilliant Belisarius been withdrawn to the city in a fit of jealousy, and there were rumours that the strong man was wearying of serving an Emperor who could do nothing but employ others and reap their glory. Antonina won her way to the heart and confidence of the girl, and betrayed to her that her husband was secretly disaffected. The artless Euphemia hastened to tell her father that there was a prospect of overthrowing Theodora, whom they both hated. Even John was deceived by the astute adventuress. It was arranged that Antonina should go to her suburban palace and meet John there during the night. We do not know that Theodora had a share in framing this diabolical plot, but it was now communicated to her by Antonina, and she at once pressed it and used her resources for carrying it out with safety. In the dead of the following night John entered the palace of the unscrupulous adventuress and listened to her whispers of treachery. Procopius says that Theodora had initiated the Emperor to the plot, and he had consented, but at the last moment sent a messenger to John not to see Antonina. This seems to be a piece of polite fiction in the interest of the Emperor; it is incredible that an astute and experienced minister would risk his neck after such a message. John went, and, in the apparently lonely palace, spoke his secret sympathy with the supposed design of Belisarius. No sooner had he uttered the words than a troop of imperial guards entered the room to arrest or assassinate him, but John also had brought soldiers and they enabled him to escape.

Had John gone straight to the palace of Justinian, he might still have saved his position. Instead, he fled nervously to the sanctuary, and Theodora hardened the mind of her husband. The wealthy and powerful noble was stripped of his estates and forced to enter the ranks of the clergy—one of the quaintest penalties of the time—in the suburb of Cyzicus. There the people whom he had oppressed might behold their once powerful enemy, the secret pagan and Sybarite, shaven and humiliated. It appears that Theodora was not yet satisfied, though she is not directly implicated by Procopius in the last act of the tragedy. The Bishop of Cyzicus was murdered, and as John was one of his many bitter enemies, he was arrested, scourged, and driven into exile and poverty. The fate of the unhappy Euphemia is unknown; she was probably compelled to enter a nunnery and weep there over the memory of the imperial tigress and her friend.

This story of perfidy, corruption and vindictiveness, which Procopius tells openly in his historical work, disposes us to believe the sequel, as it is narrated in the "Anecdotes," even if we must regard certain details of the narrative with reserve. There was with Belisarius in Persia a son of Antonina by a former husband (or lover) of the name of Photius. Bitterly ashamed of his mother's conduct, he accepted from Belisarius the charge of watching her lover Theodosius. At Ephesus he learned that Theodosius was in Constantinople, and soon caused him to fly back to Ephesus and cling to the altars which had sheltered so much vice and crime since the law of sanctuary had been established. The prelate, however, delivered Theodosius to the youth, and he was imprisoned in Cilicia.

Theodora was now eager to reward her friend and she had Photius arrested and scourged. He refused to reveal the prison in which he had placed Theodosius, but an officer was bribed to betray the secret, and the Thracian was brought to Theodora's apartments. Theodora then sent for Antonina and said: "Dear patrician, yesterday there fell into my hands a gem finer than any that mortal eye has ever seen; if you would like to see it, I will show it to you." Procopius concludes this astounding story by saying that Photius was kept for four years in the Empress's underground dungeons. Twice he escaped to the church of St Sophia, and twice he was dragged back; at length he got away from Constantinople and hid from the vindictiveness of Theodora in the robes of a monk. There are writers who flatly refuse to believe this statement, though the authentic actions of Theodora which we have described lend it some plausibility. Once more, however, the recently published works of the contemporary Bishop of Ephesus supply some confirmation. We read in them that Photius, son of Antonina, "became a monk for some cause or other"; but the pathos of Gibbon's picture of his fate is somewhat lessened when we read that he still enlivened the monastic life with his genial soldierly vices and led the troops to the plunder of the southern provinces.

I have mentioned the underground prisons of Theodora. Since it is from the "Anecdotes" alone that we learn of these dungeons, we should regard the statements with some reserve, and in this case there is additional reason for reserve. As Gibbon says: "Darkness is propitious to cruelty, but it is likewise favourable to calumny and fiction." Procopius seems to know too much of what passed in these carefully guarded places. Theodora doubtless had spies everywhere, and it would be easy enough for her to have her enemies conveyed into the palace during the night, or to some prison in remote provinces. Somewhere about this time (541), we learn from John of Ephesus, her episcopal friend Anthimus incurred the anger of the Emperor and disappeared. John assures us that Anthimus was hidden in the Empress's apartments for seven years. The two chamberlains who waited on him alone knew the secret, besides Theodora, until the day of her death. A woman with such resources could easily maintain private dungeons if she willed, and we can hardly say that it would be inconsistent with her character. But when Procopius minutely describes the fetid condition of these prisons, and tells how fiercely the prisoners were scourged, or how cords were tightened round their heads until the eyes started from their sockets, we are disposed to think that he has hastily admitted popular rumours which the judicious historian must set aside as unauthoritative.

On the other hand, a set of grave charges which Procopius combines with these statements are not without very serious confirmation. His most persistent charge against Justinian and Theodora is that they extorted money by cruel and flagrantly dishonest means. The superb buildings—the new palace, the new St Sophia, etc.—with which Justinian adorned the city absorbed stupendous sums of money; and the personal luxury and religious munificence of Theodora were such that a vast fortune would be needed to sustain them. It is equally certain that the money was largely raised by corrupt means. I have quoted the monastic writer Zonaras saying that Justinian raised money "by fair means and foul" and by "dishonest practices"; and the weighty testimony of Evagrius that the Emperor was of such "insatiable avarice" that he would share the "vile gain" of loose women impeaching wealthy men on false charges. The most that we can say for Justinian is that the money was not spent in personal luxury, and that it was extorted by subordinate officers. Agathias, another good authority, tells us how the steward Anatolius used to forge or suppress wills, and practise other dishonest arts, so that he might affix to houses and estates the strip of purple which betokened that they had become the property of the Emperor.

It is indisputable that the metropolis and the provinces suffered a most unjust and corrupt spoliation in order to sustain the splendour of the reign of Justinian and Theodora. Now Zonaras declares that the Empress was "worse than Justinian in extorting money, both by unlawful and lawful means," and that she was "especially ingenious in finding ways" to enrich herself. Wealthy men had charges of secret heresy or unnatural vice brought against them, and their fortunes passed into the coffers of Theodora. This must mean that her servants, as the informers, claimed for her the legal share of the confiscated property which went to an informer.

Here again, therefore, the charges in the "Anecdotes" are substantially confirmed. Not content with securing testaments in her favour, she had them forged or altered. She suborned witnesses to support charges of vice or heresy. The only difference from Zonaras is in the added allegation of physical cruelty, and on this point Procopius is at times explicit. A member of the blue party, Bassus, a refined and delicate youth, issued some squib upon the Empress, possibly referring to her early career. He was dragged from the church in which he had taken refuge, charged with and convicted of vice, and subjected, before an indignant crowd, to the barbaric mutilation with which such vice was then punished. His property went to Theodora—in part, I assume, for laying information. Usually it was the greens who suffered. So angry were the people that they accused Theodora of a secret (but "impotent") love of the sinister Syrian financier, Peter Barsymes, who had succeeded John of Cappadocia in the duty of governing and exploiting Constantinople. The restraint with which Procopius represents her love as "impotent" lends credit to his other charges. An accusation of an actual liaison would have been more credible than some of the stories he reproduces.

A few episodes remain in the career of Theodora from which we may confirm our impression of her remarkable personality. Unfortunately, they rest entirely on the authority of the "Anecdotes," and cannot be pressed; we know only from another, and a sound, authority that Belisarius was maliciously attacked and disgraced after his many brilliant campaigns on behalf of the Empire.

To the evils of oppression, spoliation, corruption of justice, and persecution which afflicted the Eastern Empire under Justinian and Theodora there was added in the year 542 the deadly scourge of the plague, and for several years in succession it scattered the seeds of death over the broad provinces. Justinian at length contracted it, and became dangerously ill. As he had no son, the question of the succession to the throne was very naturally discussed, and the generals Belisarius and Buza in the Persian camp incautiously expressed themselves on the rumour that Justinian was dying, or were represented to the Empress by her spies as having done so. She at once ordered them to Constantinople. Buza is said to have been lodged in her underground prisons, and Belisarius was stripped of his rank, his guard and his immense wealth. A eunuch was sent by Theodora to secure the large sums he had deposited in the east, and the chosen soldiers who formed his personal guard, and were maintained at his expense, were distributed among the army. The greatest soldier that the Eastern Empire ever possessed, the most brilliant contributor to the success of Justinian's reign, a man who had preserved his loyalty in a decade of supreme military power, he was received at the palace with cold haughtiness, and retired in deep distress to his mansion. When at length he observed the approach of a servant of the Empress, he prepared for death. Instead of death, however, Theodora's officer brought this extraordinary message: "You know what you have done to me, Belisarius, but I forgive your crimes on account of what your wife has done for me. Hope for the future through her, but know that we shall hear how you bear yourself to Antonina." And the episode closes with the great soldier kissing the feet of his perfidious wife, vowing that he will be her slave, and accepting the office of master of the stables in the imperial service which he had so gloriously illumined. Theodora had secured an enormous sum of money and intimidated an enemy.

Up to the last year of Theodora's life (548) the implacable writer of the "Anecdotes" pursues his record of her misdeeds. Ever attentive to the men who might some day dislodge her and her relatives from the palace, Theodora watched with especial jealousy the grave and distinguished nephew of the Emperor, Germanus, and his three children. His eldest daughter Justina was in her nineteenth year, yet none had dared, out of fear of Theodora, to offer marriage to her. Theodora then decided to unite the fortunes of the two houses, and secure the succession, by commanding Justina to wed her grandson Anastasius—obviously the son of an illegitimate daughter of the Empress, since it was little over twenty years since her marriage to Justinian. Justina refused, and was vindictively married by the Empress to a common officer. She then commanded the daughter of Belisarius, Joannina, to wed Anastasius. Procopius, forgetting that he has stripped Belisarius of almost all his wealth (an exaggeration), says that Theodora wanted in this way to secure the general's fortune, but we may assume that Theodora was mainly endeavouring to secure the succession to the throne for her grandson. Her own health was delicate, and Justinian was well over sixty. Belisarius shrank from the union, and even Antonina seems to have refused to further it. All knew that a struggle impended between the families of Justinian and Theodora, and it must have been the general feeling that the former would win. Theodora is said to have angrily united Joannina to her grandson in the loose popular form of marriage; indeed later rumour said that she had the young woman violated first.

Another matrimonial interference of the Empress in her later years exhibits the better features of her character. An ambitious general, Artabanes, sought and obtained the hand of Justinian's niece, whom he had delivered from peril in Africa. Soon afterwards, however, a woman appeared who claimed that she was the legitimate wife of Artabanes. She appealed to the Empress, and Theodora forced Artabanes to take back his humbler wife. Procopius tells this story in one of the historical works in which he was careful not to offend the ruling powers, and he courteously adds that "it was the nature of Theodora to befriend afflicted women." It is the only instance of her doing so that has reached us, and, ungracious as it may seem to cast a doubt upon the pure humanity of that one recorded good deed, one is compelled to suggest that it was not to her interest to see a niece of Justinian married to a successful commander.

On the 29th of June 548, after a reign of twenty-one years, Theodora died of cancer. Her body was embalmed and exposed for public veneration in the golden-roofed Triclinon of the palace. There, still dressed in the imperial purple, still bearing the magnificent diadem for a few days, she lay on a golden bed for friends and enemies to gaze upon the last state of one of the most remarkable personalities of the time.

The character of Theodora must be interpreted in so purely oriental a sense that it is difficult for the modern European to understand it. Whether Greek or Syrian in origin, she was an incarnation of the spirit of the great metropolis in whose life Syria and Greece were so singularly blended. It is useless any longer to cast doubt upon her earlier career. She was reared in that old theatrical world in which moral restraint was wholly unknown; and her beauty, vivacity and nervous strength make it probable enough that she was distinguished in it for dissoluteness. That in her later life she spent vast sums of money on the Church and philanthropy is unquestionable; nor would I doubt for a moment that she was perfectly sincere in her endless conversations with holy men. But her passionate nature, difficult position and supple intelligence gave her a genius for casuistry, and she fell into vices far worse than the vices of her youth. Quite apart from the attacks of her bitter, anonymous enemy, we have ample evidence that she was vindictive, cruel, unscrupulous, dishonest and callous. To send a bejewelled cross to the holy church at Jerusalem, or build a monastery, she would ruin and despoil an innocent man or wreck the happiness of a woman: to secure the preaching of the true faith in Christ she would depose an upright Pope on forged evidence and put a scoundrel in the most sacred chair in Christendom. It was the temper of Constantinople—to rise from vice and folly to defend the doctrines of the Church and enforce them with the dagger or the torch. The further things that are said of her in the famous "Anecdotes" must, for the serious historian, remain unproved but not improbable.

CHAPTER IV

SOPHIA

The Emperor Justinian continued for seventeen years after the death of Theodora to occupy the golden throne and keep the throne of his consort vacant. As he approached the term of his life the palace throbbed with the impassioned struggle which always disturbed the last year of a childless Emperor, and the courtiers took sides with the relatives of Theodora or of Justinian, according to their forecast of the future. On the one side was Sophia, the niece and heiress of Theodora: on the other the Emperor's nephew, Justin. Sophia, however, was diplomatic in the pursuit of her ambition. She discarded the heresy which it had been expedient to cherish while her aunt lived, accepted the hand of Justin, and settled with him in his palace by the shore, near Theodora's palace-monastery, to await impatiently the retirement of the aged Emperor.

Justinian, says the contemporary lawyer Evagrius, passed in the year 565 to "those tortures which are provided in the nether world" for rulers who despoil their subjects. The "greatness" of Justinian seems to have been discovered by his mediæval admirers; contemporary writers usually, and justly, attribute to his great general Belisarius the military triumphs which partially restored the outline of the Empire during his reign, and to the (probably) pagan lawyer Tribonian the compilation of the famous Justinian Code, leaving to the Emperor himself the odium of those unprincipled and unjustifiable extortions which weakened and distressed his subjects. However that may be, the Emperor's last years were framed in a decaying world, and the citizens of Constantinople regarded with hesitating admiration the superb edifices which he had raised. His nephew Justin was "lord of the palace" (Curopalates), and had ample opportunity to ensure the succession.

A profoundly courtly and accommodating poet of the time, Corippus, has left us a touching account of the accession of Justin and Sophia. The noble Callinicus comes one night to rouse them in their suburban palace with the distressing news that Justinian is no more. The spouses arise, and sit discussing the situation in a room looking over the moonlit Sea of Marmora, when a group of Senators enter, and urge Justin to accept the purple. He shrinks from the terrible dignity until their tears and prayers override his modesty, and, as the first faint flush of dawn outlines the houses, they walk sadly through the streets to the sacred palace. The guards and Candidates and servants line the long avenue from the iron gate to the bronze door of Daphne, and many tears are shed over the body of the late Emperor, which lies on a lofty golden catafalque. Sophia produces a piece of embroidery on which all the illustrious victories of the great Emperor are depicted. By this time the report has spread in the town, and the citizens fly to the palace. The blues and greens in festive dress, with their respective standards, line the path to St Sophia, whither they go to ask grace, and they return to the palace to put on the robes of state. Then four strong soldiers raise Justin aloft, standing on a shield, and the patriarch crowns him and Sophia, and the Emperor passes to the Hippodrome to receive the loyal greeting of his people.

When we turn from this moving description to the prosy pages of the lawyer Evagrius we find—without surprise—that Corippus has very generously drawn upon the poet's licence. Evagrius bluntly observes that Justin "took" the purple the moment his uncle was dead, and suggests that the officers of the palace were already in his service. The death of Justinian was kept secret until Justin and Sophia had been crowned and were suddenly presented to the populace in their sheen of gold and jewels. Another contemporary writer from whom we learn much, Bishop John of Ephesus, adds a very credible and instructive detail. Sophia had been a Monophysite, like her aunt Theodora, until, in the year 562, an astute bishop had pointed out to her that Justinian was reluctant to set on the throne another woman who believed that there was only one nature in Christ. By this powerful argument Sophia was happily convinced that there were two natures in Christ, and accepted the orthodox baptism. It is our first glimpse of the character of the new Empress, and is quite in harmony with all that we know of her. She was the niece of Theodora.

The new reign opened auspiciously. As the Emperor stood in the royal gallery, or kathisma, overlooking the Hippodrome, to receive the plaudits of his people, the cry was raised, and soon ran through the crowded benches, that he should undo at once the dishonesty of his predecessor. If we may believe the poet, the citizens had, with great forethought, brought with them the bills of the treasury's debts to them, and waved their tablets before the kathisma. One is tempted to believe that it was part of Justin's plan to outstrip his cousins and other rivals. The gold also was produced with theatrical promptness, and from the glittering pile heaped at his feet the Emperor discharged all the debts in full. Sophia sustained her husband's policy. We read that a few years after her accession she gathered the moneylenders of the city at her palace, paid all the debts due to them by the people, and ensured a large measure of popularity.

In virtue of the genial feeling engendered by this generous conduct the new Emperor and Empress were enabled to strengthen their throne at the expense of their rivals. The chief rival to the hopes of Justin had been another nephew of the late Emperor, Germanus, and his sons: a noble and gifted figure in comparison with the mean and petty intrigues of Justin. We saw how instinctively Theodora had hated this family. Germanus had ended his brilliant and stainless career in war, but his son Justin seems to have inherited his character and popularity, and certainly inherited his misfortunes. Obscure references to revolt in the chronicles of the time close with the curt statement that Justin and other nobles were put to death. Justin had been banished to Alexandria, and may have expressed resentment. Sophia joined with her husband in what we are tempted to regard as murder. "Justin and Sophia," says the sardonic Evagrius, "did not abate their fury against the son of Germanus" until his severed and grisly head was exhibited to them. The metaphors of the time are so true to life that the historian is often puzzled as to the exact details of such episodes. The truth is, as we shall soon realize, that the Byzantine Empire, in spite of its opulence, its art and its religious ardour, was sinking toward barbarism.

For a few years Justin and Sophia ruled with moderation and success in their decaying dominion. The administration of justice was reformed and the decoration of churches and public buildings proceeded. Another palace—the Sophian palace—was added to the growing cluster of mansions which made up the imperial town. Justin cleared a vast site in the quarter where he and Sophia had lived, built for her a palace and hippodrome, and raised two large brass statues of himself and the Empress. In this marble-lined palace, in the imperial quarters, or in the Hieria palace across the water, or the new suburban palace at Blachernæ in the north, Sophia passed the first nine years of her reign without taking any apparent part in public affairs. Then her husband lost his mind, and she began to reveal her true character.

From his early tolerance Justin had passed to the temper of the persecutor, and the groans of the Monophysites were heard throughout the Empire. Whether this new phase of activity contributed to, or resulted from, his growing insanity, and how far Sophia was implicated in it, we do not know; but by the year 574 Justin had become a dangerous maniac. Bars had to be placed at his windows, and his servants had carefully to avoid the imperial teeth; while, in his less dangerous hours, he would shriek with delight, or bark like a dog, as the servants pulled him along the corridors in a small cart fitted with a throne. The commander of the Excubitors who guarded or amused him was a tall and very handsome Thracian officer named Tiberius, whose fine bluish eyes, light hair and beard, fresh florid complexion and manly form, pleased the eye of the Empress, and she induced Justin, in a lucid hour toward the end of the year 574, to raise him to the rank of Cæsar. Writers of the time describe with great feeling this last sane act of Justin II. The Empress, the patriarch and his clergy, and the nobles and Senators, were summoned to the palace, and Justin held to them a long and deeply penitent discourse, lamenting his sins and cruelty, and recommending his wife and his Empire to the fortunate Tiberius. The scepticism of the historian is apparently silenced by the weighty assurance of Bishop John that this remarkable speech of the insane ruler was taken down in shorthand,[11] but the publication of such a statement would be by no means inconsistent with the character of Sophia, and we must interpret the narrative with some liberality.

In most of the historians we read that, when Justin died and Tiberius ascended the throne, a romantic scene was witnessed in the Hippodrome and the astute Sophia was outwitted by her handsome favourite. Sophia, it is said, proposed to marry him, but when the crowd in the Hippodrome cried, "Let us see a Roman Empress," he replied, through the herald, that an Empress already existed, and that her name was similar to that of a church in the city, the position of which he indicated. The citizens at once solved the conundrum, acclaimed his secret wife Anastasia, and laughed at the discomfiture of Sophia, who retired to her palace in anger and mortification.

The entire inaccuracy of this legend, which has found its way into Gibbon and all the earlier historians, must confirm our feeling of reserve in reading the Byzantine chroniclers. It is true that Sophia designed to marry Tiberius, and we may confidently assume that his marriage was a secret at the time when she raised him to the cæsarship. But we now know from John of Ephesus that Sophia learned of the marriage of Tiberius long before the death of her husband, and the citizens of Constantinople cannot have been unaware of it. Bishop John observes that she looked with dry eyes on the burly figure of her husband as he shrieked and laughed in his toy chariot; he was, she said, deservedly punished for his sins, and the Empire would now fall into her more capable hands. She induced the Senate to consent to the elevation of the imposing officer, put an edifying discourse into the mouth of Justin—unless one prefers the singular story of his hour of lucidity and eloquence—and bade the patriarch clothe him in the glittering insignia of a Cæsar. We can imagine her mortification when she discovered that he was already married.

The entry of Ino, wife of Tiberius, into the roll of the Byzantine Empresses is romantic enough without this discredited story of the concealment of her existence until her husband was on the throne. Tiberius was a simple provincial soldier who had won his way to the captainship of the guards and to the purple by his fascinating appearance. Gibbon represents beauty as one of his many virtues; it was certainly much more conspicuous than any other virtue he may have possessed. He came from Daphnudium, which commentators place in the province of Thrace, and it seems to have been while he was on military service in that town that he met Ino. She was then married to a soldier, and must have been older than Tiberius, since we read that he was betrothed to her daughter. The daughter died, however, and, as the husband also presently died, Tiberius gave his hand to the widow, a rustic and undistinguished matron of a frontier province. When Tiberius was promoted to the captainship of the imperial guards, Ino came to Constantinople, and lived there in obscurity with her surviving daughters, Charito and Constantina. Here the simple provincial family learned that Tiberius had been raised to the dazzling height of the cæsarship.

But it soon became apparent that Ino had, by her elevation, incurred the resentment of the all-powerful Empress. It is said that Justin, in one of his lucid hours, urged that Tiberius should take up his residence in the sacred palace, and that, since the flesh of young men was weak, Ino should reside with him. Sophia bluntly refused her consent. "Fool," Bishop John represents her as saying, "do you who have invested yourself with the insignia of royalty wish to make me as great a simpleton as yourself? As long as I live I will never give my kingdom and crown to another, nor shall another enter here." Tiberius, knowing that she might still arrest his progress toward the throne, submitted, and Ino and her daughters were installed in the splendid Hormisdas palace—now purified of Theodora's monks and hermits— which Justinian had decorated for his mistress. Such quarters as Tiberius was permitted to have in the main palace were poor and inadequate; he preferred to retire each night to the mansion by the shore.

During the four years that followed Sophia ruled with the power and rigour of an autocrat. When Tiberius, seeing the vast sums of money which she and Justin had amassed, and affecting to regard it as unjustly extorted, began to squander it on the people, she deprived him of the key of the treasury. It is not unlikely that he was trying to win popularity independently of her. When nobles, mindful of her attitude, asked if they might visit the wife of the Cæsar, she angrily told them to "be quiet," as it was "no business of theirs." It was, in fact, rumoured in the city that, as two contemporary writers assure us, she urged Tiberius to divorce his wife and prepare to marry her. We shall see later that, in spite of the rigorous teaching of the Church, a Byzantine Emperor, with the tacit connivance of the archbishop, more than once divorced his wife. As Justin lingered, and no one dared visit the trembling ladies in the Hormisdas palace, the courage of the provincial matron failed and she fled back to her native town.

In September 578, however, Justin passed the imperial crown to Tiberius, and died nine days afterwards. Sophia had more than the strength, but less than the penetration, of her aunt Theodora, and she very quickly discovered that she had misjudged the submissive Cæsar. I have already rejected the fable that he now revealed to the citizens for the first time the existence of his wife. It is more plausible to assume that his servants were at work among the citizens ensuring that, the moment he appeared in the kathisma in his stiff gold tunic, the cry should ring out: "Let us see the Roman Empress." He submitted with alacrity to the voice of the people. Officers of distinction were at once despatched to Thrace, to bring Ino to the palace, and Sophia retired in great chagrin to her quarters.

Ino, like so many of the Roman Empresses, remains a mere name to which are attached a number of singular and romantic adventures, but a little consideration of her behaviour in these adventures affords an occasional glimpse of her personality. A simple and, no doubt, quite uncultivated provincial matron, she had gladly exchanged the troubled splendours of a palace for the tranquil plainness of her former home in Daphnudium. The faithful Tiberius had occasionally visited her in her retirement, and it was doubtless understood that when the death of Justin made him free to defy Sophia she should return to the Court. The day had arrived, and her humble home in the provinces was now besieged by nobles and officers who were eager to escort her across the sea to the bronze-roofed palace. "Come in the morning, and we will start immediately," Ino told them. In the morning, however, they found that Ino and her daughters, disliking the pomp of an escort and the scenes which their passage would cause, had quietly departed during the night, and they followed in very evil temper to Constantinople.

Tiberius and the Senators and nobles met Ino at the city quay, and she was presently clothed in the gold tunic and purple mantle of the Empress. In a covered litter, accompanied by a crowd of eunuchs and chamberlains, she proceeded from the palace to the great church of St Sophia between the living hedges of the populace. It was here that her name was changed to Anastasia. Since the introduction of Empresses with provincial or pagan names a custom had arisen of changing the name at coronation, and the right to do so had been genially accorded to the people. On this occasion the ceremony was more animated than usual. The greens, standing under their banner at their appointed station, raised the cry of "Helena"; from the next station the blues raised the counter-cry of "Anastasia," and "so fiercely did they contend," says the bishop, "with rival shouts for the honour of naming her that a great and terrible riot ensued and all the people were in confusion." The blues seem to have been in the majority, and from her baptism of blood Ino emerged with the royal name of Anastasia; from the cathedral she presently returned to the sacred palace as Empress or "Queen" Antastasia.

From that moment we lose sight of the new Empress, and must imagine her peacefully vegetating in the marble-lined halls and the superb gardens of her palaces. The interest passes once more to Sophia. As soon as she realized that Tiberius had shaken off her control she removed large sums of money and much treasure from the main palace, and went to live in her Sophian palace by the Julian Port. Tiberius, knowing her temper and the vicissitudes of imperial life at Constantinople, regarded this action with distrust, and tried to disarm her. "Dwell here, and be content, as my mother," he urged, pressing her to remain in Daphne. She refused to do so, and he was content to assign her an imperial Court and make it known by decree that she was to be honoured as his "mother." He then married Charito, the daughter of Anastasia, to a distinguished officer, raised him to the rank of Cæsar, and prepared to meet the intrigues of his adopted mother.

The strong and ambitious woman chafed in the small world to which she found herself reduced and soon began to quarrel with the Emperor. Justin had begun the building of a lighthouse at the Julian Port, near the great brass statues of himself and Sophia, and Tiberius pressed Sophia to complete it. She pointed out that it was a work of public usefulness, and therefore the Emperor must undertake it. Tiberius refused, and the relations between them were strained. Here, unfortunately, our informant becomes less generous with the interesting historical matter which he mingles with his narrative of

Church affairs. He tells us only that the "proud and malignant" old Empress "set on foot plots without number against Tiberius," and was at length deprived of her imperial status and retinue. Sophia was probably still in the prime of life—Byzantine women usually married about the age of fifteen—and this drastic step would merely dispose her to more violent action, but it soon became apparent that a greater power than that of kings and queens was about to intervene. Tiberius was consumptive. In the summer of 582, after less than four years' enjoyment of his easily won honours, he felt that the end was approaching and sought a successor.

A contemporary ecclesiastical writer seems to suggest Sophia when he tells us that Tiberius died of poison, administered to him in a dish of mulberries, but we may accept the kindlier view that he was delicate and consumptive, and brought about a crisis by some indiscretion at table. A popular officer from the Persian wars named Maurice was in the city at the time, and Tiberius—passing over, for some unknown reason, the elder daughter of Anastasia and her husband—offered him the hand of the younger daughter, Constantina, and the crown. Maurice, an undistinguished provincial like Tiberius—he came from Cappadocia—was crowned on 5th August, and married Constantina a few days afterwards. It is expressly recorded that the marriage was celebrated with great magnificence. Maurice was a robust, clean-shaven, ruddy-featured young man: a man whose goodwill was as obvious as his incapacity to restore a stricken Empire. The personal features of the Empresses are never described by the Byzantine writers, but we are told that Constantina made a brave show in her bridal tunic of cloth of gold, edged with purple and sprinkled with diamonds, amongst the crowd of richly dressed nobles. The citizens honoured the new dynasty with banquets and illuminations, little dreaming of the horrible tragedy which would extinguish it in blood.

Tiberius died a week later, and Anastasia seems to have survived her husband only a few years. Sophia returned to the palace after the death of Tiberius, and spent her last years in tranquillity. But the twenty years' reign of Maurice is barren of interest for the biographer of the Empresses, and we must pass quickly over its mediocre annals to its tragic termination. Twelve months after the coronation Constantinople was again seething with joyous excitement. Constantina had a son, and it was the first time in two hundred years that a boy had been "born in the Porphyra": an appalling comment on Byzantine court life. Very costly gifts were brought to the little Theodosius, as he lay with his mother, a week or two later, under sheets of cloth of gold to receive the ladies of the city. Four years later the boy was made Cæsar, and brothers and sisters followed him into the world with great regularity, until Maurice saw a family of nine children about him, giving promise of an endless dynasty. Anastasia died a few years afterwards. Sophia is mentioned only once more in the chronicles. Fourteen or fifteen years after the coronation of Maurice we read that Sophia and Constantina presented the Emperor with a magnificent crown, and that he offended them by piously suspending it over the altar in one of the churches. We do not know in what year she died, but it is clear that she did not live to witness the horrible fate of Maurice and Constantina. No grave blunder was committed by Maurice as long as she remained in the palace, but it must have been soon after her death that he began to incur the disdain of the people and the army, and to prepare the tragedy which closed his life and that of his Empress.

The causes of that tragedy belong to history; it is enough to note here that Maurice converted the disdain of the troops into fierce anger by refusing to redeem a number of them who had fallen into the merciless hands of the barbarians. From that moment even the rabble of Constantinople could insult him with impunity. One day when he and his eldest son Theodosius were walking barefoot at the head of a religious procession, they were stoned and compelled to run for their lives. On another day the crowd found a man with some resemblance to Maurice, clothed him in black, crowned him with garlic, and drove him on an ass through the city amidst a chorus of jeering and execration. Then some troops which he had ordered to winter in the hard lands beyond the Danube revolted and marched upon Constantinople under their leader Phocas. Maurice nervously ordered games in the Hippodrome, and bade the people not be alarmed. They were not alarmed, as they had little idea of loyalty to the despised Emperor, and there was as yet no question of raising to the purple the brutal officer in command of the insurgent troops.

Phocas and his troops had now reached the outskirts of the city. One day Theodosius and his father-in-law, Germanus, were hunting in that region when a messenger of Phocas accosted them and proposed that Theodosius should replace his father on the throne, or else Germanus should take the crown. Although they refused, Maurice heard of the invitation, and accused them of conspiracy. Germanus fled to the altar, and Maurice, scourging his son for warning Germanus, sent guards to drag him from the church. This provoked a rising of the people, and Maurice fled across the water with his family. Maurice, now an old man of sixty-three, was nearly wrecked in crossing during the night, and was racked with gout. He had some years before befriended the King of Persia, and he now sent Theodosius to ask help from that monarch. The young man was, however, presently recalled by a messenger who said that his father intended to meet his fate with religious resignation. He returned to find that his father and five brothers had been butchered, and his mother and three sisters confined in a private house, at the command of the Emperor Phocas.

Phocas, a little, deformed, red-haired man of repulsive appearance and character, had at the last moment taken the purple, and won the people by showering gold among them as he drove in the imperial litter, drawn by four white horses, from the church to the palace. On the following day his wife Leontia was crowned. As she went from the palace to St Sophia another riot occurred between the blues and greens, and, when Phocas sent an officer to quell the disturbance, some of them threateningly retorted: "Maurice is still alive."[12] Soldiers were at once sent to the village on the Bay of Nicomedia which Maurice had reached with his family. The five young boys were beheaded before their father's eyes, and he was then despatched. When Theodosius returned a few days later, he fled to the church, but he in turn was dragged out by the soldiers and put to death.

Constantina and her daughters were confined "in the house of Leo," the chronicler says, and we may assume that this was a private house in the district. Unfortunately for the unhappy Empress, the new reign at once gave rise to intense disgust, and she became involved in plots to overthrow Phocas. The new Emperor was a vulgar and brutal soldier, plunging at once into an orgy of blood and licence. The Empress Leontia—probably a Syrian, as Phocas had a Syrian treasurer named Leontius—is said to have been "as bad as Phocas," but we have no detailed information about her. She was probably one of the strangest in the strange gallery of the Byzantine Empresses. Within a couple of years a plot was formed to drive this incongruous pair from the throne they had usurped, and the patrician Germanus, who was the chief conspirator, sent a eunuch to deliver Constantina and her daughters and bring them in secrecy to the cathedral. It was felt that Constantina, feeble and passive as she seems to have been throughout her stirring experiences, would be the best figure to attract the sympathies of the people. It is one of the many proofs of the appalling degradation to which the Roman Empire had sunk that the plot failed. The issue turned, not on honour and manliness, but on greed. Phocas had been liberal with money and sports, and the greens, rejecting the smaller offers of the agents of Germanus, assembled in the Hippodrome to acclaim the tyrant and revile the helpless widow of their Emperor.

Phocas turned ferociously upon the conspirators. Several nobles were put to death; Germanus and Philippicus, the brother-in-law of Maurice, were condemned to shave their heads and enlist in the ranks of the clergy. The more terrible fate seemed to be in store for Constantina and her daughters when a troop of soldiers burst into the cathedral and threatened to drag them from the altars, but the archbishop Cyriacus manfully protested, and Phocas had to swear to spare their lives before the patriarch would suffer them to leave the sanctuary. They were confined in a nunnery, apparently in or near the city.

In this confinement Constantina presently heard that the bloody reign of Phocas was becoming intolerable, and she was encouraged to enter into communication once more with Germanus. Whether or no the plot was inspired by Phocas himself, the female servant who carried the secret messages from the priestly home of Germanus to the nunnery of Constantina betrayed them to the tyrant, and he hastened to rid the Empire of the last reminders of Maurice. Constantina was tortured and compelled to name one of the patricians. By the same fearful means a number of the nobility were accused, and the city was once more driven into mourning. The hands and feet of the accused were cut off, and their mangled bodies were then burned alive in the public places. Even the daughter of Germanus, the young widow of Theodosius, was put to death. For Constantina and her daughters the brutal tyrant devised an exquisite punishment. They were taken across the water to the spot, on the Bay of Nicomedia, where Maurice and his sons had been put to death, and there the heads were struck from the bodies of Constantina and her three innocent daughters. The Empire of Rome had touched a deeper depth than it had ever done in its pagan days.

CHAPTER V

MARTINA

Over the eight years' reign of Phocas and his consort we have little disposition, and not much occasion, to linger. The Empress Leontia is characterized for us only by the one contemptuous phrase that she was "as bad as Phocas." We may trust that she equalled him neither in brutality nor licentiousness, but the slender indications suggest that she was some such low type of Syrian woman as a coarse and vicious soldier would be likely to choose for his companion. A few words must suffice to explain her exit from the imperial stage and the introduction of a fairer woman to the throne.

As the discontent increased in Constantinople, Phocas, his brutality fostered by indulgence and vice, turned upon his subjects with increasing savagery. Plots were discovered or suspected, and hands and feet and heads fell under the axes of the guards. At length Priscus heard that an upright and distinguished commander, who governed the African province, had cast off his allegiance to Phocas, and he invited Heraclius to come and seize the throne. Heraclius was too old to embark on so adventurous an enterprise, but in the spring of 609 he sent a fleet under the command of his son Heraclius and at the same time entrusted his nephew Nicetas with an army which was to range the coast of Africa and occupy Egypt. The curious statement, repeated in most historians, that whichever of the young men reached Constantinople first was to have the crown, is shown by a recently translated manuscript to be inaccurate, as we might suspect.[13] Heraclius dallied in the Mediterranean until his cousin had made progress, and it was not until 3rd October 610 that the liberating fleet, exhibiting at the prow of its commander's vessel a picture of the Virgin which angels had brought from heaven, came in sight of Constantinople. At once Phocas found a tide of desertions, and, after a feeble naval engagement on the following day, a Sunday, he fled in despair to the palace. So far was he abandoned that a citizen, whose wife he had violated, penetrated the palace during the night, dragged him to the quay, and took him on a boat to the fleet early on the Monday morning. Nicephorus, a later patriarch of Constantinople, gives us an appalling picture of his fate—and of Constantinople. He was at once cut to pieces, the member by which he had notoriously sinned was carried on a pole through the city, and his bleeding trunk was dragged through the streets and burned. Of the Empress Leontia and her fate we have no information.

The young Heraclius—he was in his thirty-sixth year, a robust, broad-chested man with fine grey eyes and light curly hair—must not be held responsible for the excesses of the Byzantine mob, though we shall not find him a man of delicate feeling. He proceeded at once, not only to assume the purple, but to provide Constantinople with an Empress. Fabia, daughter of an African noble named Rogatus, was in Constantinople with the wife of the elder Heraclius when it was announced that the African fleet lay in the Grecian waters. Phocas heard that the mother and the betrothed of his opponent were in the city, and they must have had a narrow escape from death. He was content, however, to confine them in a nunnery or penitentiary, and from this hazardous position Fabia was released to find her lover master of Constantinople. She was a beautiful and delicate girl, and the biographer must feel some impatience that the few Empresses of this more attractive character are so slenderly noticed by the chroniclers, while they dilate, as far as their prejudice against mere women will allow them, on the sins or audacities of the bolder Empresses.

Heraclius does not seem to have been eager to assume the purple, and, knowing as we do the accidents of imperial life and the degradation of the Empire, we can believe that he was sincere in offering the crown to Priscus, the son-in-law of Phocas. Priscus refused, and the long ceremonies of coronation at once proceeded. After the coronation in St Sophia he was married to Fabia, and, under the name of the Empress Eudocia, she entered the sacred palace which Leontia had vacated. But the story of Eudocia is brief and uninteresting, and we hardly make her acquaintance before a premature death removes her from the scene.

Indeed, the only details recorded of Eudocia are that she bore her husband two children in the first two years of her marriage and died of the strain. With the birth of her first child, Epiphania Eudocia, is connected one of those lively incidents which so well illustrate the character of the later Roman Empire, even under its better rulers. The patrician Priscus had refused the purple, but it came to the ears of Heraclius that he was secretly disaffected and abusive, and the Emperor chose a dramatic moment for disarming him. He invited Priscus to be godfather to the little Epiphania, and, in the midst of the ceremony, in view of the crowd of nobles and priests, charged him with his treachery. Striking Priscus on the face with a book which lay at hand—probably a Prayer Book—he directed that his head be shaven on the spot, and the great noble passed from the life of camp and Court to one of those monasteries of the Empire which harboured many such strange inmates.

In the following May (612) Eudocia bore a son, Heraclius Constantinas, and her frail constitution never recovered from the strain. She had gone during the summer to the healthier palace at Blachernæ, to the north of Constantinople, and there an attack of epilepsy carried her off in the month of August. It is painful to read that the funeral of this fine and delicate Empress was disgraced by one of the most repulsive exhibitions of Byzantine coarseness. The body was conveyed by water to the city, and borne solemnly through the streets to the great church between the mourning citizens. Just as the body was passing a certain window, a maid-servant, who was watching the procession, carelessly spat and the wind carried the spittle to the robes of the dead queen. The girl was burned alive on Eudocia's tomb for the involuntary insult, and even her mistress escaped only by concealing herself.

Two years afterwards Heraclius married again. The new Byzantine Empress, whose name stands at the head of this chapter, was one of those strong and ambitious women who generally contrive, either by their vices or their crimes, to break through the anti-feminist reserve of the later Greek writers, but in this case the prejudice is increased and we follow Martina with difficulty through her long and adventurous career. She was the niece of Heraclius, and, in spite of the support she gave to her husband in his brilliant defence of eastern Christendom against the Persians, she remains under the shadow of the sin of incest.

Historians have devised many reasons for the audacity of Heraclius in marrying his niece, but we need hardly assume more than that she had a beauty and charm which the ecclesiastical writers disdain to confess. Her father was dead, and she lived in Constantinople with her mother Maria, sister of Heraclius, who had married a second time. Young, spirited and ambitious, she welcomed the passion of the Emperor, and was prepared with him to override every ecclesiastical scruple. The archbishop Sergius, a friendly and very able counsellor of the Emperor, tried in vain to dissuade them. Heraclius coolly observed that his objections were quite natural from his episcopal point of view, but it was useless to urge them, and the patriarch discreetly stood aside and allowed another priest to marry them. According to a reliable historian the patriarch himself afterwards crowned her in the great hall of the palace, and no doubt his bold and politic action silenced the angry murmurs which arose in the Hippodrome. It was only when, in the course of time, defective children were born of the marriage—the first son was wry-necked, the second deaf—when Heraclius himself ended a brilliant career in pain and humiliation, and when Martina passed from public life under a suspicion of murder, that Constantinople discovered the action of a divine curse and darkened the memory of Martina.

So prejudiced are later historians against Martina that even Gibbon has contracted something of their feeling, and suggested that a surrender to the charms, if not the arts, of Martina explains that remarkable indolence which Heraclius betrayed during the next few years, when the advancing Persians were rending his Empire and threatening to sweep Christianity out of Asia. We need not discuss here the problem of the Emperor's alleged supineness during those years of disaster. The most recent biographer of Heraclius, Signor Pernice ("L'Imperatore Eraclio"), emphatically denies that Heraclius was indolent, and more authoritative historians, like Professor Bury, observe that the lack of funds and troops, and other internal difficulties, placed a formidable restraint on the very capable Emperor. When the war-drums beat at length, we shall find Martina, in spite of pregnancy, accompanying the Emperor in his long and arduous campaigns, and this gives us a right to assume that she supported him in the long years of preparation and organization.

At one time, three or four years after their marriage, it seemed that they would desert the sinking vessel of the Byzantine Empire and return to the tranquillity of Africa. Two devastating waves—the Persians to the south and the Avars to the north—were advancing across the impotent provinces, and it looked as though the little that was left of the Eastern Empire must soon be swallowed up in the mighty clash of their conflict. Egypt, Syria and Palestine were in the hands of the Persians, who looted and desecrated the most sacred shrines of Christendom. Famine resulted from the loss of the grain-bearing provinces, and plague followed closely upon famine. Heraclius and Martina put their treasures on a fleet of ships and resolved to transfer the throne to Africa. Then, when news came that the fleet had been destroyed in a storm, and the patriarch Sergius made the Emperor swear not to desert the city, Heraclius turned again to face his mountainous difficulties.

Raising the cry that the holy cross was in the hands of the pagans, and that the very existence of Christianity was in jeopardy, Heraclius succeeded in concentrating on a great national issue all the religious passion which had so long been expended on distracting controversies. A bargain was struck with the Church; its sacred vessels and incalculable treasures were to be put at the disposal of the

Empire, and the value returned at the close of the war. By the beginning of the year 622 the preparations were completed, the young Heraclius Constantine was appointed nominal regent of the Empire, and the real administration was entrusted to the capable hands of the archbishop and one of the patricians. On Easter Day the last stirring services were held; and on the following day the gilded imperial galley, bearing the miraculous picture of the Virgin, the brightly painted war-galleys and the hundreds of ships which bore the last part of an army of more than a hundred thousand men, sailed bravely toward the coast of Asia.

The Persian campaigns, which have put the name of Heraclius high in the list of imperial commanders, interest us because Martina set sail with her husband and accompanied him throughout the war. Unfortunately, the literary deacon of St Sophia, George of Pisidia, who tells the story of the war, shares the ecclesiastical prejudice against Martina, and never mentions her name. Congenial as the task would be, therefore, to follow the Emperor through his brilliant campaigns and imagine the spirited Martina sharing his perils and his triumphs, it is hardly a fitting task for a biographer. George of Pisidia, addressing Heraclius in the name of the clergy at St Sophia, had trusted that he would redden his black military boots in the blood of the heathen. He and Martina returned to Constantinople six months later, leaving the army in safe winter quarters, with a great victory and a brilliant march across Asia Minor to report. Martina sailed with her husband, in the following year, on his second and more dangerous campaign, and it was in the course of this campaign that she gave birth to the son Heraclius—usually called Heraclonas, to distinguish him from the father, apparently—whom we shall find tragically associated with her in her later years. She seems, indeed, to have accompanied Heraclius on all his journeys; but to what extent she kept pace with the advance of the troops—whether she reached the banks of the Euphrates and Tigris, and beheld the oriental luxury of the fallen camps and towns of the Persians—the prejudice of the deacon of St Sophia prevents us from ascertaining. She had at least the glory of accompanying her husband on one of the most brilliant, the most daring and the most profitable campaigns that ever illumined the Eastern Empire. Nor must her biographer forget to add that she bore several children during her six years' wandering over the mountains and deserts of Asia Minor, Syria, Persia and Mesopotamia. Nine children, four of whom died young, were the issue of the marriage.

Martina shared, too, the splendid triumph which crowned the victories of Heraclius. In the spring of 628 the Emperor and Empress rejoined their family at the Hieria palace, on the Asiatic coast opposite Constantinople, whither, with torches by night and olive-branches by day, the citizens sailed to greet them. Heraclius would not return to his capital until the cross was restored to his hands, and the summer was spent by the united family in the Hieria palace. Early in September the cross arrived, and they went to Constantinople for the triumph. Preceded by the cross, Heraclius rode in a chariot drawn by four elephants through the Golden Gate and along the main street of the city (the Mese) to St Sophia, amidst scenes of such rejoicing as the Empire had not witnessed since the days of Belisarius. A superb entertainment in the Hippodrome followed, and then Heraclius joined his wife in the palace.

And here ends the glory of the Emperor Heraclius; the flame that had burst forth so splendidly in a time of dejection fell just as swiftly, and Heraclius exhibited a lamentable spectacle in face of an even greater peril than the Persians. The problem of the character of Heraclius might concern us if we had any satisfactory information about the behaviour of Martina during the next few years, but as the chroniclers almost refuse to notice her until they come to what they regard as her misdeeds, we have no occasion to linger over it. Her character induces us to believe that she attempted to awaken her husband from his lethargy until she saw that this was impossible, and that she then devoted her thoughts to securing the succession for her son and the virtual rule of the Empire for herself. This, in point of fact, is suggested by the meagre indications in the chronicles.

In the spring of 629 Heraclius took the cross back to its original shrine at Jerusalem, and from that time spent nine years in the provinces of Palestine, Syria and Asia Minor. During those years the Mohammedan power became a formidable menace to the Roman Empire, and the inaction of Heraclius is a scandal to historians. His nervous system was strained to the verge of insanity, and he retreated like one paralysed with terror before the advance of the Mohammedans. Martina foresaw the end, and began to prepare for the succession. There can be no doubt that in these later years Heraclius, whose religious fervour was now greatly increased, was troubled by the cry that his "incestuous" marriage had brought these troubles on the Empire. When his nephew Theodore retreated before the invincible Arabs, and came to reproach Heraclius for his "sin," the Emperor sent him under guard to Constantinople and ordered that he should be disgraced. Some writers see in this the action of Martina, but it may quite well have been due to the broody nervousness of Heraclius himself.

It was plain that Heraclius would not stem the Mohammedan tide, and everywhere men talked of the succession. By the year 638 he and Martina were back in the Hieria palace, and the struggle deepened. Heraclius had now two children by his first wife Eudocia, and five (living) children by Martina. His eldest child, Epiphania Eudocia, had narrowly missed a romantic career. During the Persian war Heraclius had struck an alliance with the King of the Khazars, a wild people akin to the Huns, and, after gorgeously entertaining and rewarding him, had shown him a miniature of his beautiful daughter, then fifteen years old, and offered him her hand. It was only the death of the King in the next year that saved the delicate young girl from being added to the rude harem of the Hunnic prince. She was still unmarried. Her brother, Heraclius Constantinus, now twenty-six years old, was already associated in the Empire, and was the obvious heir to supreme power. But both Heraclius and Martina knew that the Emperor's death would at once set her religious enemies to work to eject her and her children from the palace, and they were anxious to secure her position by associating her eldest son, Heraclonas, in the Empire. There were, besides, a natural son of Heraclius by an early concubine, named Athalaric, and the sons of his cousin Nicetas, who had helped him to win the Empire.

Two of these possible candidates for the purple were summarily dismissed. Athalaric and the nephew Theodore were charged with conspiracy at Constantinople, their hands and feet were struck off, and they were sent into exile. It is conjectured by some writers on Martina that she dictated this heavy punishment, and that her hand is seen in the events which follow. Of this there is no proof; but there can be no doubt that she was eager to secure the succession of Heraclonas, and that Heraclius was now an almost feeble-minded patient under her care. He persistently refused to cross the strip of water from Hieria to the city, and they were compelled at length to make a bridge of boats across the narrower part of the strait, and place artificial hedges of trees along its sides, so that he could ride to Constantinople without catching sight of the sea. The young Constantine, his eldest son, had inherited the delicacy of his mother, and it was necessary to provide for the event of his death. Should his sons inherit the purple, or should it pass to "the children of incest"? The city seethed with discussion.

In the final decision we may confidently recognize the voice of Martina. On 4th July 638 Heraclonas, then a boy of fifteen years,[14] was crowned in the palace by the patriarch Sergius; a younger son, David, was raised to the same dignity shortly afterwards, and the young daughters of Martina, Augustina and Martina, were entitled Augustæ. On the 1st of January 639 three Emperors rode in the procession: Heraclius, Constantine and Heraclonas. Martina had, apparently, triumphed; but more prudent citizens must have shaken their heads in reflecting on the struggle which would inevitably follow the death of Heraclius.

The Emperor lingered for more than two years in his impotent condition, and Martina meantime found a fresh and most powerful ally. The patriarch Sergius had died soon after crowning Heraclonas, leaving his metropolitan see to a monk, Pyrrhus, whom he had raised to the higher rank of the clergy. Pyrrhus became an ally of the Empress, who may possibly have assisted in his elevation, and the alliance was the stronger because Pyrrhus secretly favoured the sect of the Monophysites. From Constantine he would receive little encouragement, whereas Martina, as events proved, was ready to allow him to impose his metaphysical distinction on the Church in return for his political support. It is even said that Martina urged her husband to send the weakly Constantine against the Mohammedans, in the hope that he would not return. Such things are easily said, and easily believed, but incapable of proof.

In February 641 Heraclius died. He suffered in his last years from dropsy, and those who are curious to know by what appalling means the medical men of the time relieved such an affliction, and how the theologians of the time placidly traced the operation of a divine curse for marrying one's niece, may read the details of his sufferings in the patriarch Nicephorus. To the last Heraclius was faithful to his beloved wife. He divided the government of the Empire equally between Constantine and Heraclonas, and he entrusted to the patriarch Pyrrhus a large sum of money to be given to Martina in the event of her enemies succeeding in driving her from power. The struggle began at once.

Martina convoked a meeting of the citizens—presumably in the Hippodrome—and had the will of Heraclius read to them. When the herald had concluded, the sullen silence was broken by a cry for the Emperors. Martina, who was evidently minded to keep the youths in the background and govern in their name, summoned the Emperors, but continued to act as mistress of the Empire. But Constantinople—a compound of inferior Greek and Roman with Syrian blood—always disliked feminine rule, and in face of the advancing Mohammedans regarded it with additional concern. "Honour to you as mother of the Emperors," the citizens cried, "but to them as Emperors and lords. You, mistress, would not be able to resist and reply to barbarians and foreigners coming against the city. God forbid that the Roman commonwealth should fall so low." We may take it that the chronicler has gathered into a speech the various murmurs which arose from the crowded benches of the Hippodrome. Plausible as the cry was, it was a grave blunder. The ailing, probably consumptive, Constantine had not the manliness of a ruler, and the palace became the theatre of the struggles of rival courtiers.

On the side of Constantine was the imperial treasurer Philagrius, and this man embittered the situation by informing the young Emperor of the money which Heraclius had left in charge of the archbishop and forcing him to pay it into the treasury. In order further to strengthen his position Philagrius represented to Constantine that his children would be in danger from Martina if he died. It is important to notice that the death of Constantine was plainly expected by all parties. Nothing is clearer than that he had inherited the delicacy of his mother, and was either epileptic or consumptive—more probably consumptive. The patriarch Nicephorus tells us that he was "chronically ill" and lived in a palace he had built at Chalcedon for the sake of his health. His Empress, Gregoria Anastasia, was a daughter of Nicetas, the young cousin who had set out from Africa with Heraclius, but we have no further information about her. For her sake and that of the children Constantine was persuaded by his intriguing courtiers to send an officer, Valentine, to the troops when he felt that his end was near. Valentine had not only a letter urging the troops to protect Constantine's children from Martina, but a large sum of money to distribute amongst them. It is strange that historians have overlooked this very obvious intrigue and so easily accepted the clerical prejudice against Martina. If Martina were unable to meet "barbarians and foreigners"—a point which might be disputed—assuredly infants could not be trusted to do so.

Constantine died about three months after the death of his father. There is no serious ground whatever for the charge that he was poisoned by agents of Martina and Pyrrhus. The patriarch Nicephorus, the best authority, knows nothing of the rumour, and the very chroniclers, of a later date, who attach importance to it admit that Constantine suffered from a chronic malady. Indeed, when we find a contemporary (and recently published) ecclesiastical writer, the Bishop of Nikin, saying that Constantine after three months' illness "vomited blood, and when he had lost all his blood he died," we may confidently acquit Martina, and conclude that the young Emperor died of consumption. The statement of Constantine's son, a boy of eleven, when he came to the throne, that Pyrrhus and Martina had been justly punished, is a mere echo of the pretext of those who deposed her. The poisoning of a consumptive youth would be a new and superfluous crime, and we have no reason to think that Martina was even normally criminal.

Martina at once assumed the government in the name of her son and expelled the hostile faction from the Court. Philagrius was visited with the most humane punishment of the time—he was forced to become a priest—and his friends were dispersed. But his emissary Valentine was in a strong position and he determined to put it to account. The large sum of money entrusted to him enabled him to purchase the devotion of an army, and he settled at Chalcedon with the ostentatious design of seeing that no evil was done to the young son of the late Emperor. Martina cleverly foiled his first move. She directed Heraclonas to become godfather to the boy, who was carefully kept in the palace at Constantinople, and to swear, with his hand on the cross, that no harm should be done to the child. Valentine then brought his troops nearer and began to ravage the suburbs and neighbourhood of the city, while his friends in Constantinople lit the flame of religious antagonism to Pyrrhus, who was unfortunately pressing his Monophysite tenets on the Church. Exasperated at the inconveniences of the siege and the heresy of the patriarch, the citizens now became restive. A mob invaded and pillaged the great church of St Sophia, and Pyrrhus was forced to abdicate. The power of Martina was now dangerously enfeebled, and she came to terms with Valentine. The ambitious officer was to be appointed "Count of the Excubitors," or commander of the heavier guards, and to be excused from rendering an account of the money entrusted to him.

The further course of the intrigue is scantily known to us, as there is here a mysterious gap of thirty years in the narrative of Nicephorus. From later chronicles we learn that, before the end of 642, the Senate deposed Martina and Heraclonas. In spite of the notorious malady of Constantine, they were found guilty of having poisoned him, with the connivance of the archbishop, and were barbarously punished. The tongue of Martina and the nose of Heraclonas were slit—the text does not imply that they were cut off—and they were expelled from Constantinople. Valentine also is said to have been expelled, so that he must have changed sides. The further course of the spirited and unfortunate Empress and her son is told in the bare phrase that they "lived a private life and were buried together in the monastery of the Lord." We do not know the place of exile, or the year of Martina's death. That her punishment was unjust and barbaric seems now to be beyond question, and there is no excuse, beyond the amiable indiscretion of her marriage, for the evil repute which chroniclers have attached to the name of the Empress Martina. She seems to have been one of the best of the Byzantine Empresses.

CHAPTER VI

THE MOST PIOUS IRENE

The revolution which drove Martina from the palace set upon the throne a boy of eleven, Constans II. The wife whom he afterwards brought to share his splendour, and by whom he had three children, is not known to us even by name. We know only that when his crimes, or violent indiscretions, had rendered him so unpopular that he passed to Sicily, he sent for his wife and children. The Senators, however, had no mind to see the Court transferred to Italy. They detained the Empress and her children, and, as the life of Constans was shortly afterwards ended by his bath-attendant felling him with a soap-dish, the unknown Empress sank into complete obscurity.

His son and successor, Constantine IV., had so clear a title to the charge of brutality that no historian has ventured to dispute it, and we will trust that the Empress Anastasia, whose features and character are unknown to us, did not greatly lament the loss of a consort who could slit the noses of his royal brothers and castrate a noble youth for deploring the execution of his father. Nor can we think that she was happier under the reign of his son, Justinian II., since the only reference to her in the chronicle of his reign is that his favourite minister, a Persian eunuch, had her flogged in the sacred palace on one occasion. Her third and last appearance in history is even more tragic; but a new and quaint type of Empress meantime enters the scene, and in order to explain her arrival we must glance for a moment at the adventures of Justinian II.

Attaining the purple at the age of sixteen, Justinian seems at first to have sinned chiefly by the very natural blunder, in a young man, of admitting corrupt and extortionate ministers. A usurper then took advantage of his unpopularity to dislodge him from the throne, and sent him, with diminished nose, into exile at Cherson, on the Black Sea. Within a year Justinian had the satisfaction of hearing that his enemy had been forced by a new usurper to retire, also with diminished nose, into the tranquil shade of a monastery, and he proposed to regain his throne. The authorities of Cherson, however, decided to conciliate the new Emperor, Tiberius III., by sending Justinian to him in chains, and he fled to the land of the Khazars, who dwelt on the other side of the Black Sea. The Khazars were a wild Asiatic people, akin to the Huns, whose manners had been somewhat softened by contact with the Byzantine civilization, and their king, or chagan, not only received the fugitive with cordiality, but bestowed on him the hand of his royal daughter.

Theodora—a name conferred on her, no doubt, by Justinian in memory of the consort of his great predecessor Justinian I.—can hardly have boasted much beauty, being a Khazar, but she was not without spirit and character. She presently learned that her father had been bribed by Tiberius to surrender Justinian, and she warned him of his danger. Sending, in succession, for the two high officials who had been charged to arrest him, Justinian strangled them with his own hands and fled to Bulgaria, leaving his wife and infant daughter in the care of her father, who very amiably sheltered them. Within a year the faithful Theodora learned that she was mistress of the mighty city of the Greeks. Justinian had offered the hand of his daughter, then one year old, and some more solid advantages to the King of Bulgaria in exchange for an army, had laid siege to Constantinople, and had, with a few soldiers, crept through the water-conduit into the town and taken it. The appalling vengeance he wrought on his enemies and on the inhabitants, even to the babies, of Cherson may be read in history. It is, comparatively, an amiable trait in his character that he did not forget the yellow-skinned princess who had lightened the dark hours of his exile. She was brought with great pomp to the city, bringing two children to their truculent father, was crowned Empress, and enjoyed for a few years the undreamt-of splendour of the imperial palaces. Happily, she did not live to see the end of her husband's savage vengeance. When a storm had threatened the life of Justinian on the Black Sea, his companions had urged him to disarm the divine wrath by forgiving his enemies. "If I spare them, may God drown me here," he had replied, with more vigour than elegance. His orgy was closed by the inevitable assassination.

We catch a third and last glimpse of the Empress Anastasia at this point. The brood of Justinian was to be exterminated, and soldiers went to the palace of Blachernæ in search of Theodora's boy. When they burst into the chapel they found the aged grandmother sitting, on guard, before the sanctuary. The six-year-old boy clung to the altar with one hand, and held a fragment of the "true cross" in the other, while his neck was loaded with the most sacred relics. But Byzantine piety was of a peculiar nature. The soldiers brushed aside the old lady, stripped the boy of his relics, took him out to the gate, and "cut his throat like a sheep."

Three Emperors followed in six years, and came to violent ends. Then Leo the Isaurian (717-740) came upon the throne, and inaugurated the famous crusade of the Iconoclasts, or breakers of images. His wife Maria is known to us only as having received the title of Empress in 718, as a reward for bringing Constantine Copronymus into the world, and having scattered gold from her litter among the people as she was borne to St Sophia for the baptism of that ill-regulated infant. Another Asiatic princess then comes faintly into view, when, in his fourteenth or fifteenth year, Constantine marries a Khazar king's daughter. The religious chroniclers would have us believe that she was endowed with much learning and piety, but the only ground of this remarkable claim is that she did not agree with her husband, as few women did, about the propriety of breaking the Virgin's statues. After eighteen years of patient expectation she ushered a feeble infant, Leo IV., into the distracted Empire, and quitted it herself shortly afterwards. The Empress Maria succeeded to her place in the arms of Constantine in 750, and in 757 she left that very doubtful felicity to the Empress Eudocia. Eudocia was pious and fertile: it is all that we know of her. Nearing her first delivery she summoned the holy nun, Anthusa—whom her husband had had publicly stripped and whipped a short time before—and, in virtue of her prayers, presented Constantine with a son and daughter, simultaneously, shortly afterwards. Four other boys followed, and Eudocia, having behaved as a good Empress ought and furnished no material to the biographer, followed her two predecessors.

Meantime the famous Irene had entered the story of Byzantine life, and once more we are in a position to make a satisfactory study of Byzantine feminism. In the year 768, seven years before the death of Constantine V., Constantinople was delighted with a succession of festivities. On 1st April Eudocia was, after ten years of industrious maternal activity, crowned Empress, or Augusta, in the "banquet-room of nineteen tables," with its golden roof and golden vessels, in the palace. On the following day, which was Easter Sunday, her eldest sons, Christopher and Nicephorus, were made Cæsars, and her third son, Nicetas, received the heavy title of nobilissimus ("most noble"), which gave the six-year-old boy a gold-embroidered mantle and a slender jewelled crown; so that the procession to church was headed by two Emperors, Constantine and young Leo, two Cæsars, and a "most noble," all flinging gold and silver among the enchanted mob. But Leo was now approaching his twentieth year and must marry. The idea was mooted first of asking the hand of the daughter of Pepin the Frank, but it is said that the Western Christians frowned on the Kensitite heresy of the Eastern Court. So Constantine then resolved to seek a beautiful and eligible lady within his own dominions, and it was announced in the late summer that the prize had been awarded to Irene, the pride of Athens.

Irene was then a beautiful, talented and spirited girl of seventeen summers. As she had, apparently, no ancestors, and as Athens had become at that time a drowsy and almost obscure provincial town, we must suppose that—as she herself afterwards acted—imperial commissioners had been sent far and wide to examine candidates for the vacancy. Irene's radiant Greek beauty, robust health, and lively intelligence pleased the officials; an imperial galley brought her to the palace of Hieria, on the Asiatic side; her qualifications were found to be adequate. There was one difficulty, and Irene gave early proof of her skill in casuistry in surmounting it. Not only was Irene a woman—and all women were on the side of the Virgin—but Athens was conservative in religion. Constantine demanded an oath, and Irene, with a large "mental reservation," to use the elegant phrase of the experts in such matters, swore on the holy cross that she would not favour the worship of images.

Her story will turn largely on the question of Iconoclasm, and a few words on the subject may be useful. The real origin of Leo the Isaurian's zeal against statues is obscure. Historians suggest the influence of the purer religion of Mohammed, but there was no cultural contact of Mohammedanism and Christianity, and an Isaurian soldier would hardly be the man to experience it if there were. When we find that the Iconoclasts went on to reject relics and monasticism and treat the Virgin in very cavalier fashion, I suggest that it was a Protestant or Rationalist movement, a spontaneous protest against the excessive superstition, clerical wealth and monastic parasitism of the time. It took strong root in the army; and we may assume that the permission to rifle wealthy churches, rather than any leaning to metaphysics, explains this zeal for advanced theology among the troops. Constantine, like his father, pressed the reform ferociously; and as monks and women were the chief recalcitrants, he fell upon the monks with grim determination. Their beards were oiled and fired: they were gathered in masses with nuns, and told to marry each other—as many did: they were forced to walk round the Hippodrome, to the delight of the mob, arm in arm with prostitutes. Even the reluctant patriarch of Constantinople was indelicately mutilated, driven on an ass round the Hippodrome, under a fire of spittle, and replaced by an obedient eunuch.

This was the Iconoclastic world into which the Athenian girl entered, armed with a mental reservation. From the palace of Hieria she went, at the beginning of September, to Constantinople, and her betrothal to Leo was celebrated in "the church of the Lighthouse."

Three months later her probation was complete; on 13th December she received the wonderful crown of the Empresses, with its cascades of pearls and diamonds, in the gold-roofed banquet-room, and was married in the chapel of St Stephen within the palace.

Constantine remained on the throne for seven years, and Irene behaved, and avoided images, with the most exemplary propriety, until, in 775, the old Emperor joined his father in the eternal home to which the religious chroniclers luridly consign him. Still for some years Irene gave no sign of strong personality, unless we may see, as is probable, her influence in the events of the following year. She had borne a son in 770, and in 776 Leo was urged to admit this boy to a share of the Empire. The Emperor was delicate, possibly consumptive, and it will be remembered that he had five half-brothers, who offered rich material for intriguing eunuchs and discontented nobles. Irene was now a young woman of twenty-five, of strong and subtle intellect, and well acquainted with Byzantine history. Her obvious interest was to secure the succession for her son and exclude the children of Eudocia. Leo at first demurred to the crowning of the boy. He submitted that, if he died, the ways of Byzantium made it not unlikely that the child would be murdered. He was answered with an assurance that the whole Court and city were prepared to swear the most solemn allegiance to his son, and in the spring of 776 he prepared to associate the younger Constantine in his imperial power. It was becoming difficult in pious Constantinople to devise an oath sufficiently sacred to be taken seriously, and Leo exacted that all orders of the citizens should swear by the cross on its most solemn festival and then place a written record of their oath on the altar of the great church. On Good Friday, therefore, the officers, Senators, courtiers and various corporations of workers and idlers in the city, swore their mighty oath by the cross to know no sovereign but Constantine VI., and on the following day, when the last son of Eudocia, Eudocimus, was made a "most noble," the written oaths were laid on the altar, to be carefully guarded by the patriarch—for a few years. On Easter Sunday Constantine was crowned in the Hippodrome in the early morning, and the glittering procession of Emperors, Cæsars, and "most nobles," moved to the church, followed at a modest distance by Irene and her eunuchs and women.

Twelve months later the imperial family and the higher orders met in the gorgeous hall of the Magnaura palace for a different ceremony. It had been "discovered" that the Cæsar Nicephorus had conspired with the eunuchs and officers, and, when Leo announced the details—there was no trial—to the audience, it was at once decided that he be degraded to the rank of the clergy and banished to Cherson. One rival was put out of the way, and Leo continued to play with his caskets of jewels—his favourite occupation— and Irene to cultivate her policy of waiting. In her service was the eunuch Stauracius, a genius of intrigue and counter-intrigue, whose watchful servants could at any time detect or manufacture a conspiracy. On one occasion only, towards the end of her husband's short reign, does Irene seem to have been indiscreet, though the indications are rather obscure.

Historians put it to the account of Leo that under him the fierce persecution of image-worshippers relaxed, but the question might be raised whether there was much occasion for persecuting. It is said that Irene secretly venerated images in her apartments and had about her a group of confidential devotees, waiting for the death of Leo; and the story runs that Leo, hearing of the conspiracy, forced his way into Irene's apartments, and discovered two sacred statues hidden under a cushion. Whether or no it is true that Irene calmly lied—or made another mental reservation—and disowned the figures of Christ and His mother, it is certain that in the last year of his life Leo had a fit of Iconoclastic wrath, and numbers of palace officials and nobles were shaved into priests, dragged ignominiously round the Hippodrome, and forced to exchange the gilded service of the Empress for the austere service of the altar.

In view of this it is not surprising that, when Leo died a few months later, there was a faint rumour that Irene had poisoned him; though the more religious chroniclers tell us that, in his infatuation for jewels, he had taken from the church the rich crown which Maurice had suspended over the altars, put it on his sacrilegious head, which at once broke into fiery carbuncles, and perished miserably. We may take it that the delicate constitution of Leo IV. came to an end after a reign of four and a half years (in 780) and the Empress Irene entered upon her long, prosperous and blood-stained reign.

Constantine VI. was ten years old at the death of his father, and the administration naturally fell to Irene and her able, if unscrupulous, ministers. When all allowance has been made for the ability of her ministers, especially the eunuch-patrician Stauracius, it must be admitted that the Empress showed conspicuous talent and vigour, and brought about a wonderful restoration of the stricken Empire. Her abjuration of the Iconoclastic tenets not only brought comparative religious peace, in the course of time, but enabled her to strengthen her rule by friendly relations with the Papacy and with Charlemagne, whose star was rising in the West. The long and exhausting war in the East was brought to a close by diplomacy, and the military victories of Stauracius restored the rule of Constantinople in Greece and Thessaly. Prosperity brightened the Empire, and it almost returned to the happy position it had enjoyed under Justinian I. But from this brighter aspect of the reign of Irene, in which it is difficult to disentangle her action from that of her ministers, we must turn to events in which her character is more clearly, if less favourably, seen.

THE EMPRESS IRENE
FROM AN IVORY PLAQUE IN THE NATIONAL MUSEUM, FLORENCE

Six weeks had not elapsed since the death of Leo when it was announced that a dangerous conspiracy had been discovered, the object of which was to put the royal half-brothers of Leo on the throne. We can well believe that there was some discontent at the rule of a woman and a child, and that the feeble sons of Eudocia were ever disposed to listen to ambitious courtiers, but the discovery was opportune. It removed at one sweep all who seemed to be in a position to dispute Irene's rule. The three Cæsars and the two "most nobles," and a crowd of nobles and officers who were suspected of favouring them, were scourged, tonsured or exiled. Indeed, lest there should be any later error as to the clerical status of the children of Eudocia, Irene forced them publicly to administer the sacraments to the people in the great church. It was Christmas Day, and a vast crowd assembled to see the royal uncles dispensing the consecrated bread under the eyes of the vigorous Empress and her son.

The cruel spectacle was resented by many, and Elpidius, whom Irene had made Governor of Sicily, rebelled. Irene ordered the local officers to send him in chains to Constantinople, and, when they refused, she sent a fleet which quickly dislodged him and punished the rebels. Unfortunately, we read that the "most pious" Empress, as the admiring chroniclers call her, so far lost her temper as to flog the wife and children of Elpidius, and drive the innocent woman, with shorn hair, into a nunnery. A more amiable way of strengthening her throne was about the same time discovered by some courtier. A marvellous ancient tombstone was brought to Constantinople, and citizens gazed with awe on the inscription: "Christ will be born of the Virgin Mary, and I believe in him. Sun, thou shalt see me again one day under the reign of Constantine and Irene." As this stone was certified to have been taken by a Thracian peasant from the tomb of some prehistoric "giant," it did much to discredit the more rationalistic Iconoclasts, who scouted the virginity of Mary, and the opposition to the divine mission of Irene.

The time was not yet ripe, however, for an open disavowal of the Iconoclasts; the heresy was too deeply rooted in the army and the more cultivated circles of the city. Irene thought for a moment of an alliance with Charlemagne, and begged the hand of his daughter Rotrud for her son. The offer was cordially received, and Byzantine eunuchs were sent to initiate the Frankish maiden into the mysteries of the Greek tongue and Greek etiquette. The fame of Charlemagne now filled the world, and the young Constantine eagerly looked for the alliance with his daughter. It would be interesting to speculate what influence such an alliance would have had on the fortunes of Europe, and there can be no doubt that Irene committed a criminal blunder in withdrawing the proposal on what we must regard as selfish grounds. The only plausible reason that can be suggested is that she feared that her son might become a monarch in reality as well as name under the influence of Charlemagne, and she was determined to be at least co-ruler. The victories which Stauracius had meantime won in Greece and Thessaly must have given her greater confidence in her own resources. In 783 she proceeded herself with a large army—not forgetting the organs and other musical instruments of the Court, the chronicler says—to pacify and restore the province of Thrace.

She now felt strong enough to restore the worship of images. At the end of the year 783 the Iconoclastic archbishop Paul mysteriously retired from his see. Irene called a meeting of the notables in the Magnaura palace, and from the marvellous golden throne she announced that Paul had been stricken with deep penitence for his opposition to images and had retired to expiate his sin. She suggested that her secretary Tarasius should be made archbishop, and the nobles and clergy faithfully echoed the name of Tarasius. The secretary then protested that he too had misgivings on the image question, and would take office only on condition that a Church council was called to decide upon it. Within a month or two Irene had brought to Constantinople a crowd of bishops and heads of monasteries, and a fiery discussion proceeded in the church of the Apostles. The Iconoclasts were, of course, in a minority. Suddenly the doors were forced, and a troop of soldiers entered, with drawn swords, and threatened to make an end to Tarasius and his monks. "We have won; thank God, those fools and brutes have done no harm," was the exultant cry of the Iconoclastic bishops—I translate literally from Theophanes[15]—and the meeting hurriedly dispersed.

Irene once more resorted to the kind of diplomacy of which she was a mistress. The rumour was spread that the Saracens were advancing, and the guards were shipped to the Asiatic side and marched toward the south. When they had reached some distance from the city, a message came from Constantinople that the war had been averted, and they might send their arms or equipment to the capital before returning themselves. They were then scattered over the provinces and the metropolitan guards were recruited from the orthodox ranks. The bishops and monks were convoked again, in the Council of

Chalcedon, and in the last sitting of the Council, which was held in the Magnaura palace, the cult of images was formally restored.

In the meantime Irene had resumed the work of finding a wife for her son. If we are right in assuming that she rejected the daughter of Charlemagne in order that Constantine should not have any strength independently of her, we can understand her next procedure. One of those innumerable "lives of the saints" which have transmitted to us a few precarious fragments of genuine and interesting information gives us a very romantic version of the rise of the next Empress. In a remote Cappadocian village dwelt a very pious man who had won a local reputation for sanctity, and impoverished his family, by his generous almsgiving. He had three daughters, whose lives and prospects must have been prosy enough in their rude village until romance entered it one day in the person of an imperial commissioner. He was one of many sent all over the Empire by Irene in search of a mate for her son, and it seemed to him that the daughters of Philaretus corresponded to the standard given to him—a standard which specified the height and the size of the feet of the candidates as well as more material features.[16] They were taken to Constantinople, with numbers of other candidates for the glass slipper, and Maria, a beautiful maiden of eighteen, was chosen for the lofty honour. It sounds like a modified version of the story of Cinderella, but it was not the first time that obscure maidens had been chosen for imperial dignity on their looks, and the most reliable authority, Theophanes, tells us that Irene sent one of her officers into distant Armenia—Maria is variously described as Cappadocian, Paphlagonian and Armenian—for the obscure girl. She was married to the Emperor in November 788, but we cannot end, as story-tellers do, by saying that she was happy ever afterwards.

Constantine was now a youth of eighteen, and had courtiers of his own. With their aid he perceived that, although rescripts went out in the names of "Constantine and Irene," the government was entirely in the hands of Irene and her ministers. He had keenly desired the daughter of Charlemagne, and he resented the forcing upon him of a village maiden. The year following his marriage was one of bitter discontent and secret whispering. Stauracius, however, or Irene, watched the conspirators closely, and in January 790 the net was drawn round them. They had intended to banish Irene to Sicily, and they now found themselves on the way to Sicily, their backs sore from the scourge and their heads marked with the odious sign of clerical office. Constantine himself was flogged, and confined for some time to the palace; it was decreed that henceforth the name of Irene should precede that of her son; and a formidable oath was imposed on the troops that they would not suffer Constantine to rule while she lived.

But the counsels of eunuchs and women, however vigorous they be in their class, are apt either to fall short of, or pass beyond, the golden mean in the game of politics. Regiment after regiment took the oath, until at last the troops in Armenia refused to submit to feminine rule. Irene sent the eunuch Alexius to persuade or coerce them. They made him their commander, spread the rebellion among other troops, and at length an army besieged the palace and dictated terms. Stauracius was scourged, tonsured and deported to Armenia; Irene was deposed and had to retire to a new palace—the Eleutherian palace—which she had built and stored with treasure for emergencies. The lament of Theophanes at this turn of the wheel, in which he sees the personal action of the devil, is equal to his naive praise of all the tricks of Irene to secure and hold power in the cause of true religion.

In spite of that zeal for true religion, the modern reader will not have followed the career of Irene up to this point with unalloyed admiration. She was essentially a casuist, the very embodiment of the Byzantine religious spirit. Chaste she undoubtedly was, though we shall presently find her acting in that regard in drastic contradiction to the teaching of the Church; she was generous, even extravagant, with money, and she showed a sincere concern for the welfare of her subjects within the limits of her own ambition; but she betrays from the start that lack of moral scrupulousness which too often accompanies fervent piety in Byzantine women, and the bitter disappointment which closes the first part of her reign will now make her more unscrupulous than ever.

It was in October 790 that Irene was deposed. Fourteen months afterwards we find her returning to imperial power and making a fearful use of it. Constantine had yielded to her pressure and that of the nobles devoted to her, and again proclaimed that she was Empress and co-ruler of the Empire. The Armenian troops at once protested against the change, and, as their commander, Alexius, was in Constantinople at the time, he was scourged and converted into an abbé malgré lui. An expedition against the Bulgarians failed shortly afterwards, and, whether the failure did really lead to a conspiracy, or the plot was invented to serve the purpose of Irene and Constantine, a terrible clearance was made of their possible opponents. Alexius and Nicephorus (the uncle of the Emperor who had been made a cleric) had their eyes cut out; and three other sons of Eudocia were brought from their clerical homes and had their tongues cut. We must not too readily implicate Irene in these barbarities. She had not returned to her former influence and activity, and it was Constantine himself who led an army against the insurgents in Armenia and made a terrible end of their rebellion. In view, however, of Irene's later behaviour, it is probable that she agreed to, if she did not inspire, these proceedings, and the authorities assure us that she now began to make selfish profit of the unpopularity of her son and encourage him in licence.

We have as yet said nothing of the imperial life of the young woman who had passed from her village home to the palace. The reason is that she seems to have been one of those admirable Empresses who impress the chroniclers only when they bear children or suffer misfortune. Maria had borne two daughters to Constantine, and the year of her misfortune was at hand. Constantine had never loved his wife and had freely sought consolation elsewhere; and in the year 794 his eye fell on a charming lady of his mother's suite. Whether this lady was too chaste or too ambitious to admit his passion irregularly, we cannot say, but we have the emphatic assurance of the authorities that Irene encouraged the passion, and supported her son in his proposal to divorce Maria, in order still further to weaken his position. If such an act seem beyond the range of a mother's ambition, I can only say that far worse is to follow.

On 3rd January 795, the unfortunate Maria was deposed from her dignity, exchanged her imperial robes for the rough black dress of a nun, and, with shorn hair, passed to a convent; and before the end of the same year the more fortunate Theodote was transferred from the service of Irene's chamber (cubicularia) to the imperial dignity. It need hardly be said that this procedure was violently opposed to the solemn teaching of the Church, which now regarded marriage as absolutely indissoluble. The courtly patriarch Tarasius, who had been converted from a very secular secretary into an archbishop, proved accommodating enough; he declined to perform the marriage, but he permitted some enterprising priest named Joseph to do so, and he sanctioned the transfer of Maria to a nunnery. But the monks of the Empire raised once more their formidable chant of execration, and showered epithets on the Emperor and the archbishop. The great monastery of Saccudion, in Bithynia, was the centre of the agitation, under its vigorous abbot Plato.[17]

The next move of Irene was to espouse the cause of the monks who fulminated against her adulterous son and his "Jezebel," and were punished for doing so. If we feel a scruple about admitting so malignant a course in a Christian mother, we must remember that these things are ascribed to her by chroniclers who are full of admiration for her piety, and that the tragic end of the story is quite beyond doubt.

Constantine lost ground, and Irene watched her opportunity. It came in the month of September 796, when mother and son went, with a large and distinguished company, to take the hot baths at Prusia. Theodote had remained behind, so as to be near the Porphyra palace, and she presently sent a message that a son was born. Constantine galloped in delight to the city, and Irene set to work. By amiable conversation and secret gifts she won a number of the officers, and the conspiracy quietly proceeded when they returned to Constantinople. The following summer Constantine set out against the Saracens, and Irene, fearing that he might return with glory and renewed popularity, for he was a skilful and vigorous soldier, determined to strike.

Constantine was recalled to the city by some false intelligence, and as he went one day (17th June) from the Hippodrome to join his wife (whose baby had recently died) in the palace of Blachernæ, he was attacked. He escaped, and fled by boat to the Asiatic side, where Theodote joined him. The position was now critical, as a number of nobles and officers were with Constantine, and Irene heard that others were daily crossing the water. For a moment she trembled and thought of sending bishops to ask her son to allow her to retire into private life, but there remained one device. Among the courtiers with Constantine were some whom she had already compromised, and she sent a secret message to these men to the effect that she would reveal their perfidy to the Emperor if they remained with him. The stratagem succeeded. In the early morning of 15th August the Emperor was brought, bound, to his palace and lodged in the Porphyra; and there, in the very palace in which he had been born, his eyes were brutally cut out by the knives of the soldiers at the ninth hour of the day. Some of the chroniclers observe that the work was done in such a way that the men really intended to kill Constantine. That is misleading, since it would have been perfectly easy to kill him, whereas we know that he lingered in confinement in the Therapia palace for some years. The truth probably is that Irene's casuistry permitted the horrible mutilation, but forbade the murder, of her son; but her agents probably concluded that if they accidentally and unintentionally killed Constantine there would be few tears shed.

It would be difficult to find a parallel to this horrible deed in the long story of the pagan Empresses, and we press on to the conclusion of Irene's reign. For several years she continued to rule the Empire in peace and prosperity. One or two feeble revolts were made, and more eyes were cut from their sockets, but the year 799 opened with little sign of trouble. Decrees went forth in the name of "Irene, the great king and autocrat of the Romans." She built convents and established charitable foundations. She gladdened the hearts of the poor by remitting taxes and import duties, and scattering money amongst them as she rode to church in a golden chariot drawn by four white horses, the reins of each held by one of the highest dignitaries of the Empire. The Pope blessed her—he had put out the eyes of his predecessor—and the great Charlemagne sent legates to ask her hand in marriage. And the blind Emperor lingered in his palace-prison with his faithful Theodote, waiting for the thunder of Jupiter.

In the year 800 the shadow of the avenger seemed to come over the palace. Irene had two powerful ministers, Stauracius (who had, of course, returned from the service of the altar) and Aetius, and their quarrels filled the palace and the heart of Irene with bitterness. In 799 she had been dangerously ill, and their intrigues had doubled. She recovered, and Stauracius determined to make a bold attempt to secure the purple. His conspiracy was discovered, and Irene, holding a council in the gold-roofed dining-hall, decreed that no military officer was to approach Stauracius. The sentence seems mild, but the truth was that, in spite of doctors and priests who lied to him even as he spat blood, Stauracius was dying. He passed away in June, and Aetius commanded the palace.

The end came in 802. Aetius had frustrated the proposal of a marriage of Charlemagne and Irene, who seems to have favoured it (she was still only in her fiftieth year), because he designed to secure the purple for his brother and thus maintain his position. But the legates of Charlemagne lingered in Constantinople, and witnessed the fall of the great Empress. On the evening of 31st October 802, when Irene lay ill in her Eleutherian palace, a group of nobles and officers knocked at the door of the Chalke and summoned the guard. They had, they said, been sent by Irene to put Nicephorus, the "chancellor of the exchequer," on the throne; she wished to forestall Aetius. In the darkness and confusion they were admitted, and they took possession of the palace and set guards round the Eleutherian palace. Almost before dawn the next morning they conveyed Nicephorus to the great church to be crowned, and, although Irene's liberality had won the people and they gathered in the square to damn Nicephorus and the archbishop and raise cheers for Irene, they were powerless. The nobles and officers were resolved to tolerate the insolence of Aetius no longer.

Irene, sick and dispirited, was incapable of making one of those spurts of energy or astute stratagems which had so often saved her. When the hypocritical Nicephorus came to visit her in her apartments, she quietly begged that she might be permitted to end her days in her Eleutherian palace. He had often been a guest at her table and grossly deceived her; even the nobles were yet to learn what a brute they had put on the throne. He promised that if she would swear on the cross to give up the whole of the imperial treasure, she should retire to her palace. It was believed that treasure was hidden in various places in that labyrinth of palaces; even the blind Constantine was brought forth to say in which wall a certain treasure was hidden. Irene swore her last oath, gave a list of the hiding-places—and was promptly imprisoned in a monastery she had built on the Princes' Islands, a group of small islands, in view of the palace, on the Sea of Marmora.

Constantinople seems to have been deeply moved, and a month later she was removed to a dismal prison on the island of Lesbos. There, under a strong guard, rigorously isolated from her friends, she spent nine miserable months reflecting on the strange career she had run since she had left Athens in the pride of her youth and beauty. She died on 9th August 803, and was buried in her monastery on the Princes' Islands.

CHAPTER VII

SAINT THEODORA

From the most pious Irene we proceed, after a passing glance at the half-dozen Empresses of less fame who come between them, to a notable Empress whose memory has actually been enshrined in the list of the canonized. Byzantine piety has at times assumed such peculiar features in the course of our story that we will not leap to the conclusion that at length we reach a woman in whom modern taste will find a realization of its standards. The restoration of the images of the Virgin and the founding of monasteries were in those days arguments powerful enough to silence the importunities of the devil's advocate. Theodora will be found to have ways that the modern woman may or may not admire, but will assuredly not be encouraged to imitate. Yet it will be something to meet a powerful Byzantine Empress whose hands are not stained with blood, and, from her romantic elevation to her tragic fall, the story of Saint Theodora will prove of no little interest.

We have left Irene dying of a broken heart in her island prison while the perfidious Nicephorus wantons on her wealth in the sacred palace. Since no wife is associated with him in the chronicles, it is not ours to determine whether he really was "the sink of all the vices," as the ecclesiastical writers say, or whether his anti-clerical spirit and his refusal to persecute heretics have not loaded the scales against him. The example of Charlemagne, who maintained an imperial harem in the heart of Christendom, seems to have affected him. When he had commanded (for his son Stauracius) one of those "beauty shows" by which the Byzantine Court often selected a royal bride, and three blushing and beautiful maidens were presented for his final decision, he is said to have appropriated two of them and imposed the third on his son. The new Empress, Theophano, was an Athenian girl, a relative of Irene, but, though she was not devoid of ambition, Fate did not afford her the opportunity enjoyed by Irene. Nicephorus fell in war after a reign of nine years, and his skull, tastefully mounted in silver, became a favourite drinking-cup of the King of Bulgaria. But his son Stauracius was gravely wounded in the same battle, and was borne back to the city in a litter in a dangerous condition.

Theophano, who was childless, saw the crown slipping from her hands as soon as she had obtained it. The Emperor's sister Procopia was married to the chief governor of the palace, a very handsome, amiable, black-haired youth, not wanting in popularity, and the soldiers and Senators whispered too loudly that he was fit to wear the purple. Stauracius, from his sickbed, petulantly ordered that the bright eyes of Michael should be cut out, and that the imperial power should pass to Theophano. Within a few weeks the army turned upon its helpless sovereign, and lodged him in a monastery. Theophano passed from the palace to a nunnery and lost the beautiful hair which had so recently helped to win her a throne; but it should be added, for the credit of Michael, that he enabled her to soften the disappointment with all the comfort that a large fortune could afford a woman with sacred vows.

Even more romance is packed into the brief story of the Empress Procopia. Rising with her father, Nicephorus, from the level of court officials to the imperial rank, she had married the handsome superintendent of the palace and had, after a fortunate escape from the vindictiveness of her brother (or of Theophano), been crowned mistress of the Roman world, in the gold-roofed triclinon on 2nd October 811. To her the Fates seemed to open a long and glorious career. Her husband had neither grit nor judgment, and she virtually undertook the administration of the Empire. Unhappily, she illustrated in a fatal degree the proverbial subservience of women to priests and monks. The policy of Nicephorus was reversed; the Church smiled under a shower of gold, while the heretics were lashed into sullen defiance in the provinces. Officers and nobles looked with disdain and irritation on this revival of clericalism, and even concerted a plot to bring the eyeless sons of Constantine VI. to the throne from their distant priestly homes. When, in the year 812, Procopia drove out at the head of the troops, who were marching against the Bulgarians, the soldiers murmured and the "simple-minded" Michael, as a contemporary calls him, was insulted. And when, in the following spring, Michael, relying on his spiritual advisers for carnal warfare, was ignominiously beaten by the Bulgarians, the soldiers offered the crown to a vigorous Armenian officer and marched on the city.

Thus in less than two years Procopia forfeited the power which, she believed, she had used so admirably. Her mild and timid husband returned to the capital to tell her that he proposed to resign and avoid a civil war. She raged in vain at his pusillanimity; the chroniclers tell us, in particular, that she dwelt with strong invective on the notion of this unlettered officer's wife appearing in the purple. While they discussed, the army reached Constantinople, and they fled, with their children, to a chapel in the palace grounds near the sea. The end was ruthless and inevitable. Michael, who was little feared, was clothed with the monastic habit which befitted him, and placed on one of the Princes' Islands, in the Sea of Marmora, from which so many kings and princes were to gaze upon the palace they had lost. His elder son was castrated. Procopia was shorn and clothed with the hated black dress of a nun, and, deprived of all her property, she lived for a few miserable years with her daughters in a convent on the fringe of the city.

The Empress Theodosia, wife of Leo the Armenian, who now ascended the throne, hardly merited all the disdain with which Procopia had depicted her in the imperial robes. She was the daughter of Arsaberes, an officer and patrician of such rank and culture that there had been an attempt to put him on the throne in the reign of Nicephorus. One of the chroniclers, however, speaks incidentally of Leo's "incestuous marriage," and we may assume that there was something wrong in the connexion. It matters little, as Theodosia remains in complete obscurity during her husband's seven years' reign. Only in the last week does she make her first, and last, appearance in history.

In spite of a sincere desire to reform the Empire, and the most energetic measures to purify and strengthen it, Leo became unpopular. Reformers were rarely popular at Constantinople, and Leo had the additional disadvantage of favouring the Iconoclasts. When fiery monks denounced his maxim of universal toleration, he resorted to violence, and hands and feet began to fall under the axes of his soldiers. At last he discovered that the Count of his guards, Michael, was at the head of a conspiracy, and he is said—many historians refuse to believe the statement—to have ordered that Michael be cast forthwith into the furnace which heated the baths of the palace. It was Christmas Eve, and the Empress was horrified to learn that the feast was to be desecrated in this way. As the soldiers conducted Michael through the palace, she rushed from her bed, with flying locks and disordered dress, and fell upon Leo "like a bacchante." He sullenly postponed the execution, muttering: "You and the children will see what comes of keeping me from sin." Michael was fettered and confined, and Leo retired with the key of the fetters in his breast.

The unknown story of Theodosia, daughter of Arsaberes, ends in a thrilling page of romance. Leo slept little, the fear that he had blundered tormenting him, and at last he went in the dead of night to the chamber in which Michael was confined. To his surprise he found Michael sleeping on the jailer's bed, instead of being chained to the wall. He retired to consider the matter, but it seems that he took no steps, and, in the early morning, he went to the chapel to chant matins with the clergy. Now a page, who had been lying in a corner of Michael's cell, had noticed the purple slippers of the man who had entered; he at once wakened Michael and his friendly jailer, and a message was hastily sent to friends in the city, threatening to betray them to Leo if they did not deliver Michael at once. It was, as I said, the depth of winter—it was now Christmas morning—and a group of singers were to enter the palace in the early hours to join with Leo in singing the service. Leo had a resonant voice, of which he was very proud. With these singers, hooded and cloaked with fur, the conspirators mingled, and made their way to the chapel, concealing their swords. They stood perplexed in the dim and cold chapel, as Leo had drawn his fur hood over his head and was unrecognizable, until at last his sonorous voice rang out, and their swords gleamed in the light of the lamp. Leo, a very powerful man, seized the cross, and defended himself for a time, but soon fell dead to the ground. Theodosia was turned adrift in the desolate Empire, her four boys were castrated—one dying under the brutal mutilation—and Michael the Stammerer, instead of passing to the furnace, sat on the golden throne, even before the fetters could be struck from his feet.

The reign of Michael introduces us at length to the woman whose name stands at the head of this chapter. Michael was the son of a Phrygian peasant, knowing more about pigs and mules than about Greek letters, says the indignant chronicler, and had risen from the lowest rank of the army. He had in early years married the daughter of an officer; though we may smile at the legend that Thecla was bestowed upon him because some soothsayer had foretold his fortune. Thecla had enjoyed a year or two of splendour and passed away, leaving a son and daughter. Second marriages were not favoured by the clergy and monks, and it is said that Michael secretly arranged with the Senators that they should press him to marry again; but when we find that he married a nun, we can hardly suppose that he was disposed to fear the clergy. His second Empress, Euphrosyne, has made no mark in history, yet she is interesting. It will be remembered that twenty years earlier the son of Irene had divorced his wife Maria, and sent her and her young daughters into a convent. It was one of these daughters who, after spending twenty years' placid existence in a religious house during all the storms that had swept through the palace, was recalled to the world, relieved of her vows by the patriarch, and married to the boorish Michael. After four or five years' further enjoyment of the palace, Michael was carried off by dysentery, and left the Empire to Euphrosyne and her stepson Theophilus. Here begins the story of the sainted Theodora, and ends the brief visit of Euphrosyne to the brighter world.

When Theophilus ascended the throne in 829 he is said to have been a widower, though still young. The chroniclers persistently state that the youngest of his five daughters married one of his officers a few years after his accession, and the only solution of this singular puzzle is said to be that an earlier wife had died and left him with several girls. He was not, at all events, married when he was crowned in 829, and, with the aid of Euphrosyne, he sought a consort. Once more matrimonial commissioners searched the city and the provinces, and every father of a beautiful girl hastened to display her charms to the imperial examiners. Some writers would confine the scrutiny to the city of Constantinople, but the fact that Theodora came from the distant province of Paphlagonia confirms the statement of George the Monk that the imperial commissioners travelled through "all regions" (of the Empire) in search of a perfect bride. The utmost that panegyric has been able to say of Theodora's parents, Marinus and Theoclista, is that they were "not ignoble." We may assume that, like the Empress Maria, the mother of Euphrosyne, she was discovered in some obscure village of Asia Minor and conducted, with fluttering heart, to the Court of the great king.

Euphrosyne added a picturesque feature to the "competition." She arranged the élite of the candidates in a line in the hall of one of the palaces, gave Theophilus a golden apple, and bade him give the apple to the lady of his choice. He first approached a maiden named Casia, or Cassia, who was not only the most beautiful of them all, but had some repute for poetical talent. "How much evil has come through woman," said the imperial prig, improvising a Greek verse. "Yet how many better things have come from woman," the young poetess modestly retorted, in verse. To her great mortification he passed on, apparently displeased with her ready tongue, and gave the apple to Theodora. Casia retired to a nunnery and to the composition of hymns, and Theodora was, on Whitsunday 830, married and crowned by the patriarch Antony in the historic chapel of St Stephen.

Euphrosyne returned to her convent immediately after the coronation. Some authorities say that she was dismissed by Theophilus, others that she retired voluntarily. It is not improbable that twenty years of religious life had made her a real nun at heart, and she retired the moment she was relieved of those reasons of State which had interrupted her solitude.

During the thirteen years of the reign of Theophilus the Empress bore her children and confined herself to the gynæceum, as a good Empress should. Two sons and five daughters are assigned to her, but, as I said, some, if not all, of these daughters of Theophilus seem to have had an earlier mother. Maria is described as the youngest, yet about the year 832, two or three years after the marriage of Theodora, she married the commander Alexis. She died shortly afterwards.

Theodora had been piously educated in the orthodox faith, and it is piquant to read the approving language of the religious writers when they describe her duping her husband and breaking her oath to him. Cardinal Baronius, who is endorsed by the Bollandists, calls her "the glory and ornament of holy womanhood ... the unique example of exalted holiness in the east." We shall follow these distinguished authorities on sanctity with some hesitation when we afterwards find Theodora encouraging her son in vice, in order that he may leave the administration to her and the clergy, and permitting him to hold drunken suppers with his mistress in her palace; but the worldly minded biographer must be less enthusiastic than they even about her earlier actions.

The first anecdote told of her is that the Emperor one day noticed a heavily laden ship making for the port of Constantinople and learned that it belonged to Theodora. He went down in great anger to the quay, and ordered the ship and its cargo to be burned. "God made me an Emperor," he cried, "and my wife and Augusta has made me a shipowner." The Bollandists merely enlarge at this point on the naughtiness of princes who wish to monopolize trade for their own profit, but I think that a better defence of Theodora can be imagined. The young Empress was probably blameless. It was a custom of courtiers to evade the duties on imports by trading in the name of the Empress, and Theodora would hardly understand the matter sufficiently to refuse her name at once.

The genial critic will also regard with some indulgence her petty mendacities in regard to the beloved images which she cherished in secret. One day her jester, or half-witted page, came suddenly into her room and found her embracing the forbidden statues. She told him that they were dolls, and Denderis went at once to tell Theophilus of the pretty dolls with which his wife played in secret. Theophilus angrily started from the table and went to her room. The fool was mistaken, she cried; she and her maids had been looking in a mirror, and the boy had taken their images in the mirror to be dolls.[18] Theophilus was not convinced. Little more could be learned from the page, who had been flogged by Theodora and told to hold his tongue about dolls, so that whenever Theophilus asked him, he said: "Hush, Emperor; nothing about dolls." But his young daughters also now began to speak of dolls, especially when they returned from visits to Theodora's mother, who had a palace at Gastria across the water. He learned from them that the old lady kept a chest full of pretty dolls, which they were encouraged to kiss and embrace when they visited her. The visits were immediately stopped, and Theodora was compelled to take the most sacred oaths that she would never favour the worship of images. Like Irene, she did so with mental reservation.

The long and vigorous reign of Theophilus ended sadly. Unsuccessful in war, indiscreet at home, and at war with the clergy, he wasted his talent in adding to the luxury of the Court. He found a wonderful mechanic and engaged him to fill the palace with expensive toys that seemed to enhance the imperial dignity. Before "Solomon's Throne" in the Magnaura palace were set lions of gilded bronze which would rise and roar at the approach of foreign ambassadors. Golden trees, with golden singing birds, invisible organs, and all kinds of mechanical barbarities were added to the rare furniture of the palace. New palaces also were built in the grounds: a semicircular hall with roof of gold and doors of bronze and silver, fountains which gave aromatic wine from their silver pipes on feast-days, summer palaces and chapels completely lined with the choicest marbles and mosaics. A superb palace was raised on the Asiatic shore in imitation of the Caliph's palace at Bagdad, and the palace at Blachernæ, in the cool northern suburb, now spread over a vast domain. But with all this facile splendour Theophilus was conscious that he failed to hold the ever-pressing enemies of the Empire, and he became morose and diseased. Theodora seems to have kept his affection to the end. In an earlier year she had detected him in criminal intimacy with one of her maids, and he had asked her forgiveness with great humility. His last act was a brutal murder in her interest. The noble Theophobos, who was married to the Emperor's sister Helena, was in jail on some suspicion. Theophilus feared that he might aspire to the throne, and ordered the head of the unfortunate noble to be brought to him. He died in January 842, leaving the Empire to Theodora and her infant son Michael.[19]

Theodora now had supreme power, and her first care was to restore the worship of images, in spite of her heavy oaths to Theophilus. In this she needed diplomacy, as well as casuistry, since the learned patriarch John, as well as the majority of the Senators, were opposed to images. There was, moreover, a Council of Regency, consisting of three of the abler officials of the Court. The first of them, Theoclistos, the eunuch "keeper of the purple ink," was an official of some ability, and so devoted to Theodora that, in spite of his condition, the gossip of the city associated the saint and the eunuch in a most unedifying manner. The second member was Manuel, an uncle of Theodora and an Iconoclast; the third her brother Bardas, a man of equal ability and unscrupulousness, who could be relied upon either to worship or to break an image according to his interest. It was to this man, in spite of notoriously immoral life, that Theodora entrusted the tutorship of the young prince; and there cannot be the slightest doubt that Michael was deliberately educated in vice and sensuality, in order to divert his attention from political power. St Theodora was to be the mother of the Nero of the Eastern Empire.

The first step was taken in the restoration of images shortly after the beginning of the Regency. Michael fell dangerously ill and at one time he was believed to be dead. The monks came from the great monastery of Studion, the most fiery centre of orthodoxy, to pray over the remains of the Iconoclast—a singular procedure—and it was presently announced that he had miraculously recovered his life and was converted to the worship of images. In this new zeal he pressed the Empress to remove the impious restriction on piety, and for a time she resisted, pleading the sanctity of her oath. Knowing Constantinople as we do, we have little difficulty in regarding the whole procedure as a comedy. At length a council was summoned in the house of Theoclistus, and the reform was sanctioned. The patriarch John was now ordered to convoke a synod; he refused, and the way in which that obstacle was removed so well illustrates the character of Constantinople, if not of Theodora, that it is worth describing.

John was one of the most learned men of his time, a genius in physical science and mechanical art. His rationalistic opposition to the popular cult of relics and statues, however, gave a dark aspect to his learning, and he was commonly regarded as a magician and a secret libertine. Men told each other of the subterraneous chamber which he had in his brother's house for entertaining nuns and other pretty women. In reality, he seems to have been a learned and conscientious man, and, even when Bardas cruelly flogged him, he refused to submit to the Empress's wish and relieve her from her oath. The report was given out from the palace that he had inflicted the marks of the scourge on himself, and had even attempted to commit suicide. He was at once deposed and confined in a monastery; and, when it was reported to Theodora, no doubt falsely, that he had there pricked the eyes out of a picture of Christ, she angrily sentenced him to lose his own eyes and to receive two hundred strokes of the loaded scourge. He had been one of the chief pillars of her husband's reign. His friends, I may add, retorted by accusing the new patriarch Methodius of rape, but decency prevents me from describing how the archbishop happily escaped the charge by proving, in open court, that St Peter had miraculously relieved him from temptations of the flesh many years before.

The new patriarch convoked a synod, and crowds of monks flocked to Constantinople from all parts to encourage the good work, and marched through the streets of Constantinople under their sacred ensigns. Theodora surprised the bishops and abbots, as they sat in conclave, by demanding that they should issue a guarantee that her husband was absolved from his sins. It was a dangerous precedent, and they protested that they had no power to give such an assurance. Theodora then explained that she had presented a sacred image to Theophilus in his last hour, and that he had embraced it fervently. Modern historians are ungallant enough to disbelieve her story, and no doubt there were many at the time who distrusted Theodora's casuistic ability, but when she proceeded to hint that image-worship would not be restored unless they satisfied her, they decreed that the sins of Theophilus had been undone by repentance. At the conclusion of the synod Theodora entertained the holy men in her Carian palace, or palace built entirely of the famous Carian marble, at Blachernæ. Near the end of the banquet, when the cakes and sweets were being served, her eye fell on the grim, disfigured face of the religious poet Theophanes. He had come from Palestine to Constantinople, during her husband's reign, to fight for the images, and Theophilus had sent him into exile with no less than twelve lines of bad verse tattooed on his face, announcing that he was a "wretched vessel of superstition." Theophanes marked the tearful gaze of the Empress, and impetuously cried that he would not forget to ask the judgment of God on Theophilus for the outrage. "Is this the way you keep your promise?" she exclaimed excitedly; and the bishops had to intervene and appease her and the martyr.

This restoration of image-worship seems to be the one virtue which ensured for Theodora a place in the Greek canon of the saints (on 11th February). That she led a chaste life we need not doubt for a moment. The rumour of amorous relations with Theoclistus is foolish gossip, and a man named Gebo, who afterwards claimed to be her natural son, was either an impostor or a lunatic. But the shallowness of her piety and weakness of her moral character are too plainly revealed in the debauching of her son by her own brother, into whose care she gave the young Emperor. The historian Finlay observes that "in the series of Byzantine Emperors from Leo III. to Michael III., only two proved utterly unfit for the duties of their station, and both appear to have been corrupted by the education they received from their mothers." When we reflect on the strange types of men whom the disordered life of the Empire brought to the throne, this is a terrible impeachment of Irene and Theodora; and it is a just impeachment. No man was less fit than her brother Bardas to train a youth, and the only conceivable palliation of Theodora's guilt is that she wished to retain power in the interest of the Church. How even that hope was mocked, and the rule of her son ended in debauchery and murder in her own house, we have next to consider.

For some ten years the Empire enjoyed comparative peace and prosperity. The Bulgarians, learning that a woman and a child ruled the Empire, made inflated demands, but Theodora met them with admirable firmness, and averted war. Her only grave blunder was the ruthless persecution of heresy. She sent officers to convert the masses of Paulicians in the eastern provinces, and, whether with her consent or no, they perpetrated horrible butcheries in the name of religion and engendered a civil war. Then, as Michael approached his sixteenth year, a series of terrible internal troubles and disorders set in.

Gladly following the example of his tutor Bardas, the young Emperor fell in love with the beautiful daughter of a high official of the Court named Inger. Eudocia Ingerina is described by one of the writers of the Court of Constantine VII.—her grandson—as "one of the most beautiful and most modest women of her time." The course of this narrative will show that she was, as most of the chroniclers say, one of the most dissolute women of the time, second only to Theodora's daughter Thecla. Whether she betrayed her laxity even at this early age, or whether Theodora merely dreaded an alliance of her son with a distinguished officer, we cannot confidently say. The chroniclers suggest that she was already the lover of Michael, and that Theodora and Theoclistus interfered. They compelled Michael to marry another Eudocia, daughter of the patrician Decapolita. We do not know the fate of this lady and may trust that she did not live to see the more sordid phases of her husband's life. It seems that very shortly after the marriage he resumed his relations with the daughter of Inger.

Bardas now began to force his ambition more openly and get rid of the members of the Council of Regency. He first, by means of Theoclistus, drove his uncle Manuel into private life, and then turned upon Theoclistus, who ventured to remonstrate with him about his notorious liaison with his own daughter-in-law. Fearing for his life Theoclistus built a house close to the palace, communicating with it by an iron door, which was carefully guarded, and continued to administer the Empire in conjunction with Theodora. There is some indication that Theodora's three sisters—Sophia, Maria and Irene—also had some share in the administration. Bardas pointed out to his pupil that he was improperly excluded by them, and suggested that Theodora intended to marry Theoclistus and have Michael's eyes put out. When, therefore, Theoclistus next went to read his report to Theodora, he was intercepted by a group of the servants of Bardas, who, in the name of the Emperor, demanded his papers. A scuffle took place, and Theoclistus was imprisoned, and presently murdered in his cell. One of the chroniclers would have us believe that one of Theodora's daughters actually witnessed the murder on behalf of her brother.

Theodora was beside herself when the news reached her that her favourite minister had been murdered. She is described as roaming about the palace with dishevelled hair, weeping and upbraiding her son and brother. The natural result was that they decided to remove her, and she saw that her rule had come to an end. She summoned the Senators and laid before them a financial statement of the affairs of the Empire. She had so well husbanded the funds left by Theophilus that a store of gold and silver amounting to many million pounds of our coinage, besides chests of jewels and other treasure, were at the disposal of the State. "I tell you this," she shrewdly added, "in order that you may not readily believe my son the Emperor if, when I have quitted the palace, he tells you that I left it empty." She saluted the Senators, laid down her power, and quitted the imperial palace. But Michael and Bardas were not content. As Theodora and her daughters went to the palace at Blachernæ they were arrested by her elder brother Petronas, shorn of their hair, and confined, in the dress of nuns, in the Carian palace at Blachernæ. They continued, however, to regard the proceedings at Court with close interest, and were transferred to the palace-monastery of Gastria across the water.

From her near exile Theodora watched the next dramatic phase of the quarrel. It was in the year 856, apparently, that Theoclistus was murdered and she forced to resign, and the next ten years witnessed a repellent development of Michael's vices. He has passed into history under the name of Michael the Drunkard, but drunkenness was not the worst of his vices. He lived in open association with Eudocia Ingerina and filled the palace with scenes that had been banished from Roman life with the death of Nero. The only point that can be urged in favour of Byzantine morals is that the drastic legislation and action of earlier Emperors had checked the spread of unnatural vice. Apart from this, Michael the Drunkard ranks with Nero and Caligula, and, in respect of some kinds of grossness, surpasses them. Only the more repellent pages of Zola's "La Terre" offer an analogy to the coarse practices which Michael rewarded in the abominable circle he gathered about him. It is enough to say that the filthiest of his friends dressed in the vestments of the archbishop, and had eleven followers dressed as metropolitan bishops; that they used the sacred vessels, with a mixture of mustard and vinegar, for their parody of the Mass; and that they paraded the streets on asses in this guise, and hailed the patriarch himself with obscene cries and gestures. The treasures left by Theodora were soon dissipated on these ruffians and on Michael's favourite charioteers, and the golden curiosities made by Theophilus were melted down to eke out the failing exchequer. And when Michael was told that the enemies of the Empire were once more pressing on its narrowed frontiers, he callously ordered that the line of signal fires, which were wont to announce the inroad of the enemy from the distant provinces, should be abandoned, so that his chariot races might not be interrupted.

Such was the spectacle which Theodora had to contemplate for ten weary years, nor can she have been unconscious how deeply she was responsible for it. At length, in 866, the infamous career of her brother came to a close, and she was free to return to the Court. A new favourite had arisen and displaced

Bardas. A handsome groom in the imperial service, Basil the Macedonian, had caught the fancy of Michael. When Bardas one day denounced a noble for not saluting him in the street, as he passed in the gorgeous robe of a Cæsar—a dignity to which Michael raised him in 865—the noble was deposed from office and Basil put in his place. Basil was married, but the besotted Emperor forced him to divorce his wife and marry Eudocia Ingerina; and, as Michael retained Eudocia as his own mistress, he brought his willing sister Thecla from her nunnery and made her the mistress of Basil. Bardas was now alarmed and perceived that either he or Basil must die. I need not enter into the sordid details. Enough to say that Basil and Michael decoyed the Cæsar from the city, after a solemn oath on the cross and the sacrament, which were held before them by the patriarch, that they had no design on his life, and murdered him. This occurred on Whit-Monday 866; on the following Saturday Basil was crowned and anointed co-Emperor of the Romans.

EUDOCIA INGERINA, WIFE OF BASIL I

To this blood-stained and sordid Court Theodora did not hesitate to return as soon as Bardas was slain. One of the chroniclers tells an anecdote which would, if one dare reproduce it in full, give some idea of the atmosphere which she breathed. Michael one day summoned her to come and receive the blessing of the patriarch, who was with him. She entered and bent in inobservant reverence before the vested figure beside her son, and she was, to the loud delight of Michael, startled by an outrage that the rudest peasant would hardly suffer to be offered to his mother. It was the infamous mock-patriarch Gryllus, perpetrating his coarsest joke.

This, however, seems to have occurred before her abdication, and she seems, after the murder of Bardas, to have lived chiefly in the Anthemian palace across the water. Unfortunately, the last scene in the squalid reign of her son shows that she still tolerated his excesses. Basil, in turn, had seen a new favourite arise and threaten his hope of inheriting the Empire. In a drunken fit Michael had put his purple slippers on a vulgar servant—a man who had formerly rowed in the galleys—for praising his chariot-driving, and brutally observed to the tearful Eudocia, who sat beside him, that the man was more fit for the purple than her husband. Basil, if not Eudocia, concluded that the Emperor must be assassinated, and before long Theodora provided them with an opportunity. I am not for a moment suggesting that Theodora was aware of their intention, but this last appearance of hers on the stage of history is a painful close of her career.

She invited Michael to sup and stay at her palace after he had spent a day hunting on the Asiatic side of the water. Such an invitation might be innocent, even virtuous, if there were a design to separate the young Emperor from his associates and, perhaps, endeavour to counsel him. But we find that his usual Court accompanied him, and the evening was spent in drunken debauch. The new favourite, Basilicius, and Michael were put to bed in a drunken condition. Basil, with whom was Eudocia, had slipped from the room and tampered with the fastenings of their doors, and in the middle of the night Theodora awoke to hear the clash of swords and cries of hurrying men; Michael and Basilicius had been murdered, and Basil and Eudocia were hastening to Constantinople to secure the palace.

The last glimpse we have of St Theodora is when she and her daughters convey the remains of the wretched Emperor to the city for interment in the great marble tombs of the kings. It was the autumn of 866, and, as the Greek Church celebrates her festival on 11th February, we may assume that she lived a few months afterwards in sad, if not penitent, obscurity. Few in modern times, even of those who share her creed, would venture to describe her as "the glory and ornament of her sex." No woman of high character could have been betrayed into the criminal blunders which Theodora committed, however exalted she may have considered her ultimate aim to be. Yet we may grant that she was rather tainted by the pitiful casuistry of her time than evil in disposition, and the historical memorial of her life-work is a sufficiently terrible punishment of her errors.

It remains briefly to dismiss the Empresses Eudocia and Thecla. On the morning after the murder Eudocia Ingerina sat proudly by the side of her husband, in the glorious robes and jewels of a reigning Empress, as he went to the great church to consecrate his Empire to Christ. She enjoyed her dignity for about fifteen years, but the only incident recorded of her is that she was detected by her husband in a liaison with a steward of the table. Thecla was discarded at the death of her brother and passed to less exalted lovers. Some years after his accession she sent a servant with a petition to Basil. "Who lives with your mistress at present?" the Emperor cynically asked. "Neatocomites," the man promptly replied.

Neatocomites was flogged and put in a monastery, and Thecla was flogged and robbed of the greater part of her fortune. It is the last glimpse we have of the family of St Theodora.

CHAPTER VIII

Basil the Macedonian, or Basil the groom, son of a Macedonian peasant of Armenian extraction, enjoyed his imperial wealth, and made excellent use of his imperial power, during nearly twenty years. His story is not one to encourage the venerable adage that honesty is the best policy. But we have dismissed his Empress, Eudocia Ingerina, whose only known features are great beauty and equally great licence in love, and we pass on to review the remarkable series of Empresses whom his son successively married. I say his son, but no historian doubts that Leo VI. was really the son of Michael the Drunkard. The temper of Eudocia Ingerina had been so accommodating that royal genealogists have to indulge largely in arithmetical calculation in order to determine the paternity of her children, or the maternity of Basil's children. Briefly, Basil's eldest son, Constantine, was probably a child of the poor Maria who had been sent back to Macedonia with her pockets full of gold, but he died before his father and will not interest us; the second son, Leo, was almost certainly the son of Michael and Eudocia, who had been transferred in a state of pregnancy from the embraces of the Emperor to the embraces of his groom; the third and fourth sons, Alexander and Stephen, were presumably born of Basil and Eudocia; and the four daughters must, in despair, be distributed over the group of parents.

When Leo had reached the age of fifteen or sixteen, his elder brother having died two years before, Basil and Eudocia sought him a wife, and we are at last so fortunate as to meet a really blameless Empress, and one whose title to her place in the calendar of the saints will not be disputed by the most irreverent historians of modern times. St Theophano has, moreover, been revealed to us more fully in recent years by the publication of ancient Greek manuscripts that were unknown in the days of Gibbon.[20] That they enlarge her virtues and attenuate the vices of her husband is only what we should expect in Byzantine writers of the time, but they enable us to give a satisfactory portrait of an imperial saint and to set it in pleasant contrast to the figures of her contemporaries and successors. Theophano is a stray lily in a garden of roses.

The first wife of Leo was the very pretty and pious daughter of a distinguished noble of the city, Constantinus Martinacius. Her mother had died in her early years, but her education had proceeded on lines of the most orthodox piety, and she had a genius for assimilating its ascetic prescriptions. The piety of her father, however, did not prevent him from putting forward his fifteen-year-old daughter when, in the winter of 881-882, Basil and Eudocia sought a mate for Leo. The city and provinces were, as usual, scoured by the special matrimonial commissioners, and Theophano was one of the dozen maids introduced into the great palace for inspection. Eudocia, a good judge, reviewed them in the Magnaura palace, and selected Theophano and two others. Eudocia's high birth probably gave her some advantage over the obscure Athenian girl and another rival who ran her close in the competition. She was exhibited to Basil, and he at once placed a ring on her young finger and ordered Leo to marry her. Much subsequent evil might have been avoided if the youth had been consulted. Either the excessive piety of Theophano was distasteful to him, or he had already set his mind on another lady. But Basil was never indulgent to Leo, whom he must have regarded as Michael's son, and the children were married with all the splendid ceremony which the Emperor Constantine describes for us, and entered upon their duty of sustaining the dynasty.

The pious Theophano soon found that life in a court was not a mere monotonous round of ceremonies. The chief friend and adviser of Basil was a compatriot—that is to say, a Macedonian of Armenian origin (Armenian colonies having been transferred, on account of the Saracens, to Macedonia)—named Stylianus Zautzes, and Zautzes had a pretty and lively daughter named Zoe. It is probable that Leo had contracted a boyish love of Zoe before he was forced to marry the young saint, and he was not of a nature to sacrifice the rose to the lily. Not very long after the marriage Theophano complained to Basil, we learn from the life of Euthymius, that her husband was making love to Zoe. Leo naturally protests to the patriarch, and no doubt protested to Basil, that his admiration was Platonic, but we shall see that he did not usually confine himself to that academic emotion. Basil believed the charge, caught Leo by the hair and flung him to the ground, and compelled Zoe to marry, out of hand, a man to whom she was more than indifferent. He was sowing a crop of tragedies.

Eudocia died about this time, and the young Theophano took her place in the rich ceremonial of the Court, walking in the endless processions and being borne in the golden litter, drawn by white horses, to the great church and the lesser shrines and palaces. Her new dignity cannot have lasted many months when a fresh and more furious storm broke upon her virtue, and she bore herself admirably. The second most intimate friend and counsellor of Basil was the abbot Theodore, of Santabaris in Phrygia, a very enterprising and peculiar monk. He was a master of magic and was regarded with the greatest awe by the Emperor. Leo ventured to urge on Basil that the man was an impostor and humbug, and the chroniclers say that the abbot turned vindictively on Leo. No one was allowed to have weapons in the company of the Emperor, but Theodore persuaded Leo that, if he kept a knife concealed in his boot when he was hunting with Basil, he might be able in an emergency to render a service and disarm Basil's anger. Leo hid a knife in his boot, and the monk promptly advised Basil to search the prince, as he feared conspiracy.

So from the palace Leo passed to prison, or confinement in the Pearl palace, and Theophano went with her little daughter Eudocia to keep him company and impress on him the duty of resignation to the divine will. The chroniclers differ as to the length of the imprisonment; some make it three months and others three years. As Zautzes and the Senators intervened and begged Basil to reconsider his verdict, I prefer to accept the shorter term. One of the chroniclers tells us that the most effective pleader for Leo was a parrot, kept in the palace, which someone taught to cry: "Poor Leo, poor Leo." At all events, Zautzes, and the patriarch Photius, and numbers of the Senators, insisted that Leo was innocent; and he was set at liberty. He was now the obvious heir to the throne. Basil could not put him aside in favour of a younger son without admitting his irregular parentage, and it is not unlikely that the old Emperor had a regard for Theophano. For a few years, therefore, the young Empress continued to rule the great palace, to which Basil had made superb additions, and to practise the high virtues which her husband so little appreciated. Then (in March 886) Basil left his purple robes to Leo, and Leo and his wife and child to the care of Zautzes.

The first concern of Leo the Philosopher—who was no philosopher at all, though he was well read in the letters of the time—was to seek Abbot Theodore of Santabaris. The monk had prudently retired to a bishopric in remote Pontus before Leo came to the throne, but he was brought to Constantinople, deposed, scourged, and exiled to Athens, where his eyes were afterwards cut out. It was the punishment he had recommended Basil to inflict on Leo. As the patriarch Photius was believed to have been in league with the monk-magician, he also was deposed, and Leo's younger brother, Stephen, was made archbishop. Leo's four sisters had already been turned into nuns by the prudent Basil, and there remained only the second brother Alexander, who was content to await the hour for his own imperial debauch.

Leo's next care was to renew his pleasant relations with the fascinating Zoe, "the most beautiful woman of her age." A few added years would have merely ripened her charms, and her father regarded with complacency her promotion to the place of imperial concubine, and continued to discharge his functions as commander of the foreign guards (hetæriarch). To Theophano only was it a grave affliction to find the palace enlivened by the fiery and beautiful oriental. She endured the outrage for some years, patiently working at her embroidery for the altars and spending long hours in prayer, until her one child died, in the winter of 892-893, and she begged Leo to allow her to retire to a convent, leaving him free to marry. Leo was not unwilling, but the patriarch Euthymius foolishly refused to consecrate her, and she languished for a few months longer in her uncongenial world.

The situation is illuminated by a passage in the chronicles which leads up to the first plot on Leo's life. Some time in 891, apparently, Leo and Zoe and Zautzes, with other members of their family, went to stay at the Damian palace in the suburbs, probably for a hunt. Theophano, the chronicler says, was not with them; she was "busy praying" in the Blachernæ palace, to which she seems to have generally retired from the dissolute Court. For some entirely obscure reason Zoe's brother and his friends concerted a plot against the life of Leo; we can hardly suppose that it was a case of outraged brothers wiping out the dishonour of their sister, seeing that Zautzes himself was a member of the house-party. Whatever the cause was, Zoe, who was sleeping with Leo, heard whispering in the garden without, and, creeping to the window, learned that her brother Tzantzes and others were about to murder Leo. These are the sober details given in the chronicles, but Byzantine history is so full of melodrama that we need not hesitate to accept them. She roused her lover, and they stole from the house and reached Constantinople. Leo suspected that Zautzes himself had been privy to the plot and was estranged from him for some months.

This seems to have been the position during the early years of Leo's reign: his wife "busy praying," or mortifying her frail body, in the quieter palace at Blachernæ, while Leo floated over the Sea of Marmora with Zoe in the great pleasure-galleys he had constructed, or wantoned in his various palaces. Theophano died in the seventh year of his reign—on 10th November 893 according to de Boor's calculations, though her festival is celebrated by the Greek Church on 16th December. The modern mind would be little impressed by an account of the miracles which her remains are said to have wrought after death, nor can one read without a certain amusement that, in the words of a later Emperor and most of the chroniclers, she deserved the aureole of sanctity by "her freedom from jealousy and her patient endurance of the contempt of Zoe." The nobles of Constantinople would not be unwilling to see such virtues consecrated by the Church. There is, however, no doubt that the daughter of Constantinus Martinacius merited her place in the calendar of the Church, and she is one of the few blameless women to gratify the biographer of the Empresses.

From the saint we pass to the sinner; from "the lilies and languors of virtue" to the "roses and raptures of vice." In the following year Leo violated all decency by taking Zoe into the sacred palace. Her husband, the patrician Theodore Guniazitza, died so opportunely that it was inevitably believed that he had been poisoned; and, although the statement is no more than a rumour, and one may hesitate to-day to admit that "an adulteress may easily become a poisoner," it cannot be said to be improbable. Leo now approached the patriarch Euthymius on the question of marrying Zoe, and the prelate again blundered, in too narrow a zeal for his ideals, and sternly resisted. He was removed to a monastery, and before the end of 894 Zoe was the legitimate Empress of the Roman world. It was, however, only to enjoy a few more hours of pleasure in the gilded palace. Her father died in the spring of 896, and Zoe followed him in the autumn or winter of the same year, having worn the crown for one year and eight months. For her the ecclesiastical chroniclers have no praise; they affirm that, when men came to lay her remains in her marble sarcophagus, the words "Miserable daughter of Babylon" were found to have been mysteriously carved on the stone. Beautiful, careless and sensual as she was, one may doubt if a single stone could be flung at her if Leo had been allowed to consult his own heart at the time of his first marriage.

Leo was now, in his thirtieth year, a widower for the second time, and he was little reconciled to that condition. Not only was his dissipated brother Alexander greedily waiting to occupy his throne, but an astrologer had assured Leo that he would yet have a son, and the message of the stars must be fulfilled. Third marriages, on the other hand, were subjected to grave ecclesiastical censure, and for several years the Emperor did not venture to take the forbidden step. Indeed, when he did begin to speak of marriage, Zoe's relatives and other disappointed courtiers took alarm and plotted against his life. Her nephew Basil had his hair oiled and fired, and all the survivors of the Zautzes family were driven from the city. The clearance made room for fresh courtiers, one of whom, a Saracen named Samonas, became the master of intrigue which we almost invariably find in the palace in each generation. One instance of his wit will suffice to make him known and to illustrate life at the Court. The commander Andronicus had taken alarm and fled to the Saracens. Leo had no wish to injure him, and he entrusted a message to that effect to a captive Saracen and bade him deliver it to Andronicus. In order to outwit Samonas, who did not wish the able officer to return and dispute his power, the message was ingeniously enclosed in a wax candle. Before he left Constantinople, however, Samonas told the Saracen that the candle contained a plot against his country, and it was never delivered to Andronicus.

At the beginning of 899 Leo braved the censures of the clergy and, apparently, sent out his commissioners in search of a bride. As a result he married, probably at Easter, a beautiful maiden from the Opsikian district—the region of Asia Minor nearest to Constantinople—named Eudocia. To his great mortification, Eudocia gave birth to a boy, but both mother and child died immediately. The majority of Christian Emperors would have resigned themselves to this third disappointment, but it seems to have increased Leo's determination. Most historians admit that it was not so much sensuality, which such a man as Leo could easily gratify, as the determination to have a son, which inspired Leo's defiance of the Church; not impossibly he also had regard to the complaisance of the Western clergy in face of the conduct of the great Frankish monarchs.

It is conjectured by de Boor that Eudocia died about Easter of the year 900, and before the end of that, or in the following, year Leo began to look for another spouse. In place of the patriarch Euthymius, who had resisted his marriage to Zoe, he had appointed a certain Nicholas, an intimate friend of his in earlier years, and he expected the new prelate to be accommodating. Nicholas, however, violently opposed the idea of a fourth marriage, and a long and stormy struggle with the Church party followed. On one occasion a man attempted the life of the Emperor in a church, and Alexander and Nicholas were strongly suspected of treachery, but no torture could wring a confession from the assailant.

Leo took a first defiant step by again admitting a lady to the palace. Zoe Carbonopsina, as she was named, seems to have had a humble origin, since her son, the imperial historian, Constantine Porphyrogenitus, cannot devise any genealogy for her. Diligent research, however, finds that she was related to the famous abbot St Epiphanius, the admiral Himerius, and the patrician Nicholas, so that we must not imagine her as a flower transplanted by imperial commissioners from some rural garden. Her later career will confirm the impression she makes on her first entry into the pages of history as mistress of the Emperor. She was a woman of great vigour and faint scruples: a less pleasant type of sinner than the Zoe who had preceded her in the halls of Daphne.

We do not know how long Zoe lived in the palace as Leo's mistress, nor is it material to seek to determine. It is enough that in the course of the year 905 she promised to become a mother, and Leo renewed his effort to provide a legitimate heir to his throne. The confused and poorly written records of the time merely tantalize us with fragmentary or conflicting statements, and one must present a connected version of the accession to the throne of Zoe Carbonopsina with some hesitation. Apparently ("Life of Euthymius") the patriarch Nicholas was at first not unfriendly. He blessed the womb which gave promise of an heir, ordered prayers in the churches, and met Zoe without a blush in the palace. These candid details need a short explanation. A bitter feud had set in between the followers of the deposed patriarch Euthymius and the followers of Nicholas, so that an admirer of the former may be trusted to say even more than the truth in regard to Nicholas. Leo seems to have promised the clergy that he would put away Zoe as soon as she gave him an heir to the throne. But the biographer of Euthymius professes to throw another light on the situation. A rising took place in the provinces, and Leo secured a letter which proved that Nicholas was involved in it. It was in order to avoid the consequences of this treachery that he submitted to Leo.

A boy, the future Emperor and writer Constantine Porphyrogenitus, saw the light in the course of the year 905—a comet appearing in the heavens, in ominous conjunction, at the time—and in the beginning of 906 he was solemnly baptized by the patriarch, and had his uncle Alexander and some of the highest Senators as godfathers. The modern reader is amazed at the spirit which will permit the heads of Church and State to gather thus in their grandest robes about the cradle of an illegitimate child, yet resist, even to death, a fourth marriage which might supply a legitimate heir to the imperial house; but Byzantine life will exhibit singular features to the end of its history. The child was baptized, and the clergy trusted to hear no more of marriage. To their great anger Leo recalled Zoe to the palace, from which she had been temporarily removed, and found a priest to marry them. At the same time Zoe was made Augusta and Basilissa (Queen) of the Empire.

The clergy now assailed Leo with every invective, and the patriarch forbade him to enter the church. One almost despairs of following the Constantinopolitans through their tangle of scruples and licences, but we find that Leo met the prelate by entering the church at a side door and sitting in a part, apparently, where the singers used to take refreshments. He also sent a request that the Roman bishop and the three patriarchs of the East would pronounce upon the validity of his marriage. When they declared in his favour, and Nicholas still resisted, Samonas consulted his large faculty for intrigue; indeed, we may confidently trace the counsel of that wily courtier, a great friend of Zoe, in the whole procedure. Nicholas was invited to dine at the Bucoleon palace, on the shore of the Sea of Marmora. In the middle of the banquet he was again pressed to withdraw, and again refused; and the chamberlain's servants dragged him down the stairs which led to the palace quay and shipped him to Asia. Euthymius now returned to the see, and, after a decent show of reluctance, recognized the marriage of Zoe. Some of his admirers recount that he was directed in a vision to overrule the law of the Church; others tell us that Leo compelled him by threatening to enact a law that every citizen might have, if he pleased, three or four simultaneous wives. If we change the word "simultaneous" into "successive" we shall not be far from the truth.

The adventurous career of Zoe Carbonopsina now ran quietly for a few years. Her boy flourished, and was, about four years later, associated in the purple with his father. The only event to ruffle the even flow of her pleasant life in the palace was one of those deadly feuds of rival courtiers which were of constant occurrence in the great palace. Samonas had introduced into her service a handsome Paphlagonian named Constantine, and, about the year 911, was alarmed to perceive that this man was supplanting him in the royal favour. He denounced Constantine to Leo for improper conduct with the Empress. In another passage the chronicler has already described Constantine as a eunuch, and it is not the only occasion on which we find this strange charge against an Empress in the chronicles; it may be added that another writer marries Constantine to a cousin of Zoe. Leo, at all events, was convinced, and ordered that Constantine be shaved and put in a monastery. He repented, however, and brought the eunuch back to the palace. In revenge Samonas drew up a libellous writing on the Emperor, and secretly put it in the church. There was great agitation in the palace, especially as an eclipse of the moon occurred at the height of the quarrel. Leo the Philosopher trembled and sent for a bishop who was better versed than he in astrology. On this occasion the reader of the stars proved correct. When Samonas intercepted him, and asked whether the darkening of the moon portended evil for him or for Leo, the bishop answered: "You." In a few days he was betrayed, and he exchanged his hope of the throne for the obscurity of a monastery.

Leo died in the next year, commending his wife and child to the Senators, who swore tearful oaths to protect her and the boy from any misconduct on the part of his successor and younger brother Alexander. But Alexander met no opposition when, as soon as he had ascended the throne, he bade Zoe leave her child and quit the palace. Even the boy had a narrow escape, as Alexander ordered that he should be castrated, but his guardians happily lied to the Emperor and represented that Constantine was too delicate to live. All knew that the reign of Constantine would be short. Although only in his twenty-first year, he had ruined his constitution by vicious indulgence, and the life he led after mounting the throne was killing him. He perished miserably from intemperance within a year, leaving his young colleague to a Council of Regents, from which he had carefully excluded Zoe.

The imperial career of Zoe was, however, by no means closed. A regency was the opportunity of a Byzantine Empress, and Zoe had, no doubt, faithful servants about her boy in the palace. He was now seven years old, and he insisted that his mother must return to the palace. She at once took the lead in the administration, and, having the support of a group of experienced statesmen and several able commanders, she must have looked forward to a long and prosperous rule. At one moment it was gravely threatened with premature extinction. One of the commanders in Asia Minor was invited by some of the disaffected nobles to seize the throne, and it seemed to the vigorous Constantine Ducas that the hour long ago promised to him by astrologers had come. He crossed the sea in the night, and had seized the anterior part of the palace before the guards were thoroughly roused. Then one of the regents flung himself upon the intruders with a troop of armed servants and sailors—there seems to have been treason among the guards—and Zoe presently learned that Ducas and, it is said, three thousand of the combatants lay in a lake of blood on the marble floor of the palace. A terrible vengeance purified Constantinople of those who were opposed to the rule of Zoe and her son. Women were shorn, boys castrated, and men hung on gallows along the Asiatic shore for all Constantinople to see.

During several years Zoe seems to have governed with vigour and judgment, but since it is impossible to disentangle her share from that of her servants and counsellors, it would be inexpedient to enter into the prosy details of the administration. A personal note is sounded when we find, in a later page of one of the chronicles, that she was intimate with the admiral, and later Emperor, Romanus. Neither of the two can be regarded as very scrupulous, but it is probable that Bishop Luidprand, who accuses her, is in this hastily retailing the gossip he picked up in Constantinople. A disappointed ambassador is apt to be a libeller.

The behaviour of Romanus in the crisis which, in the year 919, put an end to her reign does not encourage the idea of a liaison. By dexterous diplomacy Zoe had obtained peace with the Saracens and then withdrawn all her forces from Asia, to make a concentrated attack upon the Bulgarians. It was admirable, if not very subtle, policy, since at that time the Saracens and Bulgarians were the upper and nether stones that threatened to grind the Eastern capital between them. Unhappily the jealousy of her two chief commanders betrayed and ruined her. A vast army was assembled at Constantinople, new arms and equipment were supplied, and advance pay was liberally given to the soldiers. The cross was borne at their head by the clergy, and, with a last entreaty that all would be faithful to their country, Zoe sent forth the great army which was to begin the restoration of the Empire. And in a few weeks the fleet returned with the news of complete and irreparable disaster. The admiral Romanus had, out of jealousy of the land commander, failed to transfer their northern allies across the Danube; the general of the troops, Leo Phocas, too eager for glory, had attacked without his allies and been utterly routed.

Zoe at once summoned a council and proposed that her alleged lover should lose his eyes for his failure to co-operate. Romanus had, however, a firm hold on the affection of the sailors, and it was judged inexpedient to attempt to displace him. But the position of Zoe was, through no fault of hers, terribly weakened, and a change of government was openly expected. Zoe's chief hope lay in the fact that the two commanders, Leo Phocas and Romanus, could not share the power, yet neither was likely to suffer the other to occupy it, and for some time matters remained in suspense. Then the experienced intriguers of the palace began to act, and the quarrel hastened to its climax. Constantine, the favourite chamberlain, urged Zoe to build on Leo Phocas (who had married his sister) and take him into the Regency. A rival courtier, the young Emperor's tutor, Theodore, then espoused the cause of Romanus, and secretly urged him to declare himself the protector of the boy. Zoe ordered Romanus to sail with the fleet to the Black Sea, and, when Romanus pleaded that the pay was in arrears and the sailors disaffected, the chamberlain himself rowed out to the commander's vessel with the money. He did not return, and Zoe was soon alarmed to hear that the admiral had imprisoned him on the fleet.

The patriarch and Senators were summoned to the palace, and it was decided that their leaders should row out to the fleet and demand an explanation of Romanus. By this time the citizens were keenly interested in the quarrel. The fleet lay in sight of all on the Sea of Marmora, and the detention of the chief eunuch of the palace became known and seems to have pleased the people. When the patriarch and the heads of the Senate went down to the quay, they were stoned and forced to retire. Early the next morning Zoe went to the Bucoleon palace, where Constantine and his tutor lived, and demanded an explanation. Strong in the support of the admiral, whom he now induced to draw up the fleet in battle array opposite the Bucoleon palace, the tutor replied insolently that the time had come for Constantine to take the reins; the eunuch Constantine, he said, had ruined the palace and Leo Phocas had wasted the army. Zoe saw that she had lost the battle. She submitted very quietly, except that when the aggressive tutor ordered her to quit the palace she appealed to her son, and was allowed to remain.

Little remains to be told of the fourth wife of Leo the Philosopher. She was for a time an idle spectator, in the palace, of the course of events. The patriarch Nicholas sternly challenged the admiral, and, when he disavowed the charge of treason, invited him ashore to clear himself. In the historic church by the lighthouse a number of the higher officials gathered to hear Romanus swear the "direst oaths" on the true cross that he would be loyal to the young Emperor, and the reconciliation was sealed by Constantine wedding the admiral's daughter Helena in April (919), a month later. Leo Phocas had meantime retired to the provinces and raised an army. By the characteristically Byzantine device of sending a prostitute with a secret message among his troops, his force was weakened and his rebellion soon trodden out. Zoe now played her last and most desperate card, and attempted the life of Romanus. Some of the chroniclers give the charge as a rumour, but when her son observes that she was "detected" in an attempt to poison the food of Romanus, by means of one of his servants, we cannot hesitate to believe it. She was at once removed from the palace, forced to take the vows of religion, and ended her romantic life, at some unknown date, in the monastery of St Euphemia at Petrion.

CHAPTER IX

THE TAVERN-KEEPER'S DAUGHTER

It may not be inexpedient to pause for a moment to consider the general character of the period through which the romantic story of the Empresses is hurrying us. The reader may learn with some astonishment that we are now, in the tenth century, in the golden age of Byzantine history; or that, at least, the Roman Empire in the East has nearly returned to the altitude it had reached in the days of Justinian and Theodora. It is not a part of a biographer's duty to enlarge on historical themes, and the somewhat slender thread which he pursues through the web of history may lead to erroneous conclusions. Precisely on that account, however, it seems advisable to say a word in correction of the prejudice which the restricted study of one set of characters may create. It shall be brief.

The truth in regard to the Byzantine Empire seems to lie between the disdain of older historians like Gibbon and Finlay and the exaggerated claims made for it by some recent writers. I speak of character only, not of art or industry or military success. In some respects—in regard to unnatural vice, for instance—it is superior to the older Empire of the West; in ordinary licentiousness it has no superiority whatever, and the ascetic code it so pompously boasts only makes its guilt the greater; while there are persistent strains of coarseness in its character which tempt one to characterize it as barbaric. Castration and the excision of eyes continue for many centuries, under almost every Emperor and Empress, ordinary punishments of political offence; and the constant violation of the most terrible oaths that the clergy can devise, the abominable device of filling the priesthood and the monastic world with reputed criminals, the unceasing intrigues of eunuchs and officers, the sanguinary coercion of heretics, the persistent financial and administrative corruption, and the lamentable casuistry of priests and religious women, betray a new and general type of character which no amount of appreciation of Byzantine art can restore to honour. The four hundred years of Byzantine history that we have traversed, compared with the four hundred years which preceded them in Roman history, show no elevation of the type of womanhood, nor will the four centuries that remain compel us to alter this conclusion.

The young Empress Helena, daughter of Romanus, whom we introduced at the close of the last chapter is imperfectly, but not favourably, known to us. Beautiful and intelligent, she found no occasion to assert herself as long as her father lived. That unscrupulous commander had very quickly found a way to gratify his personal ambition without violating the letter of his solemn oaths. He had in March sworn on the wood of the true cross to be loyal to Constantine; in September of the same year he received, or obtained, the dignity of Cæsar, and three months later he was co-Emperor. In the following January he made his wife Theodora Empress, and in May he conferred imperial rank on his son Christopher and his wife Sophia. Later he gave the purple to his two remaining sons, and destined his fourth son,

Theophylactus, for the patriarchate. Further, "in order to prevent plots," which were frequent, he put his own name before that of Constantine, and arrogated the whole work of administration. He lived in the largest, latest and most superb palace of the imperial town—the golden-roofed Chrysotriclinon—and, plebeian as he was by birth, carried the pageantry and ceremonial of the Court to its highest point. His wife Theodora did not long survive her elevation, and Helena seems to have taken the chief place as Empress in the glittering crowd, but she escapes our scrutiny altogether until the close of the twenty-five years' reign of her father.

Romanus seems in his later years to have shown symptoms of remorse and made edifying preparations for death. His philanthropy and religious fervour alarmed his sons, who concluded, apparently, that if his repentance were carried too far they might lose their purple robes. The eldest son, Christopher, had died, and the youngest, Theophylactus, was quite happy in possession of the patriarchate; he had, it seemed to the pious, turned the cathedral into a theatre and the bishop's house into a place of debauch, and his religious duties were so far postponed to the cares of his stable of two thousand horses that he would cut a ceremony short when a groom came to the altar to whisper that a favourite mare had foaled. There remained Stephen and Constantine, whose royal position seemed to be threatened. Stephen, with the consent of his brother, deposed his father at the end of 944, and sent him into a monastery on the Princes' Islands.

Helena was the chief inspirer of the next intrigue. Constantine Porphyrogenitus had sought consolation in art and letters for the imperial power of which he had been defrauded. He was now a tall, straight, well-made man of thirty-nine, with mild blue eyes and fresh, ruddy countenance, but he had little faculty or disposition for politics, and was more interested in the pleasures of the table and the library. His attainments in art and science would have been respectable in any other than a king. Helena, however, supplied the resolution he lacked, and watched the procedure of her brothers. She concluded that they intended to displace or ignore her husband, and she stimulated him to action, or, more probably, acted herself with the aid of her head chamberlain Basil, an illegitimate son of Romanus. On the evening of 27th January the royal brothers were invited to sup with their mild-mannered and long-suffering colleague, and they found themselves dragged from their purple couches by his servants, bound, and put aboard a waiting vessel at the palace quay. Some of the authorities improbably state that they asked permission to visit their father, Romanus, in his monastery, so that Gibbon's genial picture of the father cynically greeting his sons at the shore is not without foundation. The story is unlikely, however, and they were soon despatched to remote parts.

During the fifteen years' reign of her husband Helena is known to us only for the unscrupulousness with which, in collusion with the head chamberlain Basil, she sold offices of state to the highest bidders. The interest passes to the new and singular types of Empresses who now enter the chronicles. The first is the most pathetic and remarkable figure in the whole strange gallery of the Byzantine Empresses. Helena and Constantine had a son named Romanus, and the elder Romanus, who was most assiduous at making royal matches for his descendants, had decided to marry the boy in good time. It seems not unlikely that, in his last year of life, he realized the unscrupulousness of his sons, and entertained a tardy concern about his oath. At that time the kingdom of Italy was ruled by Hugh, a violent and half-barbaric monarch, whose conjugal arrangements were calculated to furnish a rich supply of royal alliances. Romanus sent an envoy to ask the hand of one of his natural daughters, and the little Bertha, a beautiful child of tender years, was conducted to Constantinople by the Bishop of Parma and married to the boy Emperor. Romanus was five years old, and it is not likely that Bertha, or Eudocia, as she was now named, was older than he. What type of woman the little princess, offspring of a wild Teuton and his concubine, would have made, we shall never know, for she died five years afterwards. The chroniclers are careful to add that she died a virgin.

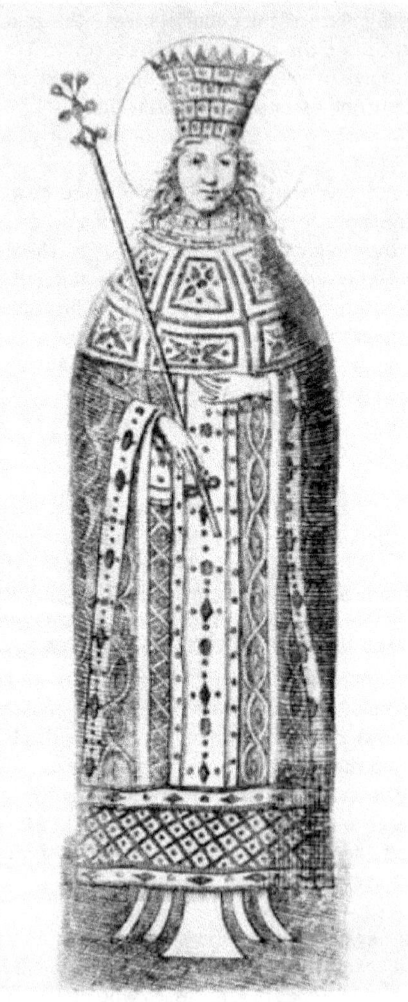

THE EMPRESS HELENA

FROM DU CANGE'S 'HISTORIA BYZANTINA'

The young prince was allowed to grow, and develop his vices, for a few years, before contracting a second marriage. It seems to have been in his eighteenth year that he took a second wife, and his choice illustrates at once the supineness of his father, the selfishness of his mother, and the unrestrained passion of the son. He married Anastaso, the daughter of a tavern-keeper named Crateros. We have seen so many types of Empresses ascend the throne that it might cause us little surprise to find a woman passing from the counter of a wine-shop to the palace, but there is grave suspicion that Theophano—the name substituted for Anastaso—was base in more than the genealogical sense of the word. She is accused of poisoning her father-in-law and her first husband, and she certainly led the assassins to the chamber of her second husband. Whatever allowance we make for the prejudice against her humble birth, authentic facts in her story show that she was licentious and criminal.

We do not know how the son of a highly cultivated Emperor made the acquaintance of a tavern-girl. It is clear that she was a young woman of singular beauty—"a kind of miracle of nature," Zonaras says—and most graceful figure, and I would conjecture that some courtier among the disreputable followers of the young prince brought her to his notice. There may have been a "beauty show," and the publican may have boldly pressed the merits of his daughter, but some attention was generally paid to birth in these matrimonial contests. A tavern-woman was still held to be equivalent to a prostitute or an actress. It is useless to speculate. Constantine idly acquiesced, and the beautiful Theophano passed from the sordid scenes of a little wine-shop to the wonderful splendours of the palace. Courtly writers afterwards discovered that there was royal blood in her veins. The only serious clue we have to her origin is that she came from Laconia, and we may regard her as a common type of Greek.

It is calculated that the marriage took place about the end of the year 956. For three years no events occur that enable us to penetrate the secluded life of the palace, though the subsequent events suggest that Helena and her daughters were disdainful of the vulgar beauty and were met with a virulent hatred. At the end of three years (August or September 959) Constantine died, and the ampler chronicles tell a circumstantial story of his being poisoned by his son Romanus and Theophano. A poison was, it is said, put in his physic. Either by accident or from suspicion he spilled most of the contents of the cup and escaped death. But his health was gravely impaired; he went to visit the monasteries of Mount Olympus, fell dangerously ill there—the chronicler says that perhaps more poison was administered—and was brought back to the palace to die.

We must regard this charge of poisoning as probably a construction put on his illness by the officials or people of Constantinople. It may or may not be true. We have no right to conclude at once that it is an historical fact, but it seems to me that some recent historians have just as little right to reject it as "improbable." Romanus was a licentious and unscrupulous man, carrying his father's amiable weakness for wine to the pitch of debauch and ruining his constitution by vice. Theophano, we shall see, was capable of murder, and her ambition would most certainly lead her to wish the older imperial family out of the way. On the other hand, there would be a prejudice against her in Constantinople, and in the mind of later writers, and we must leave this first charge against her what it is in the chronicles—a suspicion.

Her next step was to get rid of the sisters of Romanus. Helena and her five daughters still lived in the palace, or in one out of the great cluster of palaces. There were now at least eight palaces, connected by superb colonnades or separated by choice gardens and terraces, in the vast imperial domain between the Hippodrome and the Sea of Marmora; there were, in addition, several palaces on the Asiatic coast; and the palace at Blachernæ, in the cool, hilly district to the north, had in turn become a vast cluster of palaces, chapels, colonnades and terraced gardens. The mother and sisters of Romanus could therefore find ample hospitality without being compelled to witness the daily dissipation of the Emperor, his drunken banquets and his troops of lascivious actors and women, but they frowned on the kind of Court over which Theophano presided, and she persuaded her husband to remove them. He bade his five sisters adopt the monastic life. Theophano now had two sons and a daughter, and would feel safer if their royal aunts were prevented from making aristocratic marriages. The young women were, however, not at all disposed to embrace a religious life and there were furious scenes in the palace. They were removed to the monastery into which the palace of Theodora's minister, Theoclistus, had been converted, near the Hippodrome, but they seem still to have intrigued, and were separated and transferred to other monasteries.[21]

Romanus was not cruel or malignant. His temper was to live and let live, provided that no check was placed on his imperial pleasures. He merely smiled, therefore, when he heard that, in their convents, his sisters refused to exchange their silks for the hated black robe, or abstain from the delicate meats to which they had been accustomed. We shall later find one of them coming out, in spite of her vows, to marry an Emperor, to the intense mortification of Theophano, who had murdered her husband to marry him herself. Helena was the chief sufferer. She sank into melancholy and illness after the departure of her daughters, and died in September 961.

The Emperor continued for two years to enjoy his pleasures and hasten his death, leaving the care of the Empire to his very capable ministers and officers. Amongst these officers was a very singular commander named Nicephorus Phocas, whose romantic career still puzzles historians. Whether he was a profound hypocrite, or a deeply religious man fascinated and seduced by Theophano, it is difficult to determine. "God only knows," says Leo the Deacon, a chronicler of the time to whom we owe most of our knowledge. Nicephorus was a very able general of about fifty years: a dark, robust little man, with black hair and small dark eyes under thick eyebrows, a very stern look, and the chest and arms of a Hercules. He was not at all handsome, but he was one of the greatest soldiers of his time. The singular feature about his life was that, in consequence of a tragic accident of earlier years, he had adopted a very religious and ascetic life. He wore a hair shirt under his armour and linen, abstained from flesh and women as rigidly as a monk, and was understood to have vowed chastity.

It appears that, as her husband sickened, Theophano set out to seduce this remarkable soldier-monk and succeeded. The other great power in the State was Joseph Bringas, the leading civilian and statesman; but Joseph was a eunuch, and of no use to Theophano. She would marry Nicephorus. Leo the Deacon says that she admitted, or drew, the ascetic to her arms before the death of her husband, and it is not impossible, as the chief biographer of Nicephorus admits.[22] However that may be, Romanus died in 963, after a giddy reign of four years, at the age of twenty-four. Once more Theophano is charged with poisoning, and once more we must refrain from pressing the charge. The nearest authority, Leo the Deacon, leaves it an open question whether Romanus died of poison or had closed his own life prematurely by debauch; and we may do the same. Historians are too apt to conclude that because Romanus did wear himself out by his excesses, we may dismiss the charge against Theophano. Disease, on the contrary, would furnish a cloak to an artful poisoner, and Theophano certainly wished to get rid of the despotic eunuch Bringas, whom Nicephorus would quickly displace. The chief reason why we must hesitate is because Theophano was prostrate at the time and unable to master the new situation. She had given birth to a second daughter two days before the death of Romanus, and there is reason to think that Bringas and others were anxious to remove her from power. The circumstance is not decisive, as her servants might carry out a plan made at an earlier date.

As soon as Theophano recovered she entered upon the struggle with Bringas. It seems, from the movements of Nicephorus, that the Empress was in communication with him before the death of Romanus, and that at least she sent him a secret and flattering message when Romanus died. Nicephorus had disbanded the army with which he had conducted two brilliant campaigns against the Saracens, and was little equipped to contest the power of Bringas, but he went at once to the city in order to be near Theophano. Bringas had made desperate efforts to keep him away, even going so far as to propose in the council that the general's eyes should be put out for his treasonable ambition. His great victory over the Saracens and his repute for sanctity had, however, won a large body of admirers for Nicephorus, and when he entered the city in triumph, driving before his car groups of Saracen prisoners, and exhibiting the holy relics he had rescued from the hands of the heathen, citizens and soldiers and priests united in acclaiming him. A private conversation with the new patriarch Polyeuctes, a fanatical monk and eunuch, secured the favour of that prelate and his clergy, and it is even said that he ventured into the house of Bringas and revealed to that cautious statesman the hair shirt which he wore below his fine robes and the monastic heart that beat beneath it. But for his intense devotion to the young princes, he said, he would at once retire into a monastery.

If we can believe this last statement, the situation was not without humour, because Bringas presently discovered that his pious rival was being surreptitiously admitted to the Empress's apartments. Whether it is true or no that Nicephorus had previously been intimate with her, it is certain that he now became infatuated with Theophano, and received an assurance that she would marry him, if not more intimate pledges of her love. We may be confident that Theophano did not love him; he was not physically attractive to her sensual taste, and his incongruous mixture of piety and passion and deceit must have excited her disdain. He was merely the best instrument at hand for the achievement of her ambition. Then, as I said, Bringas discovered the secret meetings and renewed his attack. He invited Nicephorus to the palace. The gallant, but prudent, soldier preferred to fly to the altar of St Sophia and secure the protection of the patriarch. The Senate was convoked, the prelate warmly espoused the cause of Nicephorus, and he departed in honour to take supreme command of the army in Asia and await the orders of Theophano.

The next move of Bringas was a blunder and the beginning of his downfall. One of Nicephorus's chief officers was his nephew, John Zimiskes, the later Emperor. When we find Zimiskes murdering his uncle with the aid of Theophano, and then callously repudiating her, we shall not suppose him to be a man of tender conscience, and Bringas, no doubt, regarded him as venal. He sent a secret messenger to offer Zimiskes the supreme command if he would send his uncle in bonds to Constantinople. Zimiskes calculated that he would have the command, in any case, if his uncle became Emperor, and he showed the letter to Nicephorus, and urged him to assume the purple. They were in Cæsarea at the time, and from that city Bringas soon learned that Nicephorus had accepted the title of Emperor and would march on Constantinople.

The spirited events which followed must here be told briefly. On Sunday morning, 9th August, the advance-guard of Nicephorus's army appeared on the Asiatic shore in sight of the city, at the point where Scutari now is, and the people began to make their choice in the usual sanguinary way. The services in the great church were desecrated with riot, the battle against the guards who were faithful to Bringas was conducted in the streets, and by midnight the houses of his supporters were in flames. Theophano remained with her children behind the barrier of palace guards, listening, not unwillingly, to the increasing cries for Nicephorus. We may very well assume that she had had her share in the riot. One of the most formidable leaders of those who called for Nicephorus was the bold and ambitious Basil, the natural son of the elder Romanus. Castrated by his father, that he might never aspire to the purple, yet promoted to wealth and high office, he seems to have come to an agreement with Theophano. As soon as the battle began he led three thousand of his servants and followers, armed, into the Augusteum, and they continued all Sunday and throughout the night to hunt the soldiers of Bringas and loot the mansions of his friends.

Nicephorus had meantime reached the Hieria palace on the Asiatic side, and on the following Sunday he made his triumphant entry by the Golden Gate, and along the Mese, to St Sophia, the citizens draping their houses with the scarlet of rejoicing and adorning the way with laurel and myrtle. The patriarch

Polyeuctes met him at the cathedral, and Theophano would be present on her golden throne, in her violet mourning robes, when the crown was put on his head.

His next step must have caused a sensation in the city and entirely deceived the clergy. He sent a monk to conduct Theophano from the palace to the fortress, or higher prison, of Petrion on the Golden Horn, and maintained for a few weeks his austere aversion from wine and women. We hardly need the assurance of the chroniclers that this was done by arrangement between the two, and we may regard it as a device of Theophano. Nicephorus was now aflame like a youth. In the middle of September he "threw off the mask," in the words of the ecclesiastical chronicler, and announced that he was to marry Theophano on 20th September. His monastic advisers, he explained, had concluded that his new position demanded that he should marry. The marriage service was performed by the patriarch himself in a chapel in the grounds of the palace, and, while the Emperor went to kiss the altars at St Sophia, Theophano retired to her familiar apartments, to congratulate herself on the fortunate issue of her difficult manÅ"uvres.

And presently the Emperor returned in terrible rage to tell her that a formidable obstacle had revealed itself. When he had reached the door of the sanctuary, the patriarch Polyeuctes had barred his way and said that he would be excluded from the church for a year for contracting a second marriage. His angry protest had availed nothing; before a vast crowd of his subjects he had had to submit to the austere priest, and he was to remain in the ignominious position of a penitent for a year. Concealing their anger, they concluded the day, as usual, with a banquet to the leading officers and nobles in the gold-roofed triclinon, now restored and magnificently decorated by Constantine, and retired to discuss Polyeuctes.

The patriarch was undoubtedly a stern and conscientious priest, insisting upon a plain law of his Church. We may, however, assume that another feeling mingled with his sense of discipline. Nicephorus had, in the literal meaning, tasted blood at his matrimonial banquet, and he passionately refused to forgo the embraces of Theophano. His pious practices were wholly discarded in a day, and the clergy must have been bitterly disappointed to see him passing from their allegiance to that of the beautiful adventuress. So Polyeuctes had made a bold bid for power; and he had made a serious mistake. From that moment Nicephorus conceived, not merely a personal hatred of the patriarch, but an anti-clerical spirit, and began to restrict the wealth and power of the priests and monks. He clung to his enchanting young bride and sternly faced the clergy. In the discussion that at once filled the palace and the city some careless noble, named Stylianus, had recalled the fact that Nicephorus was godfather to one of the Empress's children, and the patriarch learned this. He at once pronounced that the marriage was invalid, as the Church regarded this spiritual relationship as an insuperable impediment to marriage, and bade the Emperor dismiss Theophano.

The feelings of Theophano during these days of disappointment and anxiety are left to our imagination. It is enough that her charms held Nicephorus to her in spite of the terrible threats of the patriarch, and it may be that it was she who approached the unfortunate Stylianus and persuaded him to commit perjury. Nicephorus gathered a council of pliant bishops and Senators, and they decided that, as the law invoked by the patriarch had been passed by the heretic Constantine Copronymus, it was not binding. Polyeuctes scorned their decision. Then Stylianus came forward to swear that Nicephorus had not been godfather to any child of Theophano, and the Emperor's father, Bardas, came forward to swear that he was the godfather. The patriarch knew that they were lying, but his clergy were anxious to escape a formidable struggle and he was forced to yield. To Theophano it was, no doubt, immaterial whether or no she was married to Nicephorus; she had a strong and devoted soldier to protect her and her children. How the pious Nicephorus reconciled himself to the situation is one of the things that "God only knows."

All that we know is that the possession of Theophano dissipated his asceticism as the summer sun disperses the mists, and he eagerly embraced a woman to whom, under the creed of his Church, he was not married.

During the six years' reign of Nicephorus the Empress had little occasion to assert her wayward personality, but it is significant that the one statement made of her is an accusation of crime. One of the sons of the older Romanus still languished in captivity, and it seemed possible, in view of the growing discontent at Constantinople, that an intrigue would be formed to put him on the throne. "Theophano," we are curtly informed, "made an end of him." There is no reason to doubt that messengers were sent to his distant prison with an order that he should be put to death, and it is more probable that the order came from Theophano than from Nicephorus. For the first year or two, however, Nicephorus prudently removed his fiery young bride from the seditious and immoral atmosphere of Constantinople, and she passed her days in unwonted innocence amid the lonely mountains of Cilicia.

The Emperor had spent a few months in an effort, by lavish entertainment, to dispel the suspicion of parsimony and meanness under which he had ascended the throne. The Hippodrome rang daily with the applause and contests of the citizens, and the winter was enlivened with great gaiety. Meantime Nicephorus was gathering an immense army for the more substantial work of driving back the Saracens, and when, in the early spring, the cosmopolitan regiments were assembled along the Asiatic shore, he announced that the Empress would accompany him to the field. He knew Theophano too well to leave her in that world of intriguing eunuchs and ambitious courtiers. A little pot-bellied man, with dark skin and little dark eyes, with short greyish beard betraying his age, and with disproportionately long arms and short legs to his stumpy figure, he felt that he was not likely to grow fonder to the heart of the fascinating Theophano during two or three years' absence. On the other hand, one must not imagine the sensual young Empress as being inconvenienced by the rough ways of a camp. The rulers of Constantinople carried their luxury even into the camp, on the occasions on which they condescended to take the field in person. Eighty horses were needed for the transport of the kitchen equipment and table silver alone, and thirty were required to convey the imperial wardrobe from town to town; while the whole countryside was laid under contribution to supply delicacies for the table. No doubt these normal glories of an imperial march would be at least doubled in view of the presence of Theophano.

They sailed from the Bucoleon port in the great gold and purple galley of the imperial family, and joined the army at Cæsarea. From that city Theophano accompanied her husband across the hills and plains of Asia Minor until they came to the beginning of the Taurus range. Here the Emperor left Theophano and her sons, in safe charge, while he led his troops into the more dangerous country beyond. At the entrance of the narrow defile which the ancients knew as the "Cilician Gates" was the massive fortress of Drizibion, a solitary and rugged castle in a wild mountainous district. It was in this quiet and cool home, removed from communication with the metropolis, that Theophano and her children spent the summer of the year 964. She would, of course, have an ample retinue of eunuchs and women, and every provision would be made for her comfort, but, whether it was the jealousy or the amorousness of Nicephorus that detained her in this healthy solitude, she would be sure to resent it. At the beginning of the winter he returned to her, with modest laurels, and may have conducted her to Cæsarea, or some other city of the plains, for the enjoyment of the winter. But the early spring called him once more to the field, and it seems that Theophano had to spend another summer in the wilds of Cilicia. It was only in the autumn of 965 that she re-entered Constantinople, to witness the splendid triumph of her husband.

In the following year Nicephorus made another campaign, and from the time of his return in the autumn of 966 the shadow of tragedy began to creep over his life. His vast armies and laborious victories had laid a heavy burden of taxation on the Empire, and, passionately as Constantinople loved to see a herd of captives driven before the royal chariot in the hour of triumph, it was little disposed to pay for remote victories. The clergy also were embittered. Nicephorus, soured by the action of the patriarch, and thus made sensible of the revolting spread of luxurious idleness under the name of monasticism, curtailed the revenues of the clergy, forbade the further conversion of mansions and palaces into monasteries, and claimed the right to appoint bishops. The people became sullen and hostile. When, on Easter Sunday, 967, Nicephorus crossed the Augusteum to go to church, they pelted him with mud and stones so violently that a group of the more sober citizens had to rescue him. It was expected that he would inflict some punishment, and when, a few weeks later, he ordered his guards to descend to the arena in the Hippodrome and begin their military evolutions, either to impress or to entertain the spectators, there was a frantic rush for the gates and many were trodden underfoot.

By the summer of 969 life in the sacred palace had become very sombre and unpleasant, and Theophano began to seek a new companion. The ardour of her husband's passion had been chilled by the terrors which now surrounded him, and, in preparation for the death which was foretold to him, he returned zealously to his monastic habits. Even the soldiers were now hostile to him, except his immediate corps of foreign mercenaries. Nicephorus relied on their formidable axes, converted the old and decaying Bucoleon palace into a massive fortress, girt the whole enclosure with a lofty castellated wall, and retired within this heavily guarded circle to spend his days and nights in prayer and penitence.

It is one of the most curious features of the story that, while he moodily punished his bravest officers for their very victories, the lithe and insidious Theophano retained his confidence. She had no longer the comparative solace of his sensual fire, and she must have looked on with deep disdain when he refused to share the imperial bed at night and, after long hours of prayer and psalm-reading, flung himself for a brief and feverish sleep on a panther-skin spread upon the ground in the corner of his chamber. But Theophano was not excluded from the Bucoleon palace, and she laid her plans to defeat his desperate entrenchments. The new partner whom she chose to encourage was the general Zimiskes, the Emperor's nephew, whom we have seen on an earlier page revealing the perfidy of Bringas to his uncle. He had been dismissed from office by Nicephorus "on account of certain suspicions"; and we have little trouble in inferring that he was suspected of liaison with Theophano and eagerness for the throne. He was, like his uncle, a very little and robust man, but much more handsome than Nicephorus; his broad chest and great brawny arms were redeemed by a fair countenance, a pair of keen and friendly blue eyes and a crown of almost golden hair. I must be pardoned for inserting such portraits of the Emperors as we have, while seeming to omit the more desirable portraits of their consorts. The Byzantine chroniclers rarely give us more than the very vaguest assurances that Empresses were "very beautiful," and so on, and the few surviving representations of them in ivory or bronze or mosaic are not portraits on which one would dare to found a physiognomical study.

In the autumn of 969 Zimiskes was living impatiently on his private estate in Armenia, when he received an assurance that Theophano had persuaded his uncle to allow him to return to Court. Whether or no it is true that he had previously enjoyed the favours of Theophano, he now certainly became her ally and accomplice. She seems to have deluded Nicephorus with diabolical duplicity. A rumour, which most historians plausibly ascribe to her, was circulated in Constantinople, to the effect that Nicephorus intended to castrate her sons and leave the crown to his brother Leo, who, on account of his extortions, was no less hated than he. On the other hand, Theophano persuaded Nicephorus that the interest of herself and her children would be best consulted if Zimiskes were recalled to the capital and compelled to marry some noble lady of the city. Nicephorus assented, and his nephew came to Constantinople. Then it seems to have been betrayed to the Emperor, probably by his brother, that Zimiskes was being secretly admitted to the Empress's apartments, and he placed restrictions on him. Zimiskes retired to his mansion at Chalcedon, on the Asiatic side, and continued to communicate with Theophano.

The culmination of the plot is a thrilling, if sordid, page of romance. On the night of 10th December Theophano visited her husband and persuaded him to leave his chamber door unfastened, as she would see him later. He still failed to suspect her, although some watchful priest had warned him of the plot. Some time before a group of tall, veiled women had presented themselves at the palace door and been admitted; and, when they had reached the secret chambers assigned to them by Theophano, it was a group of bronzed soldiers who emerged from the mantles and veils. Someone betrayed them, and Nicephorus sent an officer to explore the palace, but he, probably being in the pay of Theophano, reported that all was well, and Nicephorus turned to his long psalms. Theophano and her servants were in the upper part of the palace looking out anxiously over the Sea of Marmora. It was a dark wintry night, and the snow was falling heavily. At length a faint whistle from below told them that a boat had arrived from Chalcedon and lay under the walls. A basket (some say a ladder) was tied to a rope and lowered into the depths, and presently Zimiskes and several companions were within the palace. An Arab historian would have us believe that Theophano herself led them, with drawn swords, to her husband's room; it is more probable that, as the Greek writers say, she left this to one of her eunuchs.

For a moment the conspirators started back in alarm; the imperial bed was empty, and they fancied that the plot was known, and Nicephorus would fall on them. But the eunuch showed them the sleeping form of the Emperor on his panther-rug, and, with a cry for help to the Virgin, the strange soldier-monk passed out of the imperial world he had invaded. Basil, the astute head chamberlain, had an opportune illness at the moment, and only recovered in time to do reverence to his new sovereign. The guards alone rushed from their quarters and attacked the conspirators, but the sight of the grisly head of the late Emperor, which was exhibited at the window, induced them to sheathe their swords and accept a new paymaster. So Zimiskes proceeded gaily to the golden palace (Chrysotriclinon) to put on the purple slippers, and Theophano retired to her room to reflect on the next phase of her career: perhaps to glance now and again at the ghastly trunk of her late husband, which lay, all night and all the following day, in the snow without. This, surely, was the last crime she need commit. She was still young, and might look forward to many years of power with the robust soldier she had invited to share her throne.

Six days later Zimiskes went in state to St Sophia to receive his diadem, and found the stern patriarch Polyeuctes again boldly barring the way. He refused to crown Zimiskes except on three conditions: he must undo the anti-clerical work of his predecessor, he must deliver to justice the actual murderer of Nicephorus, and he must drive the guilty Theophano from the palace. Theophano now discovered the full brutality of her accomplice. He bowed at once to the commands of the patriarch, and the beautiful young Empress—she must still have been in her twenties, unless she was much older than her husband at the time of her first marriage—was dragged from her apartments to the Bucoleon quay and shipped to one of the dreary island prisons in the Sea of Marmora. She was furious with rage and disappointment. After a time she escaped and contrived to reach the altar in St Sophia; but even the mob of Constantinople shrank from the murderess, and her former confederate, Basil, was allowed to tear her from the altar. In her frenzy she beat the grand chamberlain with her own white hands and, reverting to the language of the tavern, poured her invectives on the "Scythian bastard."[23] Her career had been so darkened with suspicion, and had so plainly ended in murder, that her appeals fell on a cold, if not jeering, audience, and she was conveyed to distant Armenia and confined in a monastery.

The rest of the story of Theophano, as far as it is known to us, is told in the curt statement that she was recalled to Court in the reign of her eldest son, Basil, and again enjoyed the imperial position for half-a-century. John Zimiskes retained only for a few years the power for which he had paid so base a price. The marriage which he presently contracted was not much less sordid than the marriage he had intended to contract; if, indeed, he ever had a serious desire to make so dangerous a woman as Theophano the partner of his throne. He took a nun from her monastery, bade the patriarch—whose scruples had their limits—relieve her of her vows, and married her. The Empress Theodora is not clearly outlined in the chronicles, but she is not without interest. She was one of those daughters of Constantine whom her brother Romanus had forced to take the veil. Zimiskes had felt that an alliance with the late dynasty would strengthen his position, and it may be remembered that the daughters of Constantine were not at all scrupulous. They had refused to wear the black robe or eat the bread and beans of the monastery. Constantinople is said to have indulged in the most boisterous rejoicing over the marriage, and even the heavens seemed to express their satisfaction, when one of the Senators discovered in his orchard an ancient stone on which was miraculously inscribed: "Long Life to John and Theodora." There were, however, sceptics in the city, as it was recalled that a similar "discovery" had been made in the interest of Irene and her son, yet the blessing had proved illusory. The Senator was richly rewarded, but he may have lived to see the futility of his miracle. After a few years (976) the handsome chamberlain Basil bribed John's cook to put less innocent things than condiments in his dishes, and he went the beaten way of Byzantine Emperors. Theodora disappears after his death, though we can hardly suppose that she returned to her monastery.

Theophano's sons, Basil and Constantine, now became joint Emperors, and they recalled their mother from Armenia to the palace. One would be inclined to suspect that the poisoning did not come to her as a surprise, but the chroniclers do not impeach her, and we need not strive to lengthen the list of her misdeeds. She makes no further mark, for good or evil, in the chronicles. Possibly the terrible experiences of her early womanhood and seven years of sober reflection in her monastic prison had destroyed her passion for intrigue. In any case, the very vigorous administration of her elder son left her little room to interfere, and she seems to have been content with the quiet enjoyment of the position of a dowager Empress. According to George the Monk (or his continuer) she lived for fifty years after the death of her first husband—that is to say, after 963—and so she must have passed her seventieth year at the time of her death. There seems to have been no rival Empress during that time. We may trust that the character of Theophano sobered and matured, and that the forty years' silence means that she led a regular and unambitious life. However that may be, the personality she shows when she is under the full limelight on the imperial stage is one of unrestrained passion and greed. She was a tavern-keeper's daughter in the purple, an appalling instance of the lowest type of Greek beauty.

CHAPTER X

TWO IMPERIAL SISTERS

The long and prosperous reign of Basil II. (976-1025) has no further interest for us, since we find in the chronicles no reference to a wife of that hardy and brilliant soldier. His younger brother, Constantine, was more like their mother: a man of passion and greed, though with no higher ambition than that of an imperial enjoyment of wine and women, and in that enjoyment he was quite willing to await the natural death of his more sober and more distinguished brother. Although he approached his seventieth year when the undivided rule fell to him, his ways were still those of an aged and jaded, and not very refined,

Sybarite, and the three years of his reign interest us only because they show us the earlier environment of his two daughters, Zoe and Theodora, who are the next to occupy—alternately or simultaneously, according to the course of the romance—the gynæceum, or women's quarters, of the palace.

Constantine's wife, Helena, daughter of the patrician Alypius, is a mere cipher in the imperial records, and seems to have died much earlier, leaving three daughters—Eudocia, Zoe and Theodora—to grow up as they might in the palace of her voluptuous husband. Eudocia, the eldest, lost during an attack of smallpox whatever comeliness she may have had, and retired to hide her disfigured countenance under the veil of a nun. There remained Zoe and Theodora, and Constantine determined to marry one of the two to some important noble and leave the crown to him. The elder of the two was nearly fifty years old, and Theodora cannot have been much younger. It is not very clear why they had not married earlier. Their father, who could hardly be induced to take the least interest in his Empire, had wholly neglected his daughters until he held the sceptre in his hands, and felt that the time was at hand when he must relinquish it to another. He was a very large and robust man, absorbed in hunting, gambling and other less reputable pleasures, and, even when he was sole Emperor, he left the cares of state to his eunuchs and retained his imperial attention for the theatre, the banquet and the dance. In his home the sisters had, says the chronicler, "lived as they listed," and the further course of the story will make it probable that Zoe had not failed to enjoy her liberty. Theodora was less sensual, but we shall have to include both sisters in the list of Empresses who were little embarrassed by moral scruples.

In approaching their careers we have the rare advantage of an excellent guide. Michael Psellus, one of the leading philosophers and literary men of Byzantine history, not only lived at their Court, and knew them intimately, but he had a genial taste for the tattle and scandal of a court and not the least reluctance to entrust it to his graceful pen. He has been called the Voltaire of Byzantine letters on account of his brilliant, caustic and very candid way of writing the story of his times. We shall find his "Chronography" of inestimable value, provided we make due allowance for the prejudices of the politician and the amiable unscrupulousness of the anecdotist.

Zoe and Theodora were very different types of women. Zoe, who will interest us most, was a woman of fine complexion, very graceful figure and ardent passions. She had large sensuous eyes under heavy eyebrows, a mass of blonde hair, and a skin of remarkable whiteness. She was of middle height, and preferred to dress in simple robes, which exhibited her figure, rather than in the heavy and gorgeous draperies and massive jewellery of an Empress; though this simplicity of taste was limited, on one side, by a passion for perfumes and cosmetics, of which she gathered the material from all parts of the world and compounded, either with her own hands or by her maids, so industriously that her room "looked like a workshop." She took such care of her smooth and clear skin and blonde hair that even in her seventieth year she had no wrinkle or other mark of age. She retained youth also in her blood, and we shall find her remarkably amorous in her sixth decade of life. Such a woman we shall hardly expect to find richly endowed with intellect or greatly restrained by moral sentiments, yet I think that M. Diehl follows too literally the facile witticism of Psellus when he speaks of Zoe as "childish" and "silly," and I will prefer to let the story of her life tell us the limitations of her intelligence and character.

Theodora will interest us much less than Zoe, and it will suffice to say that she was in all respects different from her sister. Her tall and graceless figure and her very plain features were compensated by a stronger intelligence and greater force of character. She could be coldly stern, even cruel, on occasions, while cruelty only came to Zoe in the impulsive anger of her thwarted passions. We shall see that, when the occasion came to her, she cherished a very high ideal of public duty and used her power with an intelligence and beneficence that Psellus greatly underrates.

Such were the two daughters who, in middle age, were warned by their father that one of them must marry and inherit the Empire. The choice of Constantine first fell upon a distinguished noble named Constantine Delassenus, and a eunuch was sent to bring him from Armenia, where duty had taken him, to the Court. Much tragedy might have been prevented if that eunuch had reached his destination in time, but he was recalled by a second courier and told that the Emperor had changed his mind. It appears that the commander of the palace guards had felt that he would not have much influence on a noble like Delassenus, and he had brought to the notice of the Emperor a less young and less vigorous candidate, Romanus Argyrus, who was related to Constantine. Romanus was sixty years old, and had little to recommend him except his incompetency, which would suit the designs of the officers of the Court. He had, however, a wife living in Constantinople at the time, and it seems to have been supposed that he might not be willing to abandon her. The petty schemers of the Court were accordingly directed to bring about a separation, and, as Polyeuctes was dead, and a more accommodating patriarch held the see, no opposition was expected from the Church.

A file of soldiers entered the mansion of Romanus and told him that he had incurred the anger of the Emperor. They were, they said, to lead him to the palace for execution, and his wife was to enter a monastery. Many eyes had been put out, on slight grounds, during the three years' licentious reign of Constantine, and the threat was serious. The wife fled at once to a monastery, and Romanus was brought, in some trepidation, to the royal presence—to learn that, since his wife was now a nun, he was free to marry the Emperor's daughter and thus secure the purple. Instead of retiring to thrust a dagger in his heart, as an older Roman would probably have done, the sixty-year-old noble graciously submitted his person to the princesses. Theodora, the favourite of her father, had the first choice, but she turned away in disgust. Possibly Romanus did not regret that this gave him the hand of the more charming Zoe, who, in her forty-ninth year, fully preserved the fresh and brilliant complexion and the warm passions of a young woman. He had set out from home prepared for death, and must have been bewildered by his fortune. The clergy obligingly disentangled the somewhat complicated relation in which they stood to each other, in the eyes of the Church; they were married and crowned on 19th November 1028; and, as Constantine died three or four days afterwards, the duty, or pleasure, of governing the Empire fell on them during the first week of their singular honeymoon.

After this inauspicious beginning we shall hardly expect the reign of Romanus III. and Zoe to be one of brilliant and inspiring deeds; indeed, we may say briefly that it was merely an inglorious effort to retain the crowns they had obtained. They adopted the easy device of emptying the treasury on the common folk, the clergy and the monks. The private debts of citizens were paid by them, more churches were built or richly decorated, the clergy were relieved from taxation, and the monks—it was the very culmination of their golden age—were lodged in luxurious mansions which made their calling one of the most attractive in the Empire. The graver nobles frowned, plotted and were savagely punished, but we are interested in these conspiracies only in so far as they involve the imperial sisters.

Theodora, a spirited and intelligent woman, naturally despised the marriage which she had refused, and was regarded with suspicion and hatred by her sister. By some means Zoe put at the head of Theodora's household a Paphlagonian eunuch in her own pay, a very crafty and unscrupulous man named John, who was enjoined to watch Theodora's conduct. This very interesting person will be better known to us presently, as he was destined to be the most powerful man in Zoe's Court. For the moment it is enough to say that, about a year after the coronation, Theodora was discovered to have some share in a conspiracy which was set afoot by Constantine, a relative of the Emperor. It is curious that John also was found guilty, though whether this was merely a trick to conceal his spying, or he had really been gained by Theodora, it would be difficult to say. Theodora was expelled from the palace and confined in a building at Petrion, on the Golden Horn, which seems to have had the mixed characters of a monastery, a state prison and a fort. It was the building to which Nicephorus had consigned Theophano for a few weeks before their marriage, and would have comfortable apartments. A year later Romanus was ignominiously beaten by the Saracens and the conspiracy revived. There is no proof that Theodora took part in it, but its aim would be, no doubt, to place her on the throne. In one of those moments of energy which passion occasionally gave her, Zoe went to Petrion, and forced her royal sister to take the vows and adopt the dress of a nun.

As a number of other malcontents lost their eyes or their liberty at the same time, the throne of Zoe and Romanus seemed to be firmly established. Unfortunately, a very grave breach now took place between the imperial pair, and, as a handsome official entered the service of the palace, there happened what so commonly happens in Byzantine history under the circumstances: Zoe fell in love with the handsome servant, and Romanus died, of a mysterious complaint.

Delicacy compels me to refer the inquisitive reader to the Greek text of Psellus, or to the chronicle of the monk Zonaras, for a full explanation of the rift in the sacred palace. Briefly, Romanus had been assured by one of those soothsayers who were in such high repute at Constantinople that he would have a son, and he zealously studied and employed the whole known range of aphrodisiacs and other contrivances that might help to ensure the fulfilment of the prophecy. After two or three years of this peculiar activity he retired in despair from the struggle, leaving Zoe untouched and indignant. As she had now certainly entered her sixth decade of life, the modern reader will have but a slender sympathy with her, and will recognize a very low quality of character in her conduct. Her husband became ill, and his favourite chamberlain, Michael, was often summoned to attend him, even when Zoe shared his bed. This chamberlain was a tall, handsome, fresh-faced young man, whose form pleased the Empress, but there was a deeper intrigue in the affair; the chamberlain was a brother of the Paphlagonian eunuch John, whom we saw in charge of Theodora's mansion, and it is now necessary to present him more intelligibly.

John was a very shrewd, ambitious, vulpine provincial of mean family; he had been converted into a eunuch in early years, had held office in the employment of the Emperor Basil, and had then retired to a monastery. His character is so far removed from religious ideals that one is disposed to imagine him as having been compelled to take the black robe for some indiscretion, but it is quite possible that he adopted it voluntarily, as at this time many of the monasteries were merely luxurious colonies of bachelors living on a swollen stream of legacies. Romanus, who knew his ability, brought him from his monastery to supervise Theodora and her affairs. In spite of the curious statement that he was himself involved in the conspiracy, he was soon back at Court, and in great favour. He had five brothers and a sister, and the general character of the family may be deduced from the fact that three of the six brothers were moneylenders, two (John and Simeon) were monks, while the sister, Maria, had married a ship-caulker at the quays. John used his influence to introduce these brothers into the very lucrative service of the State. Within a few years the beau of the family became Emperor, the son of the ship-caulker also became Emperor, the ship-caulker himself became High Admiral of the Fleet, two other brothers had the rank of generals, and John became the virtual ruler of the Empire.

It was chiefly through his young and attractive-looking brother that John pushed their fortunes. Michael was a young man of large and well-proportioned figure, with that freshness of complexion which we often find in nerve-diseased or epileptic subjects. He became a favourite chamberlain of Romanus, and John presently noticed that Zoe was interested in him. Romanus was visibly failing, and Michael was at times called in to chafe his feet as he lay in bed with Zoe. "Who will believe," the monk Zonaras asks, "that he did not take the opportunity to rub Zoe's feet also?" Zoe expressed to John a lively interest in his brother, and John took care that their movements should not be hampered by any of the restrictions that normally curtailed the liberty of a Byzantine Empress. The pale Paphlagonian, in the black dress of a monk, was already the supreme master of the palace, but the most piquant feature of his position is to find him chiding the nervous hesitation of his brother and feeding the improper admiration of the Empress.

Psellus dilates, almost gloats, for pages over the development of this singular love story, in a way that hardly becomes a great exponent of Plato and Aristotle. Before long the relation of the two was known to the whole Court. Michael was loaded with jewels and other presents, and not infrequently courtiers would find him sitting, still rather nervously, on the same couch with the infatuated Empress. One day a servant entered the throne-room for some purpose, and almost fell to the ground in astonishment. Zoe had made Michael sit on the throne, had put the crown on his head and the sceptre in his hand, and was admiringly murmuring: "My darling, my flower of beauty, joy of my eyes, consoler of my soul," etc. Instead of bursting into passion at the entrance of the official, she bade him do homage to the man who would one day be his Emperor. So says, at least, the philosophic Psellus, whom many believe. It is quite certain that Zoe made flagrant love to the chamberlain, and that the Emperor knew it. His sister, Pulcheria, angrily spoke to him of the notorious scandal, but he professed to be ignorant of it and was content to exact from Michael an oath that there was no truth in the rumour. Other writers say that he overlooked the liaison because it preserved his middle-aged spouse from promiscuous irregularity.

Romanus forgot that such love affairs were apt to entail tragic consequences for the superfluous man. As Zoe's passion increased, he found himself suffering from an alarming and mysterious illness. His hair fell out in patches, his breathing was laboured, his face—a more significant symptom in an old man like Romanus—became livid and puffy. Whether this illness was really due to a slow poison, and whether the poison was administered by John or Zoe, are points which we must leave as we find them in the chronicles—uncertain. Since there is very little doubt that Romanus was murdered in the end, the theory of poison is not reckless; but Romanus was aged and worn, and the illness may have been natural. However that may be, Romanus lingered in a frightful condition until Holy Thursday of the year 1041. On that sacred day Romanus distributed to the Senators the ceremonious gifts prescribed in the ritual, and retired to the bath. From the bath he was presently removed in a dying condition to his bed. However possible it may be that he had had a serious attack of his illness in the bath, we cannot easily ignore the persistent statement that men entered the bathroom, and either strangled the Emperor or held his head under the water. Psellus gives this as a rumour, but even he seems to believe it. Both Michael and John are accused of the murder, and it is left uncertain whether Zoe was privy to the plot. Her immediate conduct will not dispose us to be eager to clear her memory of the suspicion, but we may be sure that the monk John was the soul of the plot.

Zoe came, with ostentatious (the chronicler says feigned) tears, to see that her husband was really dead or dying, though she did not await the end, which occurred soon afterwards. When we learn that she announced her intention of marrying Michael the same evening we are disposed to see in her an element of cold-blooded calculation which does not very well assort with the character we have given her. It would probably be much more correct to conceive her as nervous and confused, and simply yielding to the dictation of the monk John. Her father's eunuchs, who had remained in her service, begged her to wait some time, but John bullied and threatened, and Michael was forthwith decked in the dead man's robes and placed beside Zoe in the gold-roofed hall. The patriarch was summoned to the palace and curtly ordered to crown Michael and marry him at once to the very recent widow, in the presence of the assembled Senators. The whole scene is so repulsive that we need not hesitate to accept the last touch given to it in the chronicles. The archbishop hesitated, but a present of a hundred pounds in gold from John removed his scruples, and he invoked the blessing of God on the new imperial marriage.

THE EMPRESS ZÖE

'CONSTANTINOPLE' BY E. A. GROSVENOR

After this authentic episode it is superfluous to seek to determine the share of Zoe in the illness and death of her first husband. The monk-eunuch was capable of any crime, and it is, perhaps, not likely that he would take others into his confidence in perpetrating them. His brother Michael was a feeble-minded man, of no criminal instincts, whom we shall presently find smitten with the deepest remorse for the part he had played. Zoe also was little more than a tool in the hands of John. Had he communicated his criminal design to them, they would probably have consented, but there is no evidence that he did so. The marriage, however, is a sordid fact that no casuistry can excuse. It would, no doubt, be represented to Zoe that delay would give an opportunity for a revolution, and there were always at Constantinople nobles who were ready to aspire to the throne when so excellent a pretext was afforded. These considerations may explain, but cannot excuse, Zoe's action. She was almost, if not quite, devoid of moral feeling. The utmost we can say for her is that it was not merely her passion for Michael that gave such indecent precipitancy to a woman of fifty-four years. But she had no children to protect, and she lent herself to this disgraceful procedure merely in order to retain her royal position.

We read, therefore, without the least sympathy that, while the change made the fortune of the astute John and his brethren, it brought great disappointment and chagrin to Zoe. She had, the chronicler says, imagined that the lowly chamberlain, grateful for his elevation to the throne, would be her slave, and she at once gathered about her the former servants of her father and began to rule. But the monk had no intention of handing to her the power he had purchased so heavily. His official position was merely that of "orphanotrophos," or director of charitable institutions; his real position was that of Emperor. Most of the brothers were able men, but Michael was, as John probably took into account from the first, epileptic and incapable of self-assertion. John, therefore, took the reins in his own hands. He summarily dismissed Zoe's eunuchs and maids and put about her an army of servants in his own employment, so that she could not even go to the bath without the permission and knowledge of the eunuch. To the Empire and its affairs, it may be said, he devoted the most careful and intelligent attention. Even in the midst of a solitary carouse—for the monk was fond of wine—he would turn with alacrity to any pressing business. It was only in the dishonest enrichment of himself and his brothers, whom he at once promoted to the highest commands, that he overreached himself.

One noble only, the Constantine Delassenus who had so narrowly missed the Empire and the hand of Zoe, rebelled against this division of the Empire among a family of low-born eunuchs and money-changers, and the punishment of Delassenus so well illustrates the world in which Zoe now found herself that it may be briefly recounted. John secured the loyalty of the Senators by a generous distribution of money, and then sent a eunuch to assure Delassenus, who was in Armenia, that his conduct would be overlooked if he disarmed at once. Delassenus required some tremendous security of such a promise on the part of John, and it was left to the clergy to devise a new and particularly ponderous oath. The evolution of the oath in Byzantine life is one of the many ways in which we may trace the degradation of its character; no one had any longer the faintest confidence in oaths on the true cross or the Sacrament. A group of clerics were therefore sent with the most sacred objects in the reliquaries of Constantinople, and they marshalled before the eyes of Delassenus the cross, the napkin bearing a miraculous image of Christ, the original letter of Christ to King Abgar, and the portrait of Mary painted by St Luke. On these portentous relics an oath was taken that no punishment would be inflicted on him. He submitted; and a few months later, when the people of Antioch rose against their oppressive tax-gatherers, the revolt was subtly traced to the distant noble, and he was exiled and ruined.

Zoe tolerated the domination of the odious monk for a few years impatiently, and at length made an attempt on his life. She won one of the eunuchs whom John had placed about her, and directed him to offer John's medical attendant a vast sum of money if he would poison his master. But, by one of those convenient accidents which commonly happen in novels and in Byzantine history, the doctor's boy discovered the plot and denounced it to John. Her eunuch was drastically punished, and Zoe was treated worse than ever.

At the same time her condition became more unpleasant, because Michael's illness became worse. The popular belief in Constantinople was that a devil had invaded the Emperor, to punish him for his mendacious denial, to Romanus, of intimacy with Zoe. Men told of the suddenness with which the quiet, rosy-cheeked Emperor would be, at any moment, converted into a frothing maniac, and it was noticed that, on the rare occasions on which he appeared on the throne, purple curtains were looped in readiness about it, and servants stood to draw them round the throne if the devil should choose that moment to indulge his frolics. Even the Byzantine writers take this theory seriously; though some of them offer the alternative theory of insanity. We recognize the symptoms of epilepsy, and see that Zoe's choice had failed. Between the attacks Michael, who seems to have believed in the devil, was gloomy and penitent. He and his brothers walked barefoot through the city, at the head of processions, bearing the swaddling-clothes of the infant Christ and all the other priceless relics I have mentioned; but the only answer of the heavens was a storm of such hail that the stones crashed through the tiled roofs. He visited shrines, built churches and monasteries, showered gold on the clergy, and even gave a baptism-fee to every new-born babe; and famine, pestilence and earthquake vexed the over-burdened Empire, and men cursed Michael and his brothers.

At length dropsy was added to epilepsy, and Michael determined to resign and enter a monastery. Zoe seems by this time to have been completely cowed by the arrogant monk, and she made little opposition when he went on to provide a new and strange aspirant to the throne. His sister Maria was, as I said, married to a ship-caulker named Stephen, who had been put in command of the fleet. They had a boy named Michael, a vicious youth, but young enough to submit to his uncle's rule if he obtained the crown, and the Emperor and Zoe were persuaded or coerced to adopt this child and clothe him with the dignity of Cæsar. One of the chroniclers tells that they deceived Zoe by representing the boy as the son of a noble matron. Some such fiction may have been served to the populace, but Zoe could hardly be deceived on the point; and even the people were not long deceived, if at all, since he has passed into history as Michael the Caulker. In the chapel at Blachernæ the boy was accepted into the imperial family, after swearing the customary ponderous oaths to respect Zoe as his mother and mistress. It is not impossible that Zoe felt that this adoption of a son who was to wear the crown made her own position more secure.

Some time afterwards Michael IV. retired to a monastery, and Michael V. began to look forward to his imperial opportunities of indulgence. The next course of events is not quite clear, but it seems that the retiring Emperor felt some scruple about his action and had relegated the boy to a house without the walls. He died, refusing to see Zoe, soon afterwards (10th December 1041), and John forged a letter in his name, bidding the guards deliver the young Cæsar, and brought him to the palace. We are then told that Zoe asserted her power, bestowed the crown on the youth only on the strictest promise of obedience to her, and expelled the three brothers—John, George and Constantine—from the palace. It seems more likely that the brothers quarrelled with each other. John, promising the most absolute power to Zoe, had his younger brothers exiled, and then Constantine intrigued with the young Emperor and displaced his brother.

These details are of little moment for our purpose. By the spring of 1042, three months after the death of her husband, we find Zoe sharing the power with her adopted son and his uncle Constantine, and a fresh chapter of romance opens in her story.

Constantine, apparently, urged the youth to get rid of Zoe and rule alone. A vicious and conceited youth, he was little troubled by the oaths he had taken a few months before, but he felt it necessary to proceed cautiously. He began to slight Zoe, then to treat her with disdain and harshness. He confined her to her palace, and refused to let her control the treasury. One day he announced one of those imperial processions through the city which the people regarded as opportunities to express their feelings, and rode out alone. To his delight he was received with the liveliest rejoicing. The citizens hung their choicest silks and tapestries before their houses, and displayed their silver and other treasures on their balconies, as they were wont to do on the most festive occasions. Elated with his apparent popularity, Michael consulted his unofficial council of fast-living young sportsmen, as soon as he returned to the palace, and they decided to dismiss Zoe at once. It is said that Michael himself brutally told her of his decision, and even slapped the fair face of his adopted mother. The charge he put forward was that she was preparing a poison for him. It would not be difficult to believe, if there were any serious evidence, but it was probably only a pretext to get rid of her. That night she was put on ship at the quay, rowed to the islands and consecrated a nun.

On the following day, however, the laments of Zoe were cut short in a very unexpected manner. A boat came at its highest speed from the palace, and a royal official bade her at once return to her dignity. The people had resented the flagrant conduct of her adopted son, and he had hastily summoned her to her palace. A herald had been sent into the public square to announce that the most pious Emperor had deposed his mother and the patriarch for conspiring against his throne and would himself care for their interests in the future. From the sullen crowd a voice protested angrily that they "wanted their mother Zoe, not the son of the caulker"; it was repeated fervently on every side, and the prefect had to fly under a shower of stones. Then the crowd poured into the cathedral, from which the patriarch had not yet departed, and a noisy debate took place. A council of the clergy and Senators was then held in the church, the singular resolution was taken to bring Theodora from her convent and clothe her with the purple.

The younger sister of Zoe had, it will be recalled, been compelled by her to take the monastic vows at Petrion eleven years before, and this sudden recall to life—a recall without precedent, since she was not summoned for the purpose of marrying—gave a remarkable turn to her career. She had passed from the luxury and dissipation of her father's palace, with a brief interval of independent life, to the shade of the monastery, and now she was to spend the last fifteen years of her life on the imperial throne. She was of sterner stuff than Zoe, and the Senators must have concluded that she alone could check the audacity of the low-born Paphlagonians. This does not in itself argue any great strength of character in Theodora. We must remember that there was always a party of ambitious eunuchs or statesmen behind each of the names that is put forward by the historian.

When the news of this decision reached Michael, and the crowd stormed angrily at the gates of the palace, he sent an officer on a swift vessel to the Princes' Islands for Zoe. In the palace she was quickly stripped of her nun's robe, and clothed in her former garments. It is clear that Michael's uncle, Constantine, who was not without ability, directed the campaign in the palace. Michael was advised to take Zoe with him into the imperial lodge overlooking the Hippodrome and show the citizens, who had gathered in the enclosure, that all was well. The only reply he got was a shower of stones, arrows and epithets, and, as the chroniclers remark, the young lion became at once a timid hare, and proposed to run for shelter to the monastery at Studion, on the Asiatic side. His uncle prevented him, however, and marshalled the guards in the fore part of the palace. The battle which followed ended in a complete victory for the people. Constantine and Michael fled across the water to Studion, in the early morning of

Wednesday in Holy Week, and the new Empress Theodora was conducted into the palace over the corpses of some three thousand of the combatants.

The royal sisters, it will be understood, did not fly into each other's arms. Theodora had to thank Zoe for eleven years' confinement, and Zoe herself was very reluctant to share her power with her younger sister. However, a formal reconciliation was arranged by the Senators, and the two Empresses sat side by side to receive the homage of the leading citizens and decide what was to be done with the late Emperor and his uncle. If there were any who wondered in what spirit Theodora would wield her power after a decade of religious life, they were not left long in doubt. Zoe asked what the will of her advisers was in regard to the fugitives, and such cries as "Out with their eyes!" and "Crucify them!" rang furiously through the chamber. Zoe recoiled and pleaded for leniency, but Theodora, a much better speaker than her sister, sternly ordered the prefect to see that their eyes were put out. A great crowd crossed the sea with the officers, and saw Michael, who had hidden under the altar, and his more stoical uncle dragged from the chapel. The same crowd had applauded Michael in his procession hardly a week before; now they stood by with wild delight to see the brutal sentence carried out. It was 21st April: Michael the Caulker had reigned for four months.

For a few weeks the imperial sisters ruled their kingdom in complete harmony and with exemplary zeal. M. Diehl, too lightly following the censorious Psellus, rates the intelligence and character of both at a very low level, but that estimate is hardly supported by the facts. Few Emperors had dared to attack the administrative corruption of the Empire as Zoe and Theodora attacked it in the first freshness of their power, and as we have every reason to believe that they would have continued to attack it. For centuries the State had been the easy prey of ambitious eunuchs at Court and corrupt officials in the provinces. Zoe and Theodora issued decrees to the effect that all injustice must cease and that the law must be administered with equity. They themselves sat on the highest tribunal of the city to hear cases, and the sale of offices was strictly prohibited. The accounts of the late chief minister were examined, and Constantine, eyeless and shaven, was brought from his monastery to explain the enormous deficiency. The power of his family was broken for ever, and the miserable man disclosed that 5300 pounds of gold (nearly a quarter of a million sterling) was hidden in a cistern in his house. Legates and petitions were heard with dignity by the royal sisters, and it must have seemed to many that the Empire had, by this singular adventure, obtained juster and finer rulers than it had known for many a century. We cannot discriminate in the joint public action of the sisters, but it is clear that the strong will and intelligence of Theodora were the chief power of the administration. How drastically the Empire needed such a purification may be gathered from the fact that, when the patriarch Alexis died in the following year, a secret and dishonest hoard of gold, amounting to more than Â£100,000, was discovered in his palace.

This brilliant example of feminine rule might have been expected to disarm the old Byzantine prejudice against women, but prejudices of that nature are too deeply rooted to be displaced by facts. The cry was raised that an Emperor was needed, and Zoe once more expressed her willingness to marry. The careful chronicler tells us that her conduct was not necessarily inspired by a carnal feeling—she was now sixty-two years old—but that she may have feared that Theodora and her ministers wished to dislodge her. Her age, no less than the remarkable conditions of her third and last marriage, will easily persuade us that the motive was political. There were those who said that, as Theodora had been the chief agent in expelling Michael, the throne belonged to her alone, and Zoe sought an ally. The first noble chosen by her was Constantine Delassenus, who had almost obtained her hand and the throne fourteen years before. But Constantine, when he was invited to the Court for inspection, proved so brusque and independent that he was again dismissed. Her next choice was Constantine Catepano, a handsome officer of the palace, with whom, in spite of her age, the gossips of the Court already connected Zoe somewhat too intimately. Constantine, however, had a wife living, and this lady is said to have poisoned him as soon as she heard of the proposal to divorce her.

If we may believe the gossipy chronicles, Zoe met the disappointment with tranquillity, as she had another lover among the officials of the palace. Constantine Monomachos, a very handsome and distinguished and dissolute noble, had been exiled from Court to Mitylene by Michael IV. on the suspicion of intimacy with Zoe, and had for some years gilded the hours of his distant exile with the enjoyment of letters, the pleasures of the table and the affection of a pretty and devoted cousin. When his second wife had died, he had obeyed the injunction of the Church to refrain from a third marriage and had been content with the free companionship of the beautiful Sclerena, a sister of the distinguished noble Romanus Sclerus—a member, that is to say, of one of the proudest Byzantine families. She had followed her lover to Lesbos, used her fortune to mitigate the harshness of his exile, and was living with him at the time when Zoe recalled him to Court. "Handsome as Achilles," uniting a prodigious strength with a singular delicacy and elegance of appearance, equally devoted to the robust pleasures of the chase and the enervating delights of love, Constantine Monomachos at once returned to his place in the heart of the ageing Empress, and was invited to wed her. He is said to have stipulated beforehand that the fair Sclerena should be allowed to come to Constantinople, and Zoe genially consented. They were married, and Zoe entered upon the last and strangest part of her strange career.

While the sexless Theodora continued to rule the Empire and put out the eyes of her enemies, while Constantine revelled in the new and more exquisite luxuries of his position, Zoe seems quietly to have enjoyed the secure and restful days which her marriage obtained for her. She still, with her maids, compounded and distilled the perfumes which were almost her one luxury, but she now paid a scrupulous attention to her devotions and burned much incense before the icons. Sclerena at first dwelt apart, and Constantine set about building a magnificent palace for her, thinly veiling his liaison with the pretence of going daily to see the progress of the works. As the citizens smiled at the connexion, and Zoe seemed to be piously indifferent to it, he became bolder and asked Zoe to allow him to bring Sclerena to live in the palace. Again Zoe consented, and the ménage à trois was maintained in the most pleasant harmony. She gave Sclerena the title of Empress, embraced her, when they met, with entire goodwill, and showed her such consideration that she never visited her husband without first ascertaining if he was disengaged. Constantine occupied the central part of the palace, and his wife and mistress had apartments on each side.

Although Zoe now approached her seventieth year, she still retained the freshness of her complexion and had no wrinkles. Psellus says that a stranger would have been sure that she was still a young woman. She shared the pleasures of the gay Court, and made no protest against the frivolous Constantine emptying the treasury on his mistress. If we may believe implicitly all the details given by Psellus, there was little delicacy in the fun which enlivened the gardens or halls—for Zoe disliked the open air—of the sacred domain. Music and skilful dancing were too fine for his appreciation. He liked the broader merriment of mimes, and took especial pleasure in imitations of stammering. His chief entertainers would go so far as to represent, pantomimically, the chaste Theodora lying abed in child-birth, and Theodora herself joined in the loud laughter of Constantine as the man imitated the shrieks which befitted such an occasion. The months passed very merrily, and the treasury emptied.

And as the treasury emptied, and the citizens saw their funds passing into the marvellous palace which Constantine was building for Sclerena, clouds began to gather over the life of the epicure. One day, in the year 1044, as he rode with his guards at the head of a religious procession, a cry broke from the crowd: "We don't want Sclerena as Empress, nor to see our lawful mistresses, Zoe and Theodora, perish on her account." The cry was a spark to the spreading discontent, and the small troop of guards were surrounded by a threatening mob. Fortunately for the Emperor, the Empresses were watching the procession from the balcony, and they sent troops to rescue him. Later, a discontented noble led some Macedonian troops against the city, and encamped opposite the Blachernæ gate. Constantine disdainfully ordered a chair to be placed for him outside the gate, in order that he might see, and be seen by, the rebels. For a time they were content to sing comic songs about him—of which there must have been a good supply in the city—then they made a dash and scattered his guards, and could have penetrated into the city, possibly taken it, if they had not foolishly retired. On such slender threads did crowns hang in that singular Empire.

Sclerena relieved the growing discontent by a premature death, apparently about the year 1045, and the superb palace which had been intended for Constantine's mistress was turned into a monastery. Five years later Zoe closed her long and romantic career, at the age of seventy. Constantine mourned for her as if she had been a beloved child, and even pressed the Church to put her on the list of the canonized; he may have read how St Theodora had won the aureole largely by her freedom from jealousy. When it was found, after a time, that some curious fungi had grown about her monument, he insisted that they were heaven-sent assurances that Zoe had been admitted at once into the company of the saints. The Greek Church, however, was not persuaded to add Zoe to its quaint list of the blessed, and few will reflect on the many events which reveal her personality to us without admitting that, whether or no she was guilty of the positive crimes attributed to her, she had little or no moral feeling.

Constantine found consolation in the charms of a young Alan princess who was detained as a hostage at Constantinople. The milk-white skin and fine eyes of the unknown so fascinated him that he gave her the imperial title and emptied the remainder of the treasury upon her and the relatives who flocked to share her fortune. He was by this time a miserable wreck of his former magnificent person, and could not sit unaided on a horse, but the Court still rang with laughter and buffoonery. His favourite, a man who had been raised from the position of street buffoon to that of Court jester, became so infatuated with his wealth and privileges that he dreamed of possessing the pretty Alan princess and the purple. He was caught in Constantine's bedroom with a drawn sword. The Emperor asked why he had attempted assassination, and, when the man said that he had an irresistible passion to see himself in the crown and imperial robes, burst into laughter and ordered the attendants to put them on him. He returned to his position, and, to the amusement of Constantine, made more open love than before to the fair Circassian mistress. But the Emperor died in 1054, and his mistress returned to her previous obscurity.

When it was seen that Constantine was failing, a number of the nobles and officials conspired to put on the throne Nicephorus Bryennius, but Theodora's supporters forestalled the plot. They sent a swift vessel for her and lodged her in the sacred palace before their opponents could bring Bryennius from Bulgaria, which he governed. She seems to have been forced out of affairs during the later years of Constantine, and the sending of a boat implies, apparently, that she had retired to the suburbs. She was still, in her seventh decade of life, erect of form and clear in mind, and drastic punishment was inflicted on the conspirators. She then began again to control the affairs of the Empire as she had done in conjunction with Zoe. She personally received ambassadors and heard trials, and resumed her war on corrupt officials. Psellus is disdainful of her rule, and unjust to her. The only grave defect we can recognize is that she put the higher offices and commands at the disposal of men who were less distinguished for ability than for devotion to her. A very strong provincial aristocracy had by this time arisen in the Empire, and from their vast estates a number of able nobles and officers kept a discontented eye on the hierarchy of eunuchs at Constantinople.

Theodora, conscious of her vigour, and sustained by the prophetical assurance of a monk that she would wear the crown for a long time, maintained her power for three further years, and then became seriously ill. It is said that she chose an aged and feeble noble of the city, Michael Stratioticus, to don the purple, but one is rather disposed to see in the choice of Stratioticus the action of the Court party, whose influence was threatened by the provincial nobles. Theodora still confided in the monk's prophecy; she had the aged soldier brought to her sickbed and bound him by the direst oaths to promise obedience to herself. She died a few days later, however, on 30th August 1057, leaving the crown to the frail charge of Michael VI. The historian must regret that Theodora had not a larger opportunity to prove her value as a ruler and exhibit her personality. She was a woman of great vigour and generally high political ideals, and she incurs the reproach only of stooping at times to the common Byzantine level in securing her power. It was not she, but the contemptible Constantine, who emptied the treasury for frivolous purposes, and, in spite of the light disdain of Psellus, her rule compares most favourably with that of most of the Emperors.

CHAPTER XI

EUDOCIA

The struggle which Theodora had foreseen was not long deferred after her death, and Michael Stratioticus was compelled, after a few months of feeble imperial experiment, to retire to the private life from which he had been unwisely drawn. The great territorial nobles—one might almost say, the feudal nobles—concentrated upon the capital and put one of their number, Isaac Comnenus, upon the throne. Isaac had in earlier years married a Bulgarian princess, and her career as mistress of a large provincial domain, and then as Empress of Constantinople, suggests a very interesting study. Unfortunately, her husband's reign lasted only two years, and the events yield us only few and fleeting glimpses of the new Empress.

Æcatherina, as the best contemporary authority, Nicephorus Bryennius, calls her (though later writers often say Catherina), descended from the Bulgarian royal family, which had fallen from its high estate when "Basil the Bulgarian-slayer" had won a definitive victory over the nation. Bryennius makes her a daughter of the King Samuel, and we have in a later chronicle a picture of Samuel's daughters which would dispose us to imagine Æcatherina as a very fiery and interesting personality. When, in the presence of Basil, they were brought face to face with the woman whose husband had killed their brother, the Emperor and his officers had great difficulty in preventing a very violent and undignified scene. The dates, however, make it improbable that Æcatherina was one of the daughters of Samuel— others more probably suggest that she was his niece, or grand-niece—and in character she seems rather to have been gentle and religious. She was brought from her remote provincial home and made Augusta, but she proved to be one of the quiet and retiring Empresses who leave no mark in the chronicles. The only reference to her is that, in 1059, she encouraged her husband, who had met with a serious accident or illness, to resign, and she herself took the veil of the nun. One suspects that her husband's policy of curtailing the funds of the luxurious and innumerable monks alarmed her, and she was ready to believe that, as rumour maintained, the wild boar which led him into grave peril in 1059 was no ordinary animal. He resigned, and Æcatherina, changing her name to Helena, retired with her daughter Maria to a quiet mansion, where they practised monastic discipline and were esteemed so holy that Æcatherina was eventually buried in the cemetery of the monks of Studion.

With the next Empress, Eudocia, we return to the more familiar and more piquant type of Byzantine princess: the woman who unites with her subservience to the Church a skill in casuistry which protects her human inclinations from the harsher control of the Church's ascetic standards. Eudocia Macrembolitissa, or Eudocia the daughter of Macrembolites, a distinguished noble of Constantinople, had some beauty and no little wit, as well as good birth and breeding. In the reign of Michael IV. and Zoe she had been wooed and won by a handsome and learned, if not very warlike, commander named Constantine Ducas, and had in the subsequent twenty years of changing rulers borne three sons and three daughters to her elderly husband. Constantine was at least ten years older than she, and had no higher ambition than to be regarded as a prince of letters and rhetoric. It must, therefore, have been an agreeable surprise to Eudocia to learn, in 1059, that the retiring Emperor had transferred his crown to her husband, and she was henceforth to be the mistress of the sacred palace. She was then, probably, in her later thirties. She was entitled Augusta, and the imperial dignity was conferred also on her six children, of whom the youngest was born after her coronation.

During the eight years of her husband's reign Eudocia remained a silent witness of his futility and unpopularity. He retained his pedantry, and sought the laurels of learning and eloquence, while formidable enemies threatened the Empire on every side. In 1067 he perceived that his inglorious reign was about to end, and summoned Eudocia, the nobles and the patriarch to his couch. The nobles were commanded to swear to maintain the throne of Eudocia and her sons, and Eudocia was compelled to swear a portentous oath that she would not marry again. Possibly Constantine felt that he was not imposing a very heavy sacrifice on a woman who approached her fiftieth year, and it was plainly to the interest of his sons that she should not marry. Eudocia signed the written oath, and it was entrusted to the patriarch Xiphilin to keep in the great church.

The regency of Eudocia lasted about seven months, during which she emulated the conduct of Zoe and Theodora. She received ambassadors, heard trials and paid more direct and closer attention to the affairs of the Empire than her late husband had done. Two things, however, concerned her and illustrated the weakness of woman-rule at Constantinople. The Turks and other hostile neighbours were raiding the provinces with greater vigour, and the nobles were making this a pretext for intrigue to replace Eudocia with an Emperor. Before the year was out Eudocia decided to marry again and sought a means of evading the oath which the patriarch grimly guarded.

The story of her outwitting the patriarch is, as we find it in the later chronicles, in the finest vein of Byzantine melodrama. She took into her confidence one of the wiliest eunuchs of her Court, who assured her that it was quite easy to induce the patriarch to release her. This Xiphilin, the patriarch at the time, was himself as casuistic as he was religious. Originally a noble, he had voluntarily embraced the black robe of the monk, and had been withdrawn from the monastery to rule the Eastern Church. He had in Constantinople a brother named Bardas, whose gallantries and sybaritic ways were notorious. When the eunuch proposed the subject of marriage, Xiphilin sternly maintained that the oath was binding and that Eudocia must remain a widow, but when the astute eunuch regretted that such was his view, since it was his brother Bardas whom Eudocia wished to marry, Xiphilin reconsidered the matter. It is not for us to analyse his reasoning. It is enough that in a short time he declared to the assembled Senators that the oath was unjust and invalid, a mere wanton outrage on the part of a jealous man, and he handed the precious document back to Eudocia to destroy. His feelings may be imagined when, a few hours later, he heard that the Empress was married, not to his brother, but to Romanus Diogenes.

The contemporary writer Psellus gives a more sober version, but, although Psellus was one of Eudocia's chief ministers at the time, there can be little doubt that his vanity and policy have somewhat tempered the veracity of his narrative. Eudocia, he says, came to him in tears to complain that the cares of Empire were an intolerable burden for a single woman's shoulders, and she wished to marry. The story is, perhaps, not inconsistent with the story of her outwitting the patriarch. In any case, the second marriage of Eudocia had an element of romance.

In the state prison of Constantinople at the time was a handsome young noble and commander named Romanus Diogenes, who ran some risk of losing his head for high treason. Distinguished by birth and in person, and a man of great spirit, he reflected that the throne of the Eastern Empire had been reached by less able men than he, and cherished a daydream of wearing the purple. At the death of Constantine in 1067, when there was much discussion of the empty throne and the imperial widow, he imprudently confessed his ambition to those about him in the remote province of Thrace, which he governed; he was denounced in the capital; and he was brought in bonds to Constantinople and put on trial. He had then completed his thirtieth year: a tall, comely, broad-shouldered man, with the dark skin of a Cappadocian and very winning eyes. Constantinople looked with sympathy on the manly, but impetuous, young noble. He was connected by birth with the greatest families of the Asiatic provinces, and he pleaded that it was only his concern for the safety of the menaced Empire that had wrung from him words of dissatisfaction. His treason was, however, apparent, and he was found guilty and restored to jail.

Eudocia was probably present at the trial of Romanus, and noted the handsome form and flashing eye. She professed afterwards that the trial was unsatisfactory and must be revised, and the young commander found himself acquitted and free to return to his native province. The time was not yet ripe for the marriage project; in fact, one of the historians states that Romanus was already married, and went to join his wife and family in Cappadocia. About Christmas (1067), however, he received an order from Eudocia to return to Constantinople, and may or may not have been surprised to hear that she proposed to marry and crown him. His wife and family seem to have been deserted with great cheerfulness—unless we prefer to regard the statement in the chronicle as an error[24]—and Eudocia secretly prepared for the marriage. Senators were bribed to support the proposal, and, on 31st December, the patriarch was won by the stratagem which I have already described. That very night Romanus was introduced, fully armed, into the palace and secretly wedded to the Empress, and on the first day of the new year the young Emperor and his middle-aged Empress were ceremoniously presented to the people. For a moment it seemed as if the fierce Varangian guards were about to avenge what they regarded as a violation of the oath to the dead Constantine, but Eudocia prevailed on her elder sons to assure the guards that they had consented to the marriage, and the trouble was averted for the time.

It was, however, in face of considerable hostility that Eudocia and Romanus entered upon their task of governing the Empire. The clergy were naturally hostile, since their leader had been tricked into an ignominious concession; more distinguished nobles than Romanus envied his elevation; and courtiers who were attached to the fortunes of Eudocia's elder sons regarded the new Emperor, and the possible issue of the new marriage, with sullen distrust. Michael Psellus, the historian who boasts that he guided Eudocia's counsels in regard to the marriage, is transparently hostile to Romanus, and his historical work is largely responsible for the traditional prejudice against that brave and spirited, but injudicious and unfortunate, monarch. Psellus was not merely the chief student of philosophy in Constantinople, but an ambitious and successful courtier. His great repute in letters and philosophy gave him a commanding position in the Court of Eudocia, who had herself some literary ambition,[25] and his secret and sinuous counsels must have deeply influenced the later course of the careers of Romanus and Eudocia. A philosopher-statesman was the great ideal which Plato, whose works he revived, had urged upon the Greeks, but the fortunes of Psellus remain so even throughout the various revolutions he outlived that one is tempted to compare him rather with Talleyrand than with Plato's ideal.

EUDOCIA AND ROMANUS IV

FROM AN IVORY IN THE BIBLIOTHÈQUE NATIONALE, PARIS

Into this atmosphere of culture the robust Romanus was little fitted to enter, and some disdain must have been felt of his uncultivated ways. On the other hand, the brother of the late Constantine, John Ducas, who bore the dignity of Cæsar and jealously guarded the position of his nephews, was not less hostile to Romanus. The boys had received the purple before the death of their father, and the time was rapidly approaching when, with the assistance of their uncle and Psellus, they might begin to exercise their power. To this plan Romanus was a considerable obstacle. When we further learn that Romanus was gravely conscious of his duty to restore the strength and discipline of the army, and diverted funds from the entertainment of idle citizens to the pay and equipment of his troops, we realize that the life of the palace was preparing for one more of those tragic revolutions which punctuate the history of the Byzantine Empire.

From this Court atmosphere of pedantry and intrigue Romanus turned to the field of battle; he would strengthen his position by winning such laurels as his vigorous and warlike character seemed to promise him. Two months after his coronation a fresh invasion of the Turks was announced, and he led a large army out to meet them. After nearly a year's absence he returned with some report of victories, but there had in the same year been heavy losses, and his success was not decisive enough to override the intrigues of his opponents. Already, we are told, he found Eudocia colder. Her attitude is attributed to his arrogance and boastfulness; we may suppose that it was just as much due to an instinctive irritation when her robust husband strode into the philosophic atmosphere of the palace with the smell of the camp clinging to him and the language of war on his lips. In two or three months he was off once more to the field, leaving Eudocia to her master of philosophy and her brother-in-law. Into their hands she placed the more virile cares of State, while she enlarged libraries, cultivated men of letters and fostered the higher ambition of making verses. Her eldest son, Michael, was associated with her in her cultural work.

When Romanus returned in the following winter, still without decisive success, he seems to have concluded that it would be better to remain in Constantinople, and the campaign of the third year was entrusted to his generals, but in the spring of 1071 he again prepared to take the field. Nothing but a crushing victory over the enemies of the Empire would enable him to silence his enemies in the Court and capital. Eudocia seems by this time to have wavered between admiration of her young and manly spouse and repugnance to his more robust standards of life. She was now certainly over fifty, and had never been particularly sensuous, but we cannot doubt that she had married Romanus for love and that that love was not yet extinct. As he set out from port for his last crossing to Asia a singular dark-plumaged pigeon circled his royal galley. He directed that it should be caught and sent to the Empress; and it was said in later years that Eudocia nervously recognized in the rare bird an omen of the evil fortune that was about to befall her husband.

And in the course of the summer stragglers made their way hastily to Constantinople with the news that Romanus had been heavily defeated and his large army shattered. The Emperor himself had been slain, some said, but at length there came men who had seen him captured and borne away, a prisoner, by the Turks. The hour of the malcontents had come, and a council was summoned to discuss the situation. It was at once decided that no effort would be made to save Romanus—some of the authorities declare that it was the treachery of the Cæsar's son, acting on the instructions of his father, which led to the reverse—but the eldest son, Michael, should be appointed ruling Emperor, together with his mother.

That Eudocia at once surrendered her husband becomes quite clear from the subsequent course of events. The new administration had hardly settled to its work when Eudocia received a joyful letter from her husband announcing that he was free, and on his way to Constantinople. How the Turk had entirely falsified his repute for barbarity, treated Romanus as a brother king in misfortune, and eventually released him on promise of a ransom, is a familiar and attractive picture in the history of the time. Romanus was hastening to the arms of his beloved wife. Eudocia is described by contemporary writers as "distracted" and eager to consult those about her as to her conduct. Of wifely feeling she did not exhibit one sincere particle, and, however we may remind ourselves of the inevitable coldness of a woman in her sixth decade of life, her conduct is somewhat repellent. Had she known that the Cæsar was bent on bringing her to a common ruin with her husband, she might at least have purchased some loyalty to him, in the usual Byzantine fashion; but she was either ignorant or powerless, and she accepted the counsel that Romanus should be disowned and repelled by force from his Empire.

John Ducas, however, concluded that the opportunity was convenient for the removal of both Emperor and Empress. A decree was issued to the provinces to arrest the advance of Romanus, and the guards were marshalled. At this date the mercenary troops in charge of the palace were the famous and formidable Varangian guards, in whom modern authorities recognize the blue-eyed giants of distant Scandinavia and even of Britain. Romanus had favoured the native troops of the Empire rather than these foreign mercenaries, and they at once accepted the command of the Cæsar. One half of them went to the apartments of Michael, and declared him sole Emperor of the Romans; the other body went in search of Eudocia, with orders to transfer her to a monastery.

Eudocia at once concluded that the end of her rule had come when she heard the jubilant clash of axe on shield, the deep guttural voices, raised in song, of the northern soldiers, and their heavy tread across the gardens and terraces. Fearing for her life, she hid herself in some sort of hut in the grounds of her palace, but the door was presently flung open and she looked on the fierce hairy faces and shining weapons of the Varangians. She was prostrate with terror when the Cæsar arrived, to give her the comparative consolation that her life would be spared, but her empire was over. From the palace, spoiled of all the ensigns of royalty, we follow her along the short and painful route that we have seen so many proud rulers of the sacred palace take. At the Bucoleon quays a swift galley waited to take her to the Asiatic shore, where she was lodged in a monastery which she herself had founded. A further message soon came, ordering her to take the black veil, and the frail and unfortunate woman bade farewell to all the glories of imperial life. It was only four years since she had been left in control of the Empire by her first husband.

Shortly afterwards she was summoned to bury Romanus, and with him the last flickering hope of a return to power. He had collected an army and resolved to fight for his throne, and the troops of Ducas at length pinned him in a town of Cilicia. In order to end the civil war John now sent an assurance that the life of Romanus would be spared if he would resign his claim and enter a monastery; nay, three archbishops were sent to give him a solemn testimony that John had sworn and would fulfil his oath. Frail as the most formidable oaths had become in Eastern Christendom, Romanus opened the gates and yielded to the sons of the Cæsar. The rest of the story is a chapter of nauseous horror, and concerns us, fortunately, only in outline. Romanus was conveyed across Asia Minor, in the robe of a monk, with studied insult. Most of the chroniclers affirm that poison was administered to him, but that his powerful constitution prevented it from doing more than add to his misery. At length his eyes were cut out with more than ordinary brutality, the roughest and most elementary attention to his bleeding sockets was refused, and he was borne once more on a mule, dying by inches in the most ghastly conceivable fashion, across Asia Minor. He reached the island of Prote in time to die on the soil that was already watered by so many imperial tears, and the chroniclers add that Eudocia gave a splendid funeral to the remains of the man whom she had transferred from the jail to the palace, less than four years before, in the full pride of a magnificent manhood.

I have said that with the remains of Romanus she buried her last hope of returning to power, yet some seven years afterwards a strange message reached her in her cloister, recalling the memory, if not the hope, of imperial power. Her son Michael proved an ineffective ruler. The tradition of culture which had lingered in the palace since the days of Psellus absorbed all his energy, and he could not be diverted from the dialogues of Plato or the iridescent dreams of Plotinus by mere conspiracies against his throne or invasions of his Empire. Indeed, it was with difficulty, sometimes, that they could drag him to table or persuade him to refrain from spending the night over his books. The irony of the situation was that, while the Greek writings over which he lingered urged that a profound study of philosophy was the fittest education of monarchs, Michael remained as helpless and heedless as a boy, precisely on account of his studies. Fortunately, he had the casual inspiration to call to the palace a wily eunuch, named Nicephorus, who become the virtual ruler. Nicephoritzes—as the people, using the diminutive form of his name, called the pale and shrunken little eunuch—soon displaced the Cæsar John, and, as was the invariable custom of his kind, enriched himself at the expense of the impoverished and decaying provinces.

Under Nicephoritzes Eudocia had no chance of a return to power. He had endeavoured to persuade her first husband, the Emperor Constantine, that she was unfaithful to him, and had been driven from office during her regency. But the Empress's quarters in the palace were not vacant; a new type of Empress was added to the long and varied gallery. Shortly before his accession to the supreme throne Michael had married a princess of one of the tribes that had settled in Asia Minor. The father of the Empress Maria is conflictingly described as a king of the Iberians and the Alans, and is said to have been a ruler of great fame and power; but he is not named, and it seems that he was not powerful enough to avert or temper the tragedy of his daughter's career. Her dowry had been her beauty. I have complained at times of the lamentable indifference of the male historians of Constantinople to the physical features of the Empresses, and the lack of portraits which might bring the living figure with any fulness or accuracy before the imagination. We now, however, approach a period, the history of which has been written for us by a woman, the famous Anna Comnena, and her pen happily wanders at times back to the age of Eudocia, of which her husband, Nicephorus Bryennius, was the chief historian.

Unhappily, the art of which Anna Comnena was so patently proud did not include skill in portraiture. Maria was the most beautiful woman of her time, and, although her interests become opposed to those of Anna and her family, and the learned princess was capable of malignant hatred, Anna Comnena rises to the height of superlative when her pen delineates the figure of Maria. Her grace of form and beauty of face were beyond the artist's power to convey; though one must add that Anna not infrequently uses that formula, in order to enhance the artistic wonder of her own descriptions. Maria, she says, was tall and graceful as a cypress; her body was white as snow, save for the roses that bloomed in her cheeks, and the luminous blue eyes which shone beneath the perfect and lofty arch of her auburn eyebrows. To this vague poetical description we may add at once that the beautiful young princess was not wholly devoid of the spirit of her tribe, and was prepared for romantic adventure in support of the imperial dignity.

The seven years of Michael's reign do not interest us. The Emperor lived in the remote solitude of his exalted studies; Maria enjoyed the superb luxury of her position, and brought a prince into the world for the greater security of her throne; Eudocia languished in the royal monastery of the Virgin across the straits. Usurpers rose and fell, and the defrauded people spoke with bitterness of the young pedant who let his ministers rob them while he studied the divine maxims of Plato. Another princess, daughter of Robert of Lombardy, was introduced from the West, but she was, like Maria's son, to whom she was betrothed, a child of tender years, looking with strange blue eyes on the vast palaces she would one day govern—they said—and the boy who shyly shrank from her companionship.

At last, in 1078, a more fortunate rebel advanced on Constantinople, the clergy and nobles were bribed to espouse his cause, and Michael fled to the Blachernæ palace in the suburbs. Maria accompanied him, and what we know of her character emboldens us to fancy her urging the distracted scholar to draw a sword on behalf of his throne. His friends, however, found it impossible to move him, and, yielding to the usurper, he was conducted on an ass to the monastery at Studion, where he might prosecute his studies with even greater leisure. The new Emperor had so genial a disdain for him that he made him titular Bishop of Ephesus, and allowed him to return and live in the capital.

Maria, in accordance with custom, entered the suburban monastery at Petrion. She did not, however, take the vows of the religious life, and it was not long before the interesting news came that the new Emperor designed to marry her. Nicephorus Botaneiates was an elderly voluptuary, who had seized the throne only because so little energy was needed for the task. For the administration of public business he had two slaves of his own household, of Slavonian extraction, who at once put an end to the life of Nicephoritzes and diverted the stream of gold to their own pockets. For their master the pleasures of the table and the couch sufficed. He had brought to the throne an obscure Empress named Berdena, but she died shortly afterwards, and the aged Sybarite consulted his ministers. To their cold and impartial judgment it seemed that political considerations must rule the choice and they were divided between the claims of Maria and those of Eudocia. It is true that Nicephorus had been twice married, that Eudocia was a nun, and that Maria was not yet a widow; but such difficulties were never beyond the casuistic resources of the Constantinopolitan clergy. The Emperor must marry, since the sacred ritual of the Court demanded the presence of an Empress.

The politicians favoured the suit of Eudocia, and she was actually informed that Nicephorus wished to marry her, and expressed her cordial willingness to sacrifice her monastic estate in view of such august considerations. Nicephorus, however, was, as I said, a Sybarite, and even advanced age did not blur his experienced eye to the charms of Maria. We may, therefore, suppose that Nicephorus was neither surprised nor pained when a certain very holy monk appeared at the monastery of the Virgin and sternly forbade Eudocia to quit her black robe. It may be that the monk was one of the chaplains of the monastery; it is at least clear that his zeal did not take him to the monastery at Petrion, where Maria resided. The beautiful young Empress was recalled from her prayers and fasts and conducted to the side of the Emperor in the palace chapel. The patriarch, who seems to have had some scruples, was not summoned to perform the ceremony, and Nicephorus noticed with irritation that the priest who was called hesitated to come to the sanctuary; Nicephorus had no dispensation for a third marriage, and Maria's husband still lived. A courtier, however, had foreseen the difficulty and had a more accommodating priest at hand. The irregular knot was tied, or regarded as tied, and Maria returned to enjoy, with her son, the pleasures of the Emperor's luxurious Court.

It is, perhaps, no alleviation of the conduct of Maria, in purchasing her crown by an invalid marriage to an elderly sensualist, to say that—the chroniclers assure us—quite a number of noble ladies at Constantinople were eager to be chosen. Eudocia, her youngest daughter, Zoe, and many other ladies had been pressed upon the notice of Nicephorus. It is merely one more indication of the inferiority of character, both in men and women, in the Byzantine Empire. But Maria was not destined to enjoy long the throne which she had purchased. Contemptible as the reign of Michael had been, it was succeeded by one far more contemptible, and sullen murmurs filled the palace and the city. Men told each other how the aged Emperor, who ought to be thinking of eternity, changed his splendid robes ten times a day, anointed his jaded frame with the most costly unguents, and sat down, day after day, to the most superb banquets that the Empire could afford; while the two barbaric slaves whom he had made his chief ministers ground the despairing provinces and disgusted the nobles. Within a year or two of Maria's return to power, the customary, inevitable revolt arose, and she was driven back to her monastery.

This revolution, however, introduces us to the strong women of the Comnenian house and must commence a fresh chapter. Of Eudocia we hear no more. If we accept the statement of one of the chroniclers, that she had married in the reign of Michael IV. (1034-1041), she must now have reached her seventh decade of life, and would probably not long survive her last disappointment. Her readiness, in her later sixties, and after seven years of monastic life, to accept the embraces of a roué like Nicephorus, in return for the crown, is a sufficient measure of her character; her violation of her oath to her first husband, and her desertion of her second husband, point to the same feebly vicious and unattractive type of personality. Through the favour of Nicephorus she was permitted to leave the suburban monastery, and spend her last years in considerable comfort in the city.

CHAPTER XII

IRENE AND ANNA COMNENA

The distinguished family of the Comneni has already made its appearance in our narrative. It may be recalled that the last chapter opened with a march of the great provincial nobles upon the capital, and the placing of one of their ablest representatives, Isaac Comnenus, upon the throne. Isaac's brave life had ended in heroic foolishness. Terrified by an apparition, he embraced the monastic life, ignored the natural desire of his brother John to succeed him, and handed the crown to the Ducas family. During the reign of Eudocia the widow of John Comnenus, Anna, remained in Constantinople to guard the fortunes of her children and eventually to help them to secure the throne. She was a woman of the old Roman build, rather than Byzantine; strong, ambitious, able and despotic. The Cæsar John Ducas looked on her with just suspicion, and accused her of treasonable correspondence with Romanus, when he was struggling to regain his throne. She boldly asserted that the letters were forged, and brandished an image of Christ in the eyes of her judges; but it was expedient to condemn her, and she passed to the melancholy Princes' Islands.

Michael the Scholar released her as soon as Diogenes was dead, and she returned to Constantinople, to watch and work. She had something of the spirit of her father, who had sent so many of the enemy to the land of shades that he had won the name of Alexius Charon: her mother had been of the great family of the Delasseni. The feebleness of Michael and the insipidity of Nicephorus gave promise of a successful revolution, and Anna and her two sons were shrewd enough not to force the opportunity. The youth had first to learn the mastery of legions and to marry. There were, in fact, four women in Constantinople, all able and ambitious, who sought the throne for their children, and a stupendous amount of intrigue must have been expended. The four were: Anna Comnena, the Empresses Eudocia and Maria, and the wife of Andronicus, son of the Cæsar John Ducas. Andronicus had been fatally wounded in war, and condemned to a lingering death, and his wife pressed the Cæsar to find good alliances for her three daughters. She was one of those virile and beautiful Bulgarian princesses who had found the way to Constantinople, and her eldest daughter, Irene, was now just marriageable.

The wife of Andronicus—we do not know her name—shrewdly concluded that an alliance with the Comneni would best serve her ambition, and she pressed her father-in-law to bring about a marriage between Irene and Alexis, the elder of Anna's two sons. Alexis was a very promising and successful commander who had recently lost his first wife, and he was not unwilling to wed the fair Irene. Anna Comnena (the younger) describes the pair for us, with her usual verbosity and inexactness, premising that it is beyond the power of art to reproduce their comeliness. Alexis was, it seems, a man of medium height, with very broad shoulders and massive chest, eyes of "terrible splendour," and a look that was "at once both truculent and bland." He seems, in fact, to have been a very ordinary young man, with an extraordinary capacity for ruse and intrigue. Irene (Anna's mother) was, of course, a paragon. Her face was "like the moon," though not quite so round, and her rosy cheeks and fine blue eyes make the simile somewhat weak; her look, like that of her husband, was "at once sweet and terrible"—the look of "a Minerva of heavenly splendour"—and calm and storm succeeded each other, as on the sea, in her expressive blue eyes; her arms and hands were like carven ivory, and her constant gestures extremely graceful. In other words, Irene was a very pretty maiden of thirteen summers at the time, with a large share of the spirit and temper of her Bulgarian mother. These fragments of Anna Comnena's art may serve to illustrate Gibbon's indulgent complaint that it is more feminine than the artist herself.

The prospect of so significant a marriage released a fresh flood of intrigue. Anna, the mother of Alexis, remembered that it was John Ducas who had driven her into exile, and would not hear of a match with his daughter-in-law. The Emperor Michael regarded the marriage with distrust; his brother Constantine wanted to marry Alexis to his sister Zoe, Eudocia's youngest daughter. Through this thicket of obstacles and intrigues the wife of Andronicus fought her way with spirit, and not a little bribery, and the marriage took place. We may assume that this was in the second or third year of Nicephorus, when Irene, who was only fifteen at her coronation, cannot have been more than thirteen or fourteen years old.

The Empress Eudocia had now played her last card, and resigned herself to the life of the monastery; it remained to secure the favour of the lovely Empress Maria. Isaac Comnenus had married her cousin Irene, and had therefore the entrée of her palace. The Slavonian ministers of Nicephorus watched him and his brother with concern, but he won the affection of Maria and, by generous distribution of money, the service of her eunuchs. It was presently announced that the Empress Maria proposed to adopt the successful young commander of the troops, Alexis Comnenus, and when this ceremony had been performed both brothers were at liberty to make lengthy visits to the Empress. It is not difficult to accept the rumour that the relation of Alexis to his "mother" was not entirely filial. Alexis was no ascetic, and he notoriously strayed from his girl-wife. On the other hand, Maria had not shown much delicacy in marrying the white-haired sensualist, and the privilege of intimacy with a handsome young general of thirty-seven, her eunuchs being bribed in his and her favour, would be appreciated by her. Her mind was not strong and penetrating enough to see through the trickery of Alexis. He posed as an unambitious general, loyally devoted to her reign and that of her son.

The Emperor Nicephorus probably felt that the young men would await the natural termination of his imperial orgies before seizing the throne, and seems to have regarded them with a certain genial indifference. His ministers, however, knew that their fortunes were ruined if Alexis came to the throne, and they insisted that Nicephorus must name a successor. He chose his nephew, a handsome young noble named Synadenus. Maria was now seriously alarmed, since the accession of Synadenus would mean the monastery for her and, possibly, death for her son, and she allowed the Comneni to witness her tears. They were, they said, devoted to her cause. Nay, they swore on the holy cross that they would acknowledge no rulers but Maria and her son, and she promised, in return, that they should be informed of any step that might be contemplated against them in the palace. I am following, almost entirely, the narrative of Anna Comnena, who enlarges with the most candid pleasure on the deceit of her father, and assures us that her grandmother, Anna, was the soul of the plot. In the palace of the Comneni councils were held daily, and the virile mother directed the movements of her sons. It was a time of great anxiety. One night Nicephorus invited Alexis and Isaac to his banquet, and Anna depicts them nervously glancing round them during the meal for the guards or assassins who might have been summoned to despatch them. But Alexis, a master of ruse and insinuation, won the Emperor, and, when a charge of treason was afterwards brought against him, he easily cleared himself.

At last a message came to the mansion of the Comneni from Maria that Barilas (one of the Slav ministers) intended to seize the throne and put out the eyes of Alexis; and it was decided that the time had come for action. Alexis hastily made a tour of the city, persuading some, bribing others, until he had a large number of officers and Senators bound by secret oath to support him. Anna meantime made preparations for the flight of the family during the night. The chief weakness of their position was that a young relative of the Emperor had recently married a young girl of their family, and lived, with a tutor, in an outlying part of their mansion. Anna, regarding the tutor as a spy, locked them in their rooms when they were asleep, and before dawn the whole Comneni family set out on foot to cross the city. At that hour of the night there was little watch in Constantinople, and the nervous band—the mother, the two brothers with their wives, children, and sisters, and a few servants—passed safely and silently down the colonnaded main street as far as the Forum of Constantine, where horses awaited the men. They bade each other farewell in the darkness of the early spring morning, and the brothers galloped to the Blachernæ palace, where they broke into the stables, chose the swiftest horses, hamstrung the rest of the horses, and fled to the army which awaited them in Thrace.

The women and children made their way noiselessly back along the Mese to the cathedral. As they went along the street, the glare of a torch appeared in the distance and they found themselves inconveniently accosted by the tutor spy. Anna kept her presence of mind, however. They had heard, she said, that they were accused of some crime and they were going at once to St Sophia, but as soon as the day broke they would go to the palace to demand justice, and she begged the tutor to go on to the palace to announce their intention. As soon as he had gone, they made for the house of Bishop Nicholas, an annexe of the cathedral into which fugitives were admitted during the night. Rousing the doorkeeper, they announced themselves—they were all heavily veiled—as a party of women who had just landed at the quays from the east, and who would render thanks to the Almighty before repairing to their homes. They were admitted to the church, and, when the officers of the infuriated Emperor arrived, in the early morning, they found that nothing less than a violation of the sanctuary would put the women in the power of Nicephorus. Anna, in fact, clung to the gates of the sanctuary, and exclaimed that the soldiers would have to cut off her hands to remove her from the church, as the Slav ministers threatened. Isaac's wife Irene, an Iberian princess like her cousin Maria, followed the example of her mother-in-law, and we must imagine the younger Irene and the children standing by, with large and tearful blue eyes, taking their first lesson in Byzantine politics. Nicephorus temporized, and swore to spare their lives. Anna shrewdly stipulated that his oath should be taken on the large cross which the Sybarite Emperor always wore, and, when this had been brought and the oath guaranteed to them, the women passed from the church to the palace-fortress-monastery at Petrion, on the Golden Horn. There they were soon joined by the wife and mother-in-law of George Paleologus, a dashing young commander who had fled with the Comneni, and, by sharing their delicate meats and wines liberally with their jailers, they secured a constant account of the progress of the insurgent brothers.

They heard presently that Alexis and Isaac had safely reached the camp in Thrace, and that it had needed only a little further intrigue on the part of Alexis for the troops to proclaim him Emperor. The next news of importance was that the brothers were encamped with their troops on the higher ground without the city walls, and Nicephorus was distracted and terrified. But we may tell in few words the success of the Comneni. The formidable walls of Constantinople were held by the Varangian guards and Immortals, on whose blind fidelity a ruling (and paying) Emperor could always rely. But the extravagance of Nicephorus had in three years exhausted the treasury—its doors stood open for any man to enter the empty building—the troops were few, and uncertain mercenaries had to be enlisted in the defence. Alexis bribed the German soldiers who held the tower overlooking the Blachernæ gate, and at dawn of Maundy Thursday (1081) his troops poured into the city.

It is one of the few points in favour of Alexis that he here made a very human blunder which might have cost him his life and his ambition. Instead of holding his troops to scatter the guards, who had retreated upon the palace, he rode at once to Petrion to see that the women were safe, and his soldiers—a motley and savage crowd of Thracian and Macedonian mercenaries—spread with fiendish delight over the city, violating nuns in the monasteries and burdening themselves with wine and loot. Paleologus saved them by a bold and crafty seizure of the fleet, cutting off the Emperor's retreat to Asia. Nicephorus wavered between the vigorous counsels of his ministers and the command of the patriarch that he should abdicate and prevent civil war, but his hesitation enabled the troops to rally, and, with a melancholy farewell to his perfumed baths and opulent banquets, he suffered himself to be shipped to the opposite shore and shaved into a monk.

The Empress Maria is described as trembling in her palace during these critical days of the Holy Week, clinging to her boy Constantine, a pretty seven-year-old lad with curly golden hair and pink and white complexion. Alexis had apparently deceived her, and the Comnenian women would have little consideration for her. For some days, however, she remained in quiet possession of her apartments, and a very keen discussion took place in Constantinople as to the intentions of Alexis. He had put Irene, with her mother and sisters, in the lower and older palace, while he, his mother, brother, and other relations had taken residence in the more important Bucoleon palace, by the water. Did he propose to put away his doll-wife and wed the riper beauty? Such things had happened before, and the careful reader of Anna Comnena's discreet narrative will easily believe that that was the intention, or the disposition, of Alexis. He had treated Irene with coldness and disdain (other chroniclers tell us), and been unfaithful to her. But the little Irene had her party, or Maria had her enemies, and the indecision of Alexis was forced. Paleologus drew up the fleet before Bucoleon. When Alexis sent orders to him that the sailors must not acclaim Irene, he boldly replied that he had "not done all this for Alexis, but for Irene," and her name rolled from galley to galley. Next the Cæsar John Ducas intervened, and urged Maria to retire; probably he sought favour with Anna. Alexis still hesitated, and Irene was not crowned with him.

Speculation in the city was now seething, but a curious circumstance soon ended the hesitation of Alexis. His mother was devoted to monks generally, and one in particular she so esteemed that she insisted on his being appointed at once patriarch of Constantinople. The actual patriarch, Cosmas, swore that he would not resign in favour of the monk until he had crowned Irene, and Anna had now an additional incentive to press her son. Within a week of the coronation of Alexis the second coronation took place, and Irene began to share the bed and the throne of her husband. The last hope of Maria had gone down before her more virile and older antagonist, and she prepared to retire. Her son Constantine was clothed with the imperial dignity, and an imperial rescript, written in the red or purple ink and signed with the golden seal of the Emperor, guaranteed their safety. With this precious document Maria retired, accompanied by her son, to a somewhat remote palace in the imperial domain, and we may briefly dismiss her from the story. Some years later a pretext was found to remove her from her semi-imperial state and lodge her in a monastery. Her last recorded act is that she bethought herself of her first and real husband, who still lived in Constantinople as titular Bishop of Ephesus, and asked and obtained forgiveness.

Alexis now hastened to form about his throne a bulwark of loyal, and richly rewarded, friends, and the Court resounded with sonorous new titles and glittered with new insignia. Another noble, Nicephorus

Melissenus, had sought the throne at the same time as Alexis; he was disarmed with the dignity of Cæsar and the remote governorship of Thessalonica. Isaac received the newly created dignity of Sebastocrator; Michael Taroneita, who had married a sister of Alexis, rejoiced in the opulent name of Panhypersebastos; and younger brothers were created Protosebastos and Sebastos.[26] When we recollect that the wife of each had a corresponding title and state, we appreciate the splendour of the processions which now constantly fed the enthusiasm of Constantinople.

For a time, however, life in the palace wore a humorously mournful complexion. The appalling outrages of Alexis's troops had sown bitterness in the minds of the people, and the memory of them had to be obliterated. Any other Emperor would have at once provided a glorious series of chariot races and flung gold in showers from his chariot. Alexis Comnenus found a less expensive device; unless we care to attribute the scheme to his mother, whom he consulted. The new patriarch was humbly begged to impose a penance on all the royal inmates of the palace, and he decided that forty days of fasting and prayer would efface the stain. Alexis himself generously went beyond the letter of the penance; he slept nightly on the ground and wore a hair shirt—and took care that all the citizens knew it. His brothers, his mother and the other women of the family embraced their share of the imposition, and for five or six weeks the Bucoleon palace resembled a monastery.

When the period of mourning came to an end Alexis turned to face the numerous and pressing enemies of his Empire, and his mother became the active ruler. Her granddaughter would have us believe that the elder Anna had no ambition to wield power; she was disposed to retire at once into a monastery, and it was only in obedience to a solemn decree of Alexis that she consented to remain in the palace and use the powers of her absent son. But Anna Comnena, the royal historian, possessed in a considerable degree the faculty for ruse and duplicity which distinguished her family,[27] and we have little difficulty in seeing that the older Anna claimed and clung to power. Irene was, of course, still a negligible child. Anna at once set about the restoration of discipline in the palace, which had been so grossly neglected under Nicephorus and Maria. Hours were fixed for meals and prayers and the chanting of hymns, and her table was rarely without the blessing of some priest or monk who would discuss with her the sacred books and theological issues in which she was interested. Sober in diet, liberal to the poor and the Church, awake beyond the hours of most mortals with her long prayers, yet up early in the morning for those imperial duties which the golden bull of her son had laid on her, Anna was at least not unworthy of the power she had intrigued to secure. We must, however, not exaggerate her political influence. A few years later we find Alexis, when he sets out for the field, entrusting the reins of government to his brother, and no doubt Isaac generally controlled the administration.

Of Irene we hear little until the latter part of her husband's reign, when her services as nurse make him appreciate her value. In spite of the glowing assurances of their daughter, we perceive confidently that Irene was slighted, both by the mother and the son, and we shall ultimately find her dismissing him from the world with an assurance of her profound disdain. For two years the chronicles are silent about her, and the one reference to her in twenty years is that she bore children to her spouse. As Christmas approached in 1083 she began to feel the first pangs of travail. Alexis was expected home from his campaign against Robert Guiscard in two days, and Anna Comnena, who is not hypersensitive in her narrative, relates that the young mother signed her body with a cross and said: "Stay where you are, my boy, until your father arrives." It was not a boy, but the historian herself, who saw the light two days later, and Anna—a fierce and murderous rebel against her brother—asks us to applaud her very early practice of the virtue of obedience.

In view of this silence concerning the Empresses we will hold ourselves dispensed from following Alexis through the campaigns, plots and counter-plots of the next twenty years. Five years were spent in struggle with Robert Guiscard of Italy: five in repelling the wild Patzinaks of Scythia: five more in suppressing conspiracies, or alleged conspiracies, against the throne. It may seem ungenerous to suspect that the hard-working Alexis invented these conspiracies in order to rid his camp and Court of suspected relatives or nobles, but Byzantine historians not obscurely hint such a suspicion. One conspiracy only need be related, since Irene appears on the stage at the time.

Some years after his accession to the throne—the date is uncertain—Alexis consented to the retirement of his mother into the monastery to which, her granddaughter says, her heart had always turned. Very probably Irene, as she grew to womanhood, resented the older woman's restraint and piety, and insisted on her removal. She died, a nun, a few years afterwards. From that time Alexis drew nearer to Irene, and used to take her with him on his campaigns. In 1092 or 1093 there was trouble in Dalmatia, and Irene accompanied her husband and shared his tent in the camp. It was noticed with some alarm by the officers that Nicephorus Diogenes, son of Eudocia, who had received imperial dignity in his infancy and might aspire to regain it, pitched his tent nearer to that of the Emperor than courtesy permitted. Alexis scouted their suspicions, and retired to rest with Irene; but in the middle of the night the maid who was engaged in keeping the flies, or other insects, off the royal sleepers, aroused them with the news that Nicephorus had entered the tent with a drawn sword. One hesitates to say which is the more remarkable: that there should be no guard to the imperial tent, or that Alexis should take no notice of this attempt on his life. A few days later, Anna assures us, Nicephorus renewed the attempt, and was detected with drawn sword near the Emperor's bath. He was now put to the torture and provided a list of nobles who were obnoxious to the Emperor and were duly punished. It is interesting to find that the ex-Empress Maria was included among the conspirators, and it was possibly on this occasion that she was sent to a nunnery. But the narrated details of the conspiracy are so clumsy, and the issue proved so profitable to Alexis, that historians regard it with grave suspicion.

We come next to the page of Byzantine history which is least unfamiliar to English readers, the page restored to life by Sir Walter Scott in his "Count Robert of Paris."[28] But, profoundly important as the passage of the first Crusaders is in Byzantine history and in the biography of Alexis, we have no decent pretext to enlarge on that fascinating episode in a biography of the Empresses. We need say only that Irene trembled with her husband, or more than her husband, at the formidable tide of the invasion. Thinking to secure a few thousand spears to assist him in his warfare with the Turks, Alexis had added a pathetic, if not hypocritical, plea to the eloquence of Peter the Hermit. The response was, in 1096, a devouring and destructive army of locusts: a flood of 300,000 men, women and children, who, before they could be persuaded to cross the straits and leave their bones on the plains of Asia Minor, gravely embarrassed the Byzantine Court. In their train came a more formidable menace: Godfrey of Bouillon, Robert of Flanders, the princes of Western chivalry, with their hawks and hounds and ladies, and their vast hordes of hungry and blustering men-at-arms. Their suspicions, ferocious outbursts, disdain, and greed of wealth, called out every diplomatic resource at the command of Alexis, and few will do more than smile at his duplicity in such circumstances. At one moment, when it was rumoured in their camp without the walls that Alexis had imprisoned some of their leaders, they flung themselves against the city, and a howl of terror was heard from Blachernæ to the Sea of Marmora. How Alexis astutely drew them from the fascinations of his capital, and hovered in their rear, jackal-like, to recover the towns from which they expelled the Turk, and at last brought on a conflict of Latin and Greek, must be read in history. Seven further years of the reign of Alexis and Irene passed in these adventures.

The next decade was full of war against Bohemund, son of his former antagonist Robert Guiscard, and other Crusaders. In the course of the war, in 1105, we again catch a glimpse of Irene, who accompanied Alexis to the camp of Thessalonica. Apropos of the journey her daughter, who was now a mature eyewitness of events, depicts Irene's character in phrases which we read with some discretion. She was, it seems, so devoted to the reading of sacred books, the conversation of holy men and the discharge of her domestic duties, that she was reluctant to make these journeys; indeed, she could never appear in public without a nervous blush. It is not like the Irene whom we shall know more fully anon. But her husband needed her, and she obeyed. Plotters and conspirators surrounded him, and he suffered acutely from gout in the feet. Of the constant plots Anna offers no explanation; it is not from her that we learn how Alexis so far debased the coinage that his "gold" pieces (almost entirely bronze) were a thing of contempt throughout Europe, how he further oppressed his subjects with monopolies, and how savagely he could at times treat malcontents and heretics. His gout, however, she is eager to explain. It was due, not to any generosity of diet, but to an injury to his knee in early years, aggravated by the stupid "barbarians of the West" (the Crusaders), who kept the sacred Emperor standing for hours to listen to their unceasing torrents of talk. So Irene had to accompany her husband, to chafe his poignant limbs when the gout racked him and to scare away conspirators. She travelled with great modesty, in a litter borne by two mules and so enwrapped with purple that "her divine body was not visible."

In the following year a conspiracy was "detected" at Constantinople. A wealthy Senator named Solomon and four brothers of Saracenic origin were the chief plotters, and the treasury was enriched by their fortunes. Solomon's mansion was given to Irene, who is said to have restored it to the wife of the Senator. For once Anna admits that her father could be truculent. Anna was at a window of the palace overlooking the Forum, or the streets near it, when the soldiers and mob passed with the four brother conspirators. They were mounted on oxen, and were derisively adorned with the horns and entrails of oxen by the theatrical folk to whom they had been entrusted before their eyes were put out; from another historian we learn that the hair had already been torn, by means of pitch, from their heads and chins. Anna called her mother, and the two women forced Alexis to put an end to the horrible display and spare the prisoners' eyes.

A year or two later Irene is said to have saved her husband's life from fresh conspirators. She had again set out with him for Thessalonica, and, as they camped at Psyllus on the way, a plot was formed to murder Alexis as soon as Irene should return to the city. Alexis would not part with her, and the impatient conspirators threw a parchment in his tent, deriding him for his reluctance to take the field and urging the dismissal of Irene. Shortly afterwards a more violent diatribe was placed under their bed while they slept, but one of Irene's eunuchs was on guard and arrested the man, who betrayed the plotters. Then the death of Bohemund put an end to the war in the West, and the indefatigable Emperor turned to face the Turks and the Crusaders who had settled in the East. Irene became seriously ill when she accompanied Alexis to the Chersonesus in 1112, yet we find her with him at Philippopolis in the following year.

Irene was little more than nurse to the gouty monarch during these campaigns, yet we must, in order to understand her last fierce word to him, glance for a moment at the conduct she observed in him. She had for years seen how he conducted wars and diplomacy chiefly by guile and deceit, and she now saw how he converted heretics. A few years before he had set out to refute the tenets of the "Bogomilians," one of the many sects, mingling Eastern and Western ideas, in which age after age the protestant feeling against the superstitions and corruption of the Greek Church found expression. By the use of torture Alexis discovered that the leader of the sect was a staid and venerable monk named Basil, invited the monk to visit him in the palace, and, by a grossly hypocritical pretence that he himself leaned to the sect, induced him to talk freely of their doctrines. When he had "vomited his heresy," Alexis drew aside a curtain, and showed the man that a shorthand-writer had secretly taken down his words. Basil was imprisoned, and Alexis spent hours in argumentation with him; and a few years later the "archsatrap of Satan" and large numbers of his followers were burned alive for refusing to see the force of the imperial logic. Similar tactics were now adopted at Philippopolis, where Alexis and Irene spent the greater part of 1113. It was an important seat of the Paulicians (a modified Manichæan sect), and Alexis spent days in disputation with their leaders; when persuasion failed, he resorted to bribery and coercion.

These few instances will suffice to illustrate the relations of Irene and Alexis, and we may hasten to the final scene. The last years were occupied with a campaign against the Turks, but Alexis was now seriously ill and the enemy advanced and reviled him for his cowardice. In their camp they bore about a bed with an effigy of Alexis pretending that gouty feet prevented him from taking the field. Irene was awakened one night with the news that the Turks were upon them, and Alexis was forced to let her return to the capital. There is no doubt that she accompanied Alexis on these later campaigns only because he compelled her, and one wonders whether he was not afraid to leave her in the palace. He retreated, and recalled her at once to Nicomedia. Here she found that his own subjects were singing, on the streets, comic songs about the gout of the great Emperor and his flight before the Turks. He was undoubtedly very ill, and in the spring of 1118 he was brought back to the palace to die. Then arose a fierce struggle for the throne.

Anna Comnena, the princess born in 1083, had been betrothed, in her tender years, to the Empress Maria's pretty boy Constantine. The boy died, however, and in time she was married to the distinguished and ambitious noble, Nicephorus Bryennius, who received the title of Cæsar and then that of Panhypersebastos ("the august above all others"). Bryennius was a scholar: Anna a prodigy of female learning, a cyclopædia of arts and philosophy, a most imposing writer, and—strange to say—a spirited and ambitious princess. The brilliance of this imperial pair dazzled the Court and the capital, and it was very naturally suggested that the crowns could not be placed on wiser and more fitting heads than theirs. Such was the opinion of Irene. But Alexis and Irene had three sons (John, Andronicus and Isaac) and three daughters (Maria, Eudocia and Theodora) besides the gifted Anna, and the crown belonged, by such right as was recognized in Byzantium, to the eldest son. John was a plain, quiet youth of—as events proved—sterling character and no ostentation. His father appreciated him, though few others knew him. He observed with sullen eyes the efforts of his mother to displace him, and secretly engaged officers and nobles to support him against her; and Irene retorted by forbidding them to have any intercourse with John. This struggle was now to reach the height of passion round the deathbed of the Emperor.

The last ten pages of Anna's narrative give a vivid account of the progress of her father's illness. She was appointed to a kind of presidency over the skilled medical men who were summoned from all parts of the Empire to check the "mysterious" illness—of a gouty old man of seventy. I will quote only that, when relics failed to improve his condition, they applied a red-hot iron to his stomach—to counterpoise the pain at the extremities, perhaps—and, when this brought about no relief, removed him to the Mangana palace, near what is now known as the Seraglio Point. Irene watched her husband night and day (carefully excluding John), and, although the monks assured her that he would live to visit the Holy Sepulchre, she shed "more tears than the waters of the Nile," Anna says.

In the afternoon of 15th August 1118, Alexis lay dying on his purple couch. The description of the scene, which closes Anna's narrative, has reached us only in a torn and fragmentary condition, but the chronicle of the monk Zonaras, who lived about this date, is full and authoritative, and it is supported by the chronicle of Nicetas. Their account of that last scene in the life of Alexis shows that Anna Comnena crowns her work with a masterpiece of deliberate lying. She depicts her mother overwhelmed with sorrow at the impending loss of her husband, crying that thrones and crowns are vanity, and calling for the black robe of a nun, if not actually shearing her golden tresses, before the last breath has left her husband's body. Of the real features of the scene there is merely a faint and vague report that John is hurrying to the main palace and the city is disturbed. The truth is less touching, more dramatic.

Availing himself of a temporary absence of his mother—probably bribing the guards—John entered the room and approached the bed of the dying and speechless monarch. Alexis was still conscious; but whether he gave his ring to John, or the son detached it from his finger, the chroniclers are not agreed. No doubt Alexis was too feeble to detach and give it, and merely looked assent when John detached it; Alexis had always favoured John. By the time Irene returned John was galloping across the imperial domain to the chief palace (either Daphne or, more probably, Bucoleon), and the Empress was furious. She angrily observed to Alexis that his son was seizing the throne while he yet lived. Alexis feebly, and equivocally—though some writers say that he smiled—lifted his hands and eyes toward heaven, as if to intimate that there was the only throne about which he was now concerned. Nicephorus Bryennius was summoned, and Irene urged him to unite with her in claiming the throne. He refused, and she returned to her husband. The last words, loudly and harshly spoken, which she gave the dying man were: "Husband, while you lived, you were full of guile, saying one thing and thinking another; you are no better now that you are dying."[29] We may assume that Alexis had deceived her about the succession. He died that evening, so completely deserted that there were no ministers to perform the ceremonial services over his remains. The interest had passed to the main palace.

John had found before the door a regiment of the Varangians, who, even when he showed his father's ring, refused to allow him to enter. But they grounded their formidable two-edged axes, and stood aside, when he swore (a false oath) that his father was already dead, and had appointed him successor. He at once secured the palace and the crown, and the reign of Irene Comnena was over, the hope of Anna Comnena shattered. John would not even issue to attend the funeral of Alexis, so determined he was to hold the palace. The women were beaten by the quiet, ugly little youth they had despised, and a few words of the chroniclers dismiss them from the stage of history.

Irene, changing her name to that of Xene, retired to a monastery which she had built in the city. Curiously enough, a manuscript copy of the rules of this monastery has survived, and been published,[30] so that we have an interesting glimpse of Irene's later years and of the monastic life of the time. The inmates were to number between thirty and forty, were to sleep in a common dormitory, and were to elect a prefect. Besides the steward, who was to be a eunuch, and the two chaplains, who must be monks and eunuchs, no man was ever to enter the monastery, and the reception of visitors was strictly controlled. There was midnight office to be chanted, and the remaining offices and meals and other details were planned much as in a modern "convent" (a Latin word unknown in the East). Each nun was permitted to have a bath once a month. Irene little dreamed, when she sanctioned this ascetic scheme, that she would one day be forced to adopt it. But the last glimpse we catch of her in the chronicles suggests that she did not embrace it in all its rigour. Fifteen years later, when another Irene came from the West to wed the Emperor Manuel, she noticed, among the crowd of notabilities who welcomed her to the city, an aged lady whose dark monastic robe was relieved by strips of purple and edges of gold. When she asked the name of this royal nun, she learned that it was the widow of the great Alexis. Probably Irene tempered the diet and prayers, as well as the robe, of the monastery. She was then seventy-seven years old, and cannot have lived much longer.

Anna Comnena seems to have retained her liberty and rank at the accession of her brother. He soon proved his worthiness of the crown, and the corrupt nobles and ministers, shrinking from his inflexible justice, gathered darkly about Anna and Bryennius. Anna was the most active spirit in the plot, and it would have succeeded but for the irresolution, or humanity, of Bryennius. The doorkeeper of the palace was bribed, and John might have been murdered in his bed. When Bryennius failed to use the advantage, Anna turned upon him with fury. Nicetas tells us that she complained, "in somewhat obscene language," that Nature had made her a woman and him a man. John was content to confiscate their property; though, when he gave Anna's luxurious palace and all it contained to his Turkish minister, that strange type of Byzantine official begged his master to lay aside his anger and permit him to restore the palace to Anna. Some years later she entered her mother's monastery—probably when her husband died in 1128—and lived there at least twenty years, writing her famous work, the "Alexiad," a chronicle of her father's deeds. That work—affected, insincere and ambitious—reflects the character of its author, nor can its lavish use of the art of suppressing some facts and enlarging others efface from our memory the ignoble attitude of Irene and Anna by the bedside of the dying Alexis and toward his legitimate heir.

CHAPTER XIII

A BREATH OF CHIVALRY

Our last chapter introduced the chivalry of the West into the East, and, as numbers of the princes of the West remained and set up principalities in the East, and mingled with it in matrimonial alliance, the hope may be entertained that at last we shall witness some signal alteration of the Greek character. The more informed reader, who knows how the severe historians of recent times have washed much of the colour from "the days of chivalry," whose acquaintance with that epoch extends beyond the "Idylls of the King," will, perhaps, not expect any transformation of the character of the East. I will not anticipate the verdict. We have reached a time when the ideas and sentiments of the Western knights make a marked impression on the minds and ways of the East, and it will be interesting to see what types of women now arise. I shall therefore not confine myself rigidly, in this chapter, to those women who are fortunate enough to attain the supreme title, but include in the survey a number of princesses who, in various ways, approach the throne.

John the Handsome, as the citizens of Constantinople came to call the dark and by no means handsome young Emperor they had now obtained, does not provide us with an Empress of distinct or interesting character. His wife Irene, a daughter of Wratislav, King of Hungary, was too virtuous to leave a mark in the Byzantine chronicles. While her able and upright husband flung back the invaders from his territory, and essayed such improvement in its condition as his poor political faculty enabled him to achieve, she spent her days in prayer and the rearing of her family. Pearls and diamonds had no dangerous fascination for her; she maintained a modest demeanour in the pomp of the palace and gave the superfluous wealth to the poor and the monks. After bringing five children into the world, she died about six years after her coronation, and John remained a widower for the twenty further years of his arduous and exemplary reign. In the winter of 1142-1143, as he spent the truce from campaigning in hunting in Asia Minor, he accidentally poisoned himself with an arrow, nominated his youngest son Manuel for the succession, and died a few days afterwards.

Of his four sons: two—Alexis and Andronicus—had died before their father: two—Isaac and Manuel— survived. Manuel was in the field with his father, and he at once sent to Constantinople his father's able

Turkish minister to secure the throne for him, while he remained to care for and convey the royal remains. The Turk was vigorous, and not unfamiliar with Byzantine history. Before a soul in Constantinople had heard of the Emperor's death he lodged the elder son, Isaac, in a safe monastery, promised an enormous sum of money to the clergy, and had the path to the throne lined with subservient courtiers when Manuel arrived. A shower of gold upon the city completed the preparation, and Manuel I., a tall, handsome, vigorous and fairly cultivated youth, took in hand the reins of the Empire. The spirit of Western chivalry had found an apt pupil in Manuel, and his robust frame, reckless daring, and fiery passions made him at once a brother of the Crusaders and their Eastern descendants. For generations men told of his feats of strength and boldness.

His first Empress was the daughter of the Count of Sulzbach, an important Bavarian noble, and sister to the wife of Conrad, the ruling Emperor of Germany. Bertha had been betrothed to Manuel before the death of his father, and some time after his coronation she was conducted from the humble castle of her father to the world-famed splendour of Constantinople. Her name was to be changed to Irene, and she must have had a momentary shudder when an aged lady, whose dark nun's robe was faintly edged with royal purple and gold, was introduced to her, among the welcoming crowd, as the great Irene who had once occupied the throne. But the impression was effaced by the brilliance of the marriage ceremonies and the manly beauty of her imperial husband. He returned at once to the field and spent a considerable time in expelling the Persian invaders. After that he remained a few years in his capital, attempting to reform the Court and the administration, and the royal spouses came to know, and probably dislike, each other.

Manuel had the vices, as well as the virtues, of a Western knight; Irene had no vices, and her virtues were old-fashioned. The emergence of these modest and tender young women, such as the last two Irenes, from the Courts of central Europe warns us to refrain from thinking that chivalry everywhere meant gaiety and licence of conduct. Irene had no love of luxury or of the breaking of lances. Such comeliness as she had she declined to adorn with perfumes and fine silks, placing her ideal in the practice of Church virtues and the quiet performance of a mother's duties. But Manuel had the eye and the blood of unrestrained youth, and he soon wandered from his cold and passive spouse to other women of the Court. His elder brother, Andronicus, had left three fascinating daughters, and two of these were of a temper to welcome the freer and livelier spirit which Manuel encouraged. The eldest of the three, Maria, confined herself to a sober marriage, but Theodora became the acknowledged lover of the Emperor (her uncle), and the youngest, Eudocia, was even more flagrantly connected with the Emperor's cousin, Andronicus, one of the most handsome, most daring and most unscrupulous nobles of the time. Andronicus, who in time ascended the throne, will engage us, with his lady-loves, presently. For the moment we have only to note that the Comneni princesses lived at Court without a pretence of restraint. Manuel frowned when he heard that his cousin met what little expostulation was made with the cheerful assurance that he felt it his duty to imitate the example and copy the taste of his sovereign; but Manuel had himself too little self-control to dismiss Theodora.

The clergy were at the time too corrupt and subservient to interfere, and the courtiers are contemptuously dismissed by the historian Finlay as "a herd of knaves." The chief minister, a keen financier and most successful extortioner, was known to sell in the market, even two or three times over, the choice fish or game which suitors presented to him. The favourite minister, John Camateros, was a handsome man of gigantic stature, who enjoyed the repute of drinking more wine, and retaining a clearer head, than any man of his time. He won a bet off the Emperor by emptying at two draughts an immense porphyry vase full of water.

Such were the character and pursuits of the Court into which the virtuous Irene had entered, and in which she remained a silent and despised figure for fourteen years. The second Crusade, led by her brother-in-law, Conrad, passed through Constantinople, on its way to destruction, without altering her condition. Manuel was not less unwilling than his people to cheat the despised Westerners, and further seeds of bitterness were sown in the soil of the time. Irene lingered on for some years, while Manuel waged his endless campaigns against Sicilians, Servians, Scythians and Turks, or flung himself into hunts and tournaments for the entertainment of his mistress and her friends. Then, about the year 1158, Irene died, leaving a young daughter (a second daughter having died in infancy) to the care of her boisterous spouse.

For his second wife Manuel turned to the Latin nobility who had settled in Syria. During a recent campaign in the east he had joined with the Latins in a tournament at Antioch, and made a deep impression on them by his personal bravery, the golden trappings of his charger, and the embroidered silk tunics and mantles of his suite. He begged Baldwin III., King of Jerusalem, to choose for him a bride among the Latin nobility, and professed that he would abide by Baldwin's choice. Baldwin selected Melisend, sister of Raymond, Count of Tripoli (on the Phœnician coast), and legates were sent to obtain the ready consent of her father and inquire carefully into the lady's morals and physical condition. The sad story of Melisend's disappointment is very differently told by the Greek and the Latin historians. According to the Eastern writers Melisend passed the tests of Manuel's legates, and for some months the city of Tripoli was enlivened by the preparations for her exalted marriage. The most splendid clothing, plate and jewels that the family and principality of Raymond could provide were contributed to her trousseau, and no less than twelve large galleys, laden with her treasures, lay beside the imperial trireme at the quays. The day of departure came, and the princess bade farewell to her proud relatives; but the ships had not advanced far from port when Melisend became so ill that they were forced to return. She recovered, and they set sail again, but the mysterious illness returned, and as often as they attempted to convey her across the seas she became livid with sickness or burning with fever. The legates then made a closer inquiry—of a local soothsayer—found that there was a grave flaw in the genealogical tree of the princess, and departed without her.

There is no doubt that this story is a malignant untruth published by the Greeks in order to cover the heartless vacillation of their Emperor. The Latin historian of the time in the East, William of Tyre, tells a simpler story. Manuel's legates lingered at Tripoli, month after month, until Raymond angrily asked them either to convey his daughter or refund the cost of the preparations. They then fled secretly, offering no reason whatever for the desertion, and the only consolation afforded to the wounded Melisend was that her father handed over her twelve bridal galleys to a band of pirates, and sent them to spread their terrible ravages along the Greek coasts and islands. We know little of Melisend; she may have been a woman of mature years, and one of the most lamentable signs of the abandonment of the times was the eagerness of monarchs and nobles for child brides. Manuel had discovered a child of ravishing beauty in the Court of Antioch.

Maria, daughter of Raymond of Poitou, the prince of Antioch, must have been in her early teens when Manuel's legates reported her beauty to him. Her mother, Constance, and stepfather, Reginald of Chatillon, a French adventurer, eagerly welcomed the alliance with the powerful Manuel, and the young girl was conveyed on a gilded galley to Constantinople and married to Manuel, in or about 1161, with the utmost splendour. She received the imperial title, but she naturally escapes the notice of chroniclers during the next ten years, and we may assume that Manuel continued to entertain his more mature niece, who bore him a son and was rewarded with one of the most luxurious palaces in the city. Corrupt as Constantinople was, an illegitimate son could not hope to wear the purple, and Manuel was concerned about the succession. He betrothed his daughter Maria (daughter of Irene) to the younger brother of the King of Hungary, but six years later Maria retired to the Porphyra palace, and Manuel, a keen student of astrology, consulted the heavens with feverish anxiety. The conjunction of the planets was auspicious at the hour of delivery, the child proved to be a son and heir, and the wildest rejoicing filled the Court and city. From that time Maria became "mistress" in reality as well as name, and Theodora passes from the chronicles. The Hungarian prince, who awaited his marriage and elevation at the Court, was wedded to Philippa of Antioch, and the nobles were summoned to swear allegiance to Maria and the infant Alexis. The princess Maria, Manuel's daughter, was now thrust aside as of no political importance, and was suffered to continue, "celibate and sad," at the Court until the leisure of old age permitted her father to reflect on his neglect of her.

Ten further years of warfare occupy the chronicles, and leave no room for the mention of princesses and Empresses. Then the tireless and restless monarch begins to show signs of age, and we prepare for the crisis which so frequently brings the imperial women more prominently before us. Manuel's last campaign had been overcast by grave disasters; he had lost the vigour of youth and had never possessed any large and orderly power of controlling events. Weary and saddened, he concluded an indecisive peace with the Turk, and returned to ensure the succession to the throne. His legitimate son Alexis was now, in the year 1180,[31] turned twelve years old, and therefore, in view of the political circumstances and the lax feeling of the time, fit for marriage. Some years before Manuel had learned from one of the Crusaders that Louis of France had a beautiful young daughter, and legates were sent to ask her hand for Alexis. One reads with strange feelings that the child was only seven years old when, in the spring of 1180, she was wedded to Alexis in the ancient palace of Daphne. We shall see to what a sordid fate this premature marriage to a helpless boy exposed her. From the Latin writers we learn that her name was Agnes, but it seems to have been changed to Anna (as the Greeks always call her) at her marriage. She at once received the imperial title, and must have seemed a strange young figure in the stiff gold-cloth garments and rich jewels of a Byzantine Empress.

It is interesting to notice that the thought of matrimony reminded Manuel of his "celibate and sad" daughter Maria. She was now in her thirty-first year. A spouse was found for her in a handsome seventeen-year-old Western youth, Reyner, son of the Marquis of Montferrat, and they were married with pomp at the Blachernæ palace. But the character of Maria will presently become clearer to us, and we shall see that it does not call for sympathy.

Weary and ill as Manuel was, he had by no means the idea that he was preparing for death in making these arrangements. The astrologers, in whom he put supreme confidence, assured him that he would yet live fourteen years, and he looked forward to rising from his bed and once more dashing with lance and sword against the Turks or Persians. A few months spent in his capital must have shaken his confidence. Thirty-five years of strenuous war had added no material security to his Empire and had alienated his subjects. Vast sums had been wrung from them, but they had passed into the purses of soldiers, foreigners, monks and astrologers, and the civil framework of the vast Empire was in a state of decay. Men spoke with bitterness of the superb palaces, their ceilings plated with gold, their walls lined with mosaic representations of the Emperor's victories, which Manuel had added to the imperial town. He grew sombre, his illness increased, and, one day in September, he felt his own pulse and concluded that he was sinking. Impetuous to the last, he slapped his thigh and called for the robe of a monk. He at once exchanged his purple for the rough cloth, gave his signature to a condemnation of astrology, and bade farewell to the world. He died a few days later; and the shadow of tragedy began to creep over the gold-roofed halls in which his young widow, and the child-bride of his son, played with the imperial toys while men looked on with dark and selfish designs.

The character of the Empress Maria is obscured for us by the somewhat conflicting reports or suggestions of the authorities. Finlay says that she at once retired to a monastery, and, although I can find no direct authority for this, she is so frequently named "Xene" in later passages that one may conclude that she took the veil and changed her name. The next statement about her, however, is little in accord with this. The central and most powerful person at the Court after the death of Manuel was Alexis, brother of the sisters Theodora and Eudocia whose amours had enlivened the Court. Now advanced in years, but ambitious, covetous and luxurious, he became the virtual ruler of the Empire. A somewhat repulsive picture is drawn of his efforts to maintain himself in sufficient health to enjoy the sensual rewards of his position, and it is added that he contracted a liaison with Manuel's young widow. We are quite free to reject this sordid suggestion, as a calumny of those who sought to displace her or of those who afterwards murdered her, but it must be recollected that we have arrived at a period of grosser immorality than ever. It is essential only to observe that she was closely allied to Alexis (the minister) and was accused of intimacy with him.

The Emperor Alexis, who was only thirteen years old at his coronation, was a flippant and heedless boy. The base and astute intriguers about him encouraged him to spend his time in hunting or drinking or dressing in imperial finery. On the other hand, his sister Maria (the daughter of Manuel) now began to display a dangerous ambition and an unscrupulous character. The supposed intimacy of the Empress and Alexis alarmed her; she feared, or affected to fear, that Alexis would marry Maria and seize the throne. She therefore conspired with her relatives, and sent assassins to make an end of Alexis, as he hunted in the country. Presently, however, a messenger returned, not with the head of the minister, but with the news that he had discovered the plot and was returning to wreak his vengeance. Maria and her young husband fled to St Sophia, and, as the crowd gathered in the church at the news, she loudly and bitterly harangued them on the scandalous vices of the Empress and the licentious dotage of her uncle. A judicious distribution of money opened the ears of the clergy and the mob to her charges, and she grew bolder. When the Emperor, or his minister, threatened to drag her from the church, she enlisted a troop of Italian gladiators and Iberian soldiers, and, before the clergy could follow her furious proceedings, turned the cathedral into a fortified citadel, and egged on the mob to loot the mansions of Alexis and his friends. On 7th May the troops issued from the palace, and a bloody battle was fought at the entrance to St Sophia, but the horrified clergy now intervened, and Maria and her husband were allowed to return in safety to the palace.

On this squabble of hawks there now descended a veritable eagle of intrigue, and a brief account of his story will greatly add to our knowledge of the noble women of the time. I have previously mentioned that, while Manuel made love to his niece Theodora, her sister Eudocia was the mistress of Manuel's cousin Andronicus, one of the most romantic figures in history. Andronicus Comnenus, in whom the great line of the Comneni comes to an appalling end, was one of the most handsome, most robust, most fascinating and most unscrupulous men of his age. Tall and massive of build, tender and engaging in countenance, endowed with a voice of singular strength and sweetness and an easy flow of language, he could enslave any woman on whom his heart was set; and it was set on many. Sober in diet and drink, he would avoid the revels and carouses of his brother officers, and spend hours of delight in reading the rugged epistles of St Paul. But in the enjoyment of love or the pursuit of ambition he recognized no moral principle whatever, and few men ever crowded more adventure into a single career.

His father was the elder brother of the Emperor John, Manuel's father, and, on the accession of Manuel, he was called to Court. He was married, but he admitted with equal freedom the devotion of his pretty cousin Eudocia and that of other ladies of less distinction. His wife seems to have cheerfully recognized that large need of his nature, and the lips of Manuel were sealed by his own love affair; but there were men and women of the family who cherished the older ideas, and Andronicus nearly lost his life at an early date. After failing in Armenia—for he was a lax and unskilful general—he was appointed governor of some of the chief towns on the Hungarian frontier. Hither the devoted Eudocia accompanied him, and she lay in his arms, one night, in the tent when it was announced that her brother and brother-in-law were approaching with drawn swords. She pressed him to disguise himself in some of her garments, but he buckled on his immense sword, slit the canvas of the tent, and was deep in the neighbouring forest when the young men arrived.

He was next detected in treasonable correspondence with the Hungarians. Manuel overlooked his crime, but Andronicus went on to make two attempts on the life of his cousin, and wore so brazen a face when he was charged, that he was sent in chains to Constantinople and lodged in a strong tower connected with the palace. Here he one day discovered an old and forgotten passage, almost filled with rubbish, which branched from his prison. He scooped out a hiding-place in it with his hands, entered it, and concealed the entrance. When the furious search of the guards had ended, and messengers had been despatched over the Empire with orders to arrest the fugitive, the Emperor, suspecting that his cousin's wife had aided him to escape, ordered her to be lodged in the tower. No sooner had the jailers left her than the poor woman was terrified, and then delighted, to see the burly form of her missing husband emerge from a heap of rubbish, and they fell into each other's arms. For a long time husband and wife lived together in the prison, but at length Andronicus escaped. His splendid frame betrayed him, and he was recaptured and enclosed in a more formidable prison. Once more he escaped and was caught, and for nine years he remained in prison.

At length he induced the boy who brought his meals to take an impression in wax of the key of his prison while the jailers enjoyed their midday siesta, the impression was sent to his faithful wife and son (the fruit of his earlier confinement in the tower), and a key and a rope were stealthily conveyed to him. He escaped at sundown, lay in the long grass in the garden for two days, until the search was abandoned, and then took a boat at the quay by night and reached his wife's house, where his fetters were struck off. He returned to his boat, rowed to a district beyond the walls where a horse awaited him, and set out in the direction of Russia. Once again he was captured, but, as the soldiers conducted him through a forest during the night, he feigned illness and retired a few yards. After repeating the trick a few times, so that they watched him less closely, he put his mantle and hat on his stick, so that the soldiers seemed to perceive his figure crouching in the dark, and plunged into the forest. He reached Scythia in safety, and was after a time recalled by Manuel, pardoned, and, after striking a few heavy blows in the wars, was made Governor of Cilicia. Here a fresh chapter of his love stories opened. Eudocia had married after the vigorous intervention of her brother, and his wife seems to have entered a monastery.

Endowed by Manuel with the rich revenues of the island of Cyprus, as well as the poorer proceeds of his province, he entered with alacrity the gay circle of the Latin nobles at Antioch, clothed himself in the finest embroidered silks, and kept about him a handsome suite of young courtiers. It was not long before his fascinating manner and brilliant appearance won the heart of the Princess Philippa of Antioch, a sister of the Empress Maria, and she proved to be no more scrupulous than the Greek ladies had been. William of Tyre says that he married her, but the Greek writers speak of the relation as a scandal, and the sequel favours their view. Manuel was enraged at this outrage, and because Andronicus dallied in Antioch instead of taking the field against the Armenians, and he sent a noble to replace Andronicus in his office and in the affections of Philippa. The young princess scorned the meaner figure of the new governor, but Andronicus was alarmed and, quitting his new love with a light heart and taking with him all the imperial funds he could secure, he fled to Palestine.

In the town of Acre, to which he soon repaired, he found a pretty and wealthy widow with whom he could claim a cousinship, and we are introduced to another branch of the Comneni family. Eudocia and Theodora, the frail ladies who have previously engaged our attention, were the daughters of Manuel's brother Andronicus. A third brother, Isaac, had left six daughters, of whom the eldest, Theodora, had been married in her fourteenth year to Baldwin III., King of Jerusalem. Baldwin had died four years afterwards, and the young widow had received the town of Acre as her estate. She was still in her early twenties, in the ripest development of her charms and her passions, when the handsome Andronicus came to tell the story of his misfortunes. From mutual consolation they quickly passed to love, and Manuel was once more infuriated to hear that his scapegrace cousin was openly fouling the honour of the family in the friendly kingdom of the Latins. He sent to Acre a secret and pressing request that the beaux yeux of his cousin should be cut out, and his dangerous person forwarded to Constantinople. But the letter fell into the hands of Theodora, she showed it to her lover, and the devoted pair packed their treasures and fled to Damascus and on to Mesopotamia.

A few years, in which several children were born, were spent in this extraordinary exile by the rivers of Babylon, where the passionate love of the young ex-queen endured without regret the rude accommodation of a camp in what was almost a desert. Andronicus turned brigand when their money and jewels failed, and, at the head of his little band of Arabs, raided the territory of his imperial cousin and even carried off the Christian inhabitants to be sold as slaves. His queen and he laughed at the anathema which the Greek Church laid on them. At last the Governor of Trebizond, at the request of Manuel, enticed Theodora from the camp and captured her, and Andronicus sought pardon once more. We may honour the reluctance of Manuel to shed the blood of his subjects, but in the case of Andronicus it was an almost criminal weakness. That astute adventurer put a heavy iron chain round his neck, covered it with his mantle, and sank on his knees at a respectful distance from his cousin's throne. When he was pressed to come forward to receive a cousinly embrace, he opened his cloak and protested that he must be dragged by the chain to the feet of the Emperor. The comedy ended in his receiving a wealthy appointment, but he was separated from Theodora and sent into a comfortable exile on the southern shores of the Black Sea.

Such was the man who, after the death of Manuel, came forward as the champion of the moral principle and Byzantine honour. Manuel's daughter Maria, "the virago," as Nicetas calls her, appealed to him to end the scandalous rule of the Empress Maria and her reputed lover. Age had made him cautious, however, and he allowed the conflicting parties to exhaust themselves, and the young Emperor fully to reveal his incapacity and unworthiness. Then he began to write indignant letters on the state of the Court to the patriarch and to the provincial authorities. In his great anxiety for the welfare of the Empire he left his exile and moved nearer to Constantinople, winning many to his side by his tears and his venerable appearance. He was now a white-haired old man, approaching his seventieth year, his still robust and magnificent frame made more attractive by the apparent sobering of his character. At length he reached Chalcedon, and the citizens of Constantinople went across the straits in crowds to hail the deliverer of the Empire, or of the Emperor, as he was careful to say. The sins of Andronicus had faded in the memories of their fathers, and they returned to the city to praise his loyalty and his demeanour. Before long they arrested the minister Alexis and put out his eyes. It remained to disarm the clergy, who had been forced to excommunicate him for enslaving Christians. When the patriarch came over to visit him, the wily hypocrite fell at his feet and kissed them, protesting that the archbishop had saved the Emperor, to whose cause he was devoted.

In brief, Andronicus was presently installed in the palace, and a ruthless suppression of his opponents began. Eyes were cut from their sockets, the jails were filled with nobles, and confiscated property swelled his treasury. The Princess Maria, who had appealed to him, and must now have seen her error, perished with her vigorous husband; one of their eunuchs was bribed by Andronicus to poison their food. The clergy next discovered his hypocrisy. He ordered the patriarch to marry his illegitimate daughter Irene to Manuel's illegitimate son Alexis—the natural children of two sisters—and, when he refused, deposed him and found some other bishop complaisant enough to perform the ceremony. The nobles hastily plotted to displace him, but it was too late. Another batch of condemnations routed his opponents and enriched his purse. The people, it is lamentable to find, supported his every deed with enthusiasm, and were not slow to take up the cry of "Andronicus Emperor" which his creatures soon whispered in their ears.

It was the late summer of 1183, only three years after the death of Manuel. The foolish young Alexis still caroused and hunted in frivolous unconcern, but his mother now saw that the end of her reign approached, and might come in dreadful form. She was transferred to a suburban palace, and her life was embittered by calumny and petty persecution. It is in view of these circumstances that we must hesitate to accept the charge of misconduct with the minister Alexis; she seems to have been one of the best of the princesses of the time, though her personality never comes clearly before us. Presently Andronicus charged her with treachery. Her sister, Philippa, was, after being detached from Andronicus, married to the King of Hungary, and it is not impossible that some letters were exchanged between them in regard to the monster who now aimed at the throne. Philippa would retain little tenderness for him since he had fled straight from her arms to those of Theodora. Maria was, of course, found guilty, and lodged in a dungeon. Her son, little dreaming how soon he would follow her, signed the death-warrant, and in the month of August 1183 her sufferings came to an end. A high commander of the army and a eunuch of the Court strangled her with a bowtring.

Alexis lightheartedly pursued his pleasures for a few weeks, until he heard about him the cry of "Andronicus Emperor." He nervously applauded it, and offered a share of his throne; and, with feigned reluctance, Andronicus yielded to the general demand and was crowned by the clergy in St Sophia. When, in the course of the coronation Mass, the chalice was brought to him containing the consecrated wine, he took it in his hands and swore on the living body of Christ that he accepted the crown only in order to assist Alexis. A few days later the youth was strangled by his orders, and, when the lifeless body was placed at his feet, he kicked it and observed that it was the child of a perjurer and a whore. One further detail will complete the picture of the degradation of the Eastern Empire. Two high officials of the Court took the body out in a boat, flung it in the sea, and sang gay songs as they returned to the Bucoleon quay. One of them became Archbishop of Bulgaria.

The two years' reign of the Emperor Andronicus was an orgy of bloodshed, spoliation and vice. Perhaps the most abominable detail of it is that he at once married the child-widow of Alexis, Anna, the beautiful daughter of Louis VII. She had not yet completed her twelfth year, yet she now became the daily and—one fears—nightly companion of an erotic old man of seventy, whose devices to maintain his virility are hardly less repulsive than his murders. It is in one sense a relief to know that little Anna was only one member of a veritable harem of singing and dancing girls, and some nobler women, who filled the palaces, especially the pleasure-palaces on the Asiatic coast, of the repulsive monarch. Powerful in frame and fresh in countenance to the end, Andronicus maintained even in the palace his sobriety and moderation at table in order to preserve his youthful vigour. He was, if ever a man was, an erotomaniac, one of the strangest personalities in the whole of Byzantine history. He brought about several excellent reforms in the administration of the failing Empire, and had, almost to the end, the enthusiastic attachment of his people; but his brutality in the punishment of rebels, who were numerous, was too appalling to be described, and his conduct in many ways approached insanity. He raised a statue in the city to his first wife; she was represented as a nun accompanied by a handsome youth.

We hasten through this welter of brutality and licence to the natural termination. Deliverers of the Empire arose in various places, and were either savagely crushed or showed a savagery equal to that of Andronicus. The natural son of Manuel, whom he had married to his daughter Irene, rebelled; his secretary was burned alive in the Hippodrome, his eyes were removed, and Irene was banished for shedding tears over his fate. A nephew of his mistress Theodora (of Acre) rebelled, and captured the island of Cyprus, and Andronicus impotently ordered the two innocent nobles who were Isaac's sureties to be stoned to death by their fellow-nobles in the palace; but Isaac proved as savage and licentious as Andronicus. Then another Alexis Comnenus, a grand-nephew of Manuel, fled to the West for assistance, and the Sicilian army set sail for Constantinople; but the soldiers merely fell like a fresh flood of savagery on the miserable Greeks. At last a deliverer arose, almost by accident, in the city.

Sorcery and astrology were at that time as rife in the Eastern Empire as they had been in the worst days of ancient Rome; the clergy were deeply corrupted and were almost idle (and wealthy) spectators of the vices and superstitions of Court and people. One of the more astute of these diviners was consulted as to the successor of Andronicus, and, by a device which was a thousand years old in the Roman world, he caused the letters I.S. to appear in answer to the inquiry. When Andronicus heard the result of the consultation, he concluded that Isaac of Cyprus, his rival in power and licentiousness, was the fated individual, and felt confident as long as that tyrant was unable to leave his island. But the prediction also assigned a very near date for the succession, and the chief minister of Andronicus was concerned. There was in the city a timid and unambitious noble, of a provincial family, named Isaac Angelus, and the minister insisted that this was the man designated by the diviner. Andronicus cheerfully ridiculed the idea, placed his little wife upon the royal galley, and went with her to join his gay ladies in one of the palaces across the water. It was the early autumn of the second year of his reign (1185).

Within a few days a messenger from the palace broke into their pleasant dalliance with the news that Constantinople was aflame with revolt, and Andronicus, taking with him his wife and a favourite courtesan, made with all speed for Bucoleon. It appeared that after his departure his minister had gone in person to arrest Isaac Angelus, and, in a surprising fit of boldness, the noble had drawn his sword and buried it in the body of the minister. He fled at once to St Sophia, and the people, flocking to see the man who had slain the hated minister, made him a hero in spite of himself, and burst open the prisons that all the victims of Andronicus might come and support him. He still shrank, even when they offered him the crown, and his elderly uncle, John Ducas, cheerfully presented his own bald head to receive it. "No more bald heads, especially with forked beards," cried the people—as those were features of Andronicus—and the trembling Isaac was crowned.

At this point Andronicus and his companions reached the palace, only to discover that there were no royal troops to defend the throne. In impotent rage Andronicus snatched a bow, and, from one of the towers or balconies of the palace which overlooked the square, sent a few arrows into the crowd, but they burst into the palace, and he returned in haste to his galley. With his twelve-year-old wife and his favourite, Maraptica, he made with all speed for the Black Sea, but his popularity had turned to hatred throughout the Empire, and he was dragged from the ship at the first port and sent in chains to Isaac. His right hand and eye were removed, and he was delivered to the vengeance of the mob, whose savage torture and execution of the adventurous prince must be read in the dead language in which they are described.

The young daughter of Louis of France will come again upon the imperial stage at a later date. Already, in her thirteenth year, the widow of two murdered Emperors, she was destined to wed and lose an ambitious soldier, Branas, and for the third time, almost before she reached womanhood, weep over the bloody corpse of a husband. Nor were her sufferings to end here. We shall see that she remained in Constantinople, and it was reserved for her to witness the final tragedy which the chivalry of the West was to bring upon her adopted country.

CHAPTER XIV

EUPHROSYNE DUCÆNA

The new Emperor, whom so extraordinary a chance had raised to the throne, was a worthless and entirely incompetent man of thirty summers, with the courage of a mouse, the vanity of a peacock, and the small cunning of a Byzantine mediocrity. Finlay contemptuously observes that he was "a fair specimen of the Byzantine nobility of his age." He had accepted the control of an Empire which only a Hercules could save from ruin; and he proceeded to extort money from its distracted citizens for the building of palaces and decoration of churches, to surround himself with a hedge of actors and actresses which shut out the misery of his provinces, to cast the cares of government upon a crowd of praying and feasting monks, and to place his ideal of monarchy in the possession of endless wardrobes and the enjoyment of stupendous banquets.

He was an upstart in epicureanism, and it is therefore not strange that he followed the recent and abominable practice of taking a child to wife. An earlier wife, of whom he had a son named Alexis and two daughters, had died, and, when he came to the throne, there was the customary scanning of the lists of royal families in order to secure an Empress. His choice fell on the nine-year-old daughter of Bela, King of Hungary, and the wondering maiden was brought to Constantinople by his resplendent officers and eunuchs and prepared for the impressive ceremonies of an imperial marriage. The tender little Margaret became the Empress Maria, and was entrusted to the care of the troop of strange beings whom she would learn to call her eunuchs. She would not be old enough to know that Isaac provoked a dangerous revolt at once by imposing the cost of his marriage on the overburdened provinces: or to perceive that the vast aggregation of palaces had, for the first time in Byzantine history, been looted by the mob. Isaac had ignobly lingered in the Blachernæ palace while the people of Constantinople, after despatching Andronicus, had wandered through the imperial apartments and stolen all the money and portable treasures they contained. One pious looter had even carried off the autograph letter of Christ to King Abgar. But Isaac, as soon as his throne was secure, repented of his liberality, and, by means of extortion and spoliation and adulteration of the coinage, contrived even to surpass the luxury and parade of his predecessor.

Maria will not interest us until, in her womanhood, she begins to encounter the adventures of a fallen Empress, and one or two anecdotes will serve to describe the kind of life she endured during the ten years' reign (1185-1195) of her husband. Isaac was a florid-faced, red-haired young man with imperial appetites. His banquets consisted, Nicetas says, of "a mountain of bread, a forest of game, a sea of fishes and an ocean of wine," at which he sat, richly perfumed and clothed with the conscious gorgeousness of a peacock, amidst a crowd of female relatives, and other females who were not relatives. When the dishes were removed, the choicest mimes and conjurers and musicians of the Empire were summoned to entertain him and his guests. It is narrated that one famous comedian, when he was for the first time admitted into the presence of this cohort of wine-flushed ladies, bowed to the Emperor and said: "Let us make the acquaintance of these first, and then you may bring the rest."

Nearly his whole reign was filled by a great revolt of the Wallachians and Bulgarians, and in 1195 he set out to take the field in person against them. One day he rode out from the camp to hunt, and had not proceeded far when he heard an alarming tumult in his rear. He found that his brother Alexis, who had astutely awaited his opportunity, was being acclaimed Emperor, and, without a struggle, he galloped across the country. He was captured, blinded and imprisoned; and his young wife now gives place to a more interesting type of Empress. Maria remained in Constantinople, and will re-enter the story presently.

Euphrosyne Ducæna—that is to say, Euphrosyne of the famous Ducas family, into which some ancestor of hers had married—was an energetic and ambitious woman of middle age at the time of her accession. Her father, Gregory Camaterus, had been an imperial secretary, and had taken advantage of his favoured position to marry into the nobility. Euphrosyne must have been born some time before 1150, in the reign of Manuel, and have witnessed the later series of revolutions and assassinations. In time she married the elder brother of Isaac Angelus, a provincial noble of no distinction or wealth, and, during the bloody reign of Andronicus, Alexis had taken refuge among the Turks. Even whole populations gladly put themselves under the Turks or Saracens to escape the vices of their Christian rulers. We cannot, however, say if Euphrosyne accompanied her husband or remained in Constantinople. At last Alexis heard the strange news that his brother was on the throne, and he hastened to Constantinople. He was arrested on the way by the Prince of Antioch, ransomed by Isaac, and promoted to high office and wealth. He was a more energetic, more handsome and superficially more attractive man than his younger brother, but his slender list of virtues did not include gratitude.

He had communicated to Euphrosyne, if not received from her, his design of seizing the crown, and she threw herself ardently into the work of preparing the city. She was a woman of great ability, of persuasive tongue, and still not without beauty; and it was not difficult to persuade Senators and priests that Isaac was a disgrace to the purple. Her own husband was little, if at all, better, but he had the advantage of an imposing exterior and of concealing his real character. When a messenger reached her with the news that Alexis was declared, she bribed a priest to proclaim him from the pulpit of the cathedral, and promised heavy rewards to the nobles who would support him. Alexis himself was following the same line of lavishing offices (even if they had to be created) and money on his supporters. As a result Euphrosyne was able to occupy the palace almost without opposition, and the Senators hastened to kiss her slippers and lie at her feet, while she "stroked the bellies of the pigs," in the scornful language of Nicetas, who was a Court official of the time—on the wrong side. She announced that the new Emperor would adopt the name of Comnenus, instead of Angelus. It was an indiscretion, as the artisans of the city said that they had had enough of the Comneni, and met in the Forum to place a crown on the head of a popular astrologer of the hour. But Euphrosyne sent a troop of her obedient nobles to scatter the rabble and their king, and in a few days welcomed Alexis to his golden throne. People shook their heads, however, when, as Alexis came out of St Sophia wearing the crown, his fiery Arab at first refused to let him mount, and then plunged so violently that the crown fell off and was broken.

The people of Constantinople soon discovered that they had exchanged brother for brother. Alexis emptied the war-chest, which Isaac had at length filled, into the pockets of his supporters, leaving the Bulgarians and other foes to raid the provinces. He hastened to don the gorgeous golden robes, and to restore the opulent banquets and merry parties of his predecessor, and soon "knew no more about the cares of his Empire than the inhabitants of Thule." Euphrosyne is said to have equalled him in luxury and display, but she had some idea of statesmanship. She promptly undertook to rule the Empire, and we can well believe that, even when she incurs the censure of Nicetas for going about in a golden litter borne on the shoulders of distinguished nobles, she was acting from policy. She ignored her husband, overruled his decrees, placed her own relatives in office, and had her own lovers. When important ambassadors were to be received, she had her throne placed beside that of the Emperor, and Senators had to visit and pay homage at her palace as well as at that of Alexis. Her husband was happy in his imperial lake of luxury, and for a time took no notice. If a noble offered him a sum of money for the office of ploughing the sand he accepted it cheerfully. Euphrosyne, however, forbade the selling of offices, and made a sincere effort to arrest that diversion of funds from public purposes which had been wasting the blood of the Empire for centuries.

Her integrity as a ruler soon excited the hostility of the vicious nobles, and a struggle began which makes it difficult for us to judge certain aspects of the character of Euphrosyne. The rule at Constantinople was to impeach the morals of an Empress when her public virtue was beyond question, and this the angry nobles proceeded to do. She had ventured to appoint a first minister on the mere ground of ability, and her brother Basil, her son-in-law and other nobles plotted to restrict her power. They approached Alexis and whispered that Euphrosyne was criminally intimate with a handsome young officer named Vatatzes, and that he might before long find his throne occupied by her paramour.

Nicetas, who was at the Court, has clearly no doubt about the liaison, and we must admit that Euphrosyne's family is not distinguished for asceticism. Her youngest daughter, Eudocia, had been married in 1185 to the King of Servia, and had, after a few years, been driven from the Court, naked, for her misconduct, and brought back in shame to Constantinople. Euphrosyne's brother Basil, who owed his office to her, was her chief accuser. Alexis, at all events, was convinced. He sent for the head of Vatatzes, who was in Bithynia at the time, and, when it was brought, addressed it, says Nicetas, "in words which cannot be included in this history." Euphrosyne trembled, and appealed to her courtiers to intercede. Alexis had gone to Thrace for a time, and he returned to find the Court divided into two parties over the affair. Some said that she was guilty; some were for punishing the libellers.

He went with Euphrosyne to the Blachernæ palace, and his dark demeanour and refusal to sleep with her made her fear that her head would be the next to fall. She therefore demanded a trial of the charge, but Alexis merely handed her maids and eunuchs to the official torturer, and they could only obtain release from their horrible sufferings by declaring her guilty. Alexis was not normally a cruel man; very little blood was shed in his reign. But the suggestion that Euphrosyne meditated taking from him his throne and his splendid pleasures alarmed him. He stripped her of her gold and purple, dressed her in the rough tunic of a common prostitute, and handed her to two barbaric slaves to be conveyed to the Nematorea monastery, near the entrance to the Black Sea. There, guarded by two uncivilized slaves who could hardly speak Greek, she looked back with bitterness on the two or three years of power and the ingratitude of her brother and son-in-law. But Constantinople pitied her, or at least despised her opponents. Basil and Andronicus were assailed in the street with jeers and popular songs, and began to repent. They had not, they pleaded, imagined that the luxurious Emperor had energy enough to take such a step; they had wished only to restrict the power of Euphrosyne. They and others now pleaded with the Emperor to reconsider his decision, and, after a solitary confinement of six months, Euphrosyne returned in triumph to the palace and wielded more power than ever. It is pleasant to read that Alexis found himself incapable of ruling without her judicious aid; and that she took no vengeance whatever on her accusers.

In the following year Alexis fell seriously ill, and the question of successor was opened. He suffered much from gout and despised physicians. Unfortunately his own ideas of medical treatment were much more crude than those of the doctors of the time. He ordered his servants to cauterize his gouty limbs with red-hot irons, and passed into a dangerous condition. As he had no sons, a wide field was opened for competitors, owing to the abominable Byzantine system, which knew neither the hereditary principle nor serious election, and the palace was enlivened by the intrigues of a score of aspirants. None of them seemed to have the faintest suspicion that the Byzantine Empire was within five years of its first destruction. However, to Euphrosyne's relief, Alexis recovered, and, as the earlier husbands of his elder daughters died (Eudocia was still in Servia), they were wedded to distinguished nobles, and the year ended with prolonged gaieties at the Blachernæ palace.

A long absence of the Emperor in Thrace left the supreme power in the hands of Euphrosyne, and, as so many Byzantine women had done, she held the reins with a firmer and more skilful hand than her husband. The only defect noted by the censorious Nicetas is that she was lenient to members of her own family. Fraudulent officials she punished with a severity that was rarely witnessed in the East, but the admiral Michael Stryphnus, who had married her sister, was permitted to indulge criminal malpractices, for which the Empire would soon pay a heavy price. He sold even the stores and equipment of the existing galleys, and they rotted in the harbours, while pirates spread terror throughout the Mediterranean and the Black Sea. These were not crimes at which the short-sighted Emperor could cavil. Not only did he cheat his people by creating and selling sinecures, but he resorted to practices which amounted to piracy. He once sent six galleys of the fleet into the Black Sea for the ostensible purpose of salving a wreck, but with secret orders to board and loot every vessel they met. Large numbers of mercantile galleys were returning with cargoes from the Black Sea ports, often in charge of the merchants themselves, some of whom were flung overboard for resisting. The others returned to Constantinople in great anger, and, although they stood at the door of St Sophia, candle in hand, when the Emperor came to pray, he merely laughed at their complaints. From the clergy such sufferers received little sympathy; the patriarch was a brother of Euphrosyne. The city was full of violence and knavery: the seas were scoured by pirates: the remoter provinces were ground between the imperial tax-gatherers and the foreign raiders.

Yet in this melancholy putrescence of the once mighty Empire Alexis and Euphrosyne maintained all the glamour of the imperial Court. Euphrosyne is the only Empress whom we find engaging in the chase as the Emperors did. Nicetas describes her setting out amid large companies of nobles, a falcon resting on her gold-embroidered glove, or a kennel of dogs rushing at her virile call. It is even said that she believed in, and practised, the incantations and divinations which had become generally popular among the decaying people. Her magic seems to have taken some unfamiliar form, since she had the snout cut off a famous bronze boar in the Hippodrome, had a beautiful marble statue of Hercules flogged, and ordered mutilations of other works of art that reminded Constantinople of better days. She seems to have been an able and well-disposed woman tainted by the perversity of her age.

The Empire was sinking rapidly, living on its capital, yet suffering the roads and bridges and forts to fall to ruin, the helpless provinces to writhe under the heel of every invader, and the funds that should have been spent on defence to be wasted in courtly luxury and the maintenance of a crowd of ignoble parasites. An anecdote of the time (about the year 1200) shows to what an extraordinary degree the funds had been diverted from the army. There was in Constantinople a descendant of the Comneni who, from his barrel-like shape, went by the name of John the Fat. This paltry and contemptible conspirator won a few followers among the nobility, went with them into the cathedral, and put upon his own head one of the imperial crowns that hung over the altar. The report ran through the city and a great crowd assembled and conducted the waddling and perspiring John to the palace. Alexis and Euphrosyne seem to have been at Blachernæ, or in one of the Asiatic palaces, but the strange thing is that there seem to have been no guards whatever, where former Emperors had kept whole regiments of Scholarians and Excubitors or, at the later date, Varangians. We know that there were still Varangians in the imperial service, but they seem to have been too few to defend the numerous palaces. However, John the Fat had not wit or grit enough to secure the palace when he had entered, and, as darkness came on, a few imperial soldiers penetrated to his apartments and killed him.

At length, in the year 1202, the Empire passed into the penumbra of its great tragedy. Isaac II., the younger brother whom Alexis had displaced and blinded, had lived in Constantinople, in a humble mansion near the shore, during the seven years that followed his deposition, and was regarded with so little concern that no watch was kept upon his movements. It was not noticed that the Latin soldiers who lived in, or constantly passed through, Constantinople were frequent visitors at his house, and it was not known that the letters he wrote to his daughter Irene, who had married Philip of Germany, were treasonable in their import. But the blind and neglected brother was dreaming of a return to his imperial debauches. It is probable that Maria, who would now be a comely young woman of sixteen, lived with him, but of that we are not assured; she was somewhere in Constantinople. At length the time seemed ripe for his effort, and he sent his son Alexis, a youth as ardently and unscrupulously bent on returning to power as he, to the Court of Philip and Irene in Sicily.

It was the eve of the fourth Crusade, and the knights of the West were gathering for a fresh effort to break the power of the Turk, and to gather loot by the way. To these noble buccaneers the Emperor Philip introduced the young Alexis and proposed that they should restore him and his father to their throne. Neither East nor West attracts our sympathy for a moment. The Angeli brothers were squabbling for the right to indulge their sordid tastes on an imperial scale, and the younger Alexis had no more serious ideal. The Venetians, who had an important voice in the matter, sought their own profit and a discharge of their debts, and there can be little doubt that the Western knights, as a body, were allured by the vague hope of plundering, in one way or another, the richest and most splendid city in Europe. An infamous bargain was struck. The princes of Western chivalry did not hesitate to accept from the frivolous and irresponsible youth a promise of the payment of 200,000 silver marks, a year's supply of provisions to their troops and other preposterous rewards for dethroning Alexis. Even the papacy had its share in the sordid bargain; the Greek Church was to be forced to submit to the Vatican.

In the month of April (1203) the fourth Crusade set sail in one hundred and seventy large vessels, and some smaller ships, for Constantinople. Alexis awoke from his dreams to find that a score of worn triremes was all the navy he possessed, and he must resign himself to meet a siege of his capital. The vivid story of the fall of Constantinople cannot be told here. Toward the end of June the Crusaders landed near Chalcedon and gazed with covetous eyes, most of them for the first time, at the innumerable spires of churches—schismatical churches, and therefore fair prey—that rose above the clustered houses, the princely villas that shone between the cypresses in the wealthier suburbs, and the bronze roofs and marble walls of the superb palaces which glittered in the sun among the vast imperial gardens on either side of the Sea of Marmora. When the news of their sailing had reached Alexis he had made it a table joke; now he and his trembled within the walls of their capital. By the middle of July the Crusaders were encamped outside the land walls; the Venetians lay beneath the walls which girt the shores; and the great assault began. Alexis, from a tower of the Blachernæ palace, saw the double-edged axes of the brave English Varangians scatter the Germans and Italians, but he learned that the Venetians had broken in. Packing his treasures and his money, he took ship at dawn of the following day, with his daughter Irene, and fled to Thrace, where a retreat had been prudently prepared for such an emergency. George Acropolites, whose chronicle now opens, says that he took Euphrosyne, but Nicetas, an eyewitness, more correctly observes that the imperial egoist deserted his wife, his city and his Empire.

In their anger at the flight of Alexis the people now swept aside Euphrosyne and her relatives, and turned to Isaac, for whom the eunuch-treasurer secured the Varangians. He was brought to the palace and proclaimed, and Euphrosyne, her discredited daughter, Eudocia, and other relatives, were put in confinement. The Latins were informed that the object of their expedition had been attained, and when Isaac had ratified the preposterous contract signed by his son, the young Alexis rode proudly into the city between Baldwin of Flanders, almost the one noble of the crusading party, and the blind, but astute and formidable, Doge of Venice. One of the Latin knights, Villehardouin, has left us a vivid narrative of the conquest, and enlightened us as to the fate of some of the imperial women we have encountered. When the Latins entered the Blachernæ palace they found the eyeless monarch sitting on his golden throne in robes "the like of which you would seek in vain throughout the world." By his side sat the "most fair lady," Maria, who, we may therefore conclude, had faithfully clung to her husband in his blindness and humiliation. And amongst the crowd of fine ladies, superbly dressed and glittering with jewels, who stood about the throne, was Agnes, or Anna, the beautiful and pathetic widow of the Emperor Alexis, the Emperor Andronicus, and the would-be Emperor Branas. She was still only thirty years old. Her presence in the palace suggests that she had accepted some office in it under Isaac and Maria.

But the joy and confidence of the returning throng were doomed to be speedily overcast. The end was merely postponed for a month or two. The Empire had, in its most solemn crisis, received a worthless and despicable pair of rulers, and the Latins pressed for their pound of flesh. Isaac, blind, gouty and weak-minded, spent his days among monks and astrologers, who, while they devoured the choicest dishes that the palace could afford, assured him that he had entered upon a long and glorious reign, that his gout would quickly disappear, and that his eyes would be miraculously restored to their arid sockets. The younger Alexis drank and gambled with the experienced knights of the fourth Crusade. When the leaders of the Crusade pressed for the payment of their reward, all the wealth of Euphrosyne and her relatives was confiscated—Alexis had left little to seize—the jewels and plate of the palaces were pledged, even the precious reliquaries of the churches and monasteries and the great silver lamps of St Sophia were appropriated; yet the jaws of the West still stood wide open, and the Latin troops lingered and demanded food and drink. The fugitive Alexis had, in the meantime, raised an army in Thrace, and the citizens of Constantinople were embittered and disaffected. In August a quarrel with some of Baldwin's soldiers had led to a conflagration which, it being the height of summer, had burned for two days and destroyed nearly half the city. The clergy and people met in the cathedral to appoint a new Emperor, but, though some undistinguished officer afterwards accepted the title from the mob, no serious aspirant dare take the crown in face of the hostile Latins.

Isaac died in the midst of the turmoil, and the young Empress Maria lost her crown almost as soon as she had received it. We shall see presently that she found consolation among the Crusaders, but it is necessary first to follow the adventurous fortune of Euphrosyne and her daughter. The young Alexis, distracted and feeble as ever, proposed to leave the city and join the Westerners in their camp without the walls. As he prepared for flight there came to him a fiery and ambitious young officer who felt that the time was opportune for laying his own hand on the sacred crown. Alexis Ducas Murtzuphlus—his last name, or nickname, was due to the fact that he had a peculiar connexion of the bushy eyebrows which stood out over his crafty eyes—was one of the party in the city who, to the applause of the crowd, urged direct war upon the Latins, and his popularity emboldened him to remove Alexis and ally himself with Euphrosyne. By a liberal outlay of money he secured the Varangian guards, and he then approached Alexis and whispered to him that his leaning to the Latins had exasperated the citizens. When Alexis trembled, the adventurer offered to lodge him in a secure retreat until the rage of the people should have calmed. It is hardly necessary to add that the young Emperor was conducted to one of the dungeons of the palace, where his egregious folly was presently ended with a bowstring.

Euphrosyne and her daughter were now delivered from their confinement and restored to the palace, and, as Murtzuphlus had the characteristic looseness of his age in regard to conjugal matters—he had already discarded two wives—he soon sought and obtained the affection of Eudocia. The contemporary courtier and writer Nicetas says that Eudocia was merely his mistress, but others say that he married Eudocia and it is difficult, as the sequel will show, to determine the point. Probably he did, after a time, marry Euphrosyne's daughter, and he then set to work to defend the city against the Crusaders. The issue is one of the great pages of history, but its details do not concern us. On 9th April the Latins moved their formidable rams and catapults and towers against the walls, and the Venetians drew up their vessels along the Golden Horn. Three days later, after a furious assault, amid showers of mighty stones and the blaze of burning houses, the heroes of the cross burst into the city and began that historic ravage which puts them for all time far below the moral level of the Turks they had set out to combat.

Murtzuphlus, finding his troops discouraged, had retired to the Bucoleon palace, where Euphrosyne and Eudocia awaited the issue. He had lost, he said; and from the palace quay, where the stone lion and bull, which gave the place its name, had witnessed so many flights, they took ship and sped in the direction of Thrace. The ex-Emperor Alexis would surely welcome his wife and daughter, and he would feel little tenderness in regard to the murder of his perfidious nephew. Murtzuphlus arrived in confidence at the ex-Emperor's new home, and was received in apparent friendliness. For some reason, however, which is not very clear, Alexis concealed under his friendly appearance a deadly and murderous hatred of the adventurer. It seems to me that, if a marriage had really taken place between Eudocia and Murtzuphlus, Alexis regarded it as invalid. He ordered a bath to be prepared for his daughter and Murtzuphlus, and, when the young officer had entered it, sent in his servants to put out his eyes. Eudocia, we are told, stood at the door angrily upbraiding her father, and he turned upon her with language which leaves little doubt as to her character. I may add that the blind adventurer was captured by the Latins, as he wandered miserably about the provinces. He was taken to Constantinople and flung from the top of one of the loftiest columns in one of the public squares of the city.

In order to follow the further fortunes of our ex-Empresses we must turn back for a moment to Constantinople. After they had allowed their soldiers to loot and rape with impunity—to perpetrate, with the aid of their camp-followers and prostitutes, a veritable orgy of desecration in the most sacred shrine of the Greeks—for several days, the leaders of the Crusade met to divide the spoil. Twelve electors, chosen from amongst themselves, were in future to appoint the Latin Emperor of Constantinople, and its territories were to be distributed among his feudal supporters and the Venetians. Baldwin of Flanders was chosen to be the first Emperor of the new series. His most serious competitor was the commander of the army, Boniface, Marquis of Montferrat, who had occupied the Bucoleon palace, but the shrewd Doge of Venice had preferred to set on the throne a prince whose native seat was at a safer distance from Venice and Greece. Boniface had to be content with the title of

King of Saloniki and such territory in Macedonia and Greece as he could wrest from, and hold against, the Greeks.

Among the noble dames whom Boniface found in the Bucoleon palace were Agnes, the widow of Andronicus and daughter of Louis of France, and Maria, the widow of Isaac. It is the last appearance in the chronicles of the unfortunate daughter of King Louis; we must assume that she spent the rest of her life in quiet attachment to the Latin Court. The Hungarian princess Maria was destined to enter once more the field of royal ambitions. She had not yet reached her thirtieth year, and her beauty won the heart, possibly an alliance with her supported the policy, of the ambitious Marquis. He married Maria in Constantinople, and started with his queen for Thessalonica, the seat of the new kingdom. How at the outset he nearly forfeited it by a civil war with Baldwin must be read elsewhere. The quarrel was adjusted and they settled in Thessalonica. And at their Court in that city there presently appeared the ex-Emperor Alexis, with his wife and daughter, soliciting peace and friendship.

Alexis had now concluded that the recovery of the Byzantine Empire was impossible and he was prepared to submit. He was compelled to lay aside such ensigns of royalty as he still wore, and a pleasant residence was afforded him and his family in Thessalonica. Nicetas makes the singular statement (followed at a later date by Ephraem) that Boniface sent Alexis and Euphrosyne "across the sea to the Prince of Germany." It is clear that this is incorrect. They lived for some months at Thessalonica, and it is one of the few traits we have of Maria's character that she received with kindly hospitality the man who had deposed and blinded her husband. But the tranquil life of a retired monarch did not suit Alexis, and we have already seen that his base character was devoid of gratitude. He was detected in an intrigue with the citizens of Thessalonica, and Euphrosyne and Eudocia had to accompany him once more in his wandering.

The next page in their career is singularly adventurous, but scantily preserved. As they wandered over the Greek province they met Leo Sgurus, a Peloponnesian noble who had been governor, under the Byzantine Empire, of part of Greece. He clung to his little power in the chaos which followed the fall of Constantinople, and Alexis decided to join him. The troops of Boniface were steadily restricting his range, and, shortly after the alliance with him of the imperial family, his life was little better than that of a brigand. He lived in the decaying old citadel of Corinth, and marched out periodically at the head of his men to forage and to harass the Latin troops. In this quaint home the imperial family found shelter for a few further months, and Eudocia married Sgurus. It was the fourth romantic marriage of that adventurous princess, and was destined to be as unfortunate as its predecessors. In her early girlhood she had been sent, while still immature, to wed the King of Servia. He had adopted the robe of the monk soon afterwards, and his son and successor, a fiery, brutal youth, had claimed the pretty young bride of his father and married her. After some years she had, on a charge of misconduct, been thrust out of the Servian capital, her sole garment a narrow strip of cloth round her loins, and had had to await, in the castle of a sympathetic noble, the arrival of clothes and a litter from her father. Then, as we saw, she married the already married Murtzuphlus, and shared his adventures for a few months. Now she found herself the wife of an outlaw, living in the rude and dilapidated chambers of the old Acropolis. But Sgurus was shortly afterwards captured by the troops of Boniface, and we lose sight of the unfortunate Eudocia. She was probably still in her early twenties, yet the widow of two kings, an Emperor, and an adventurer. Such was life in mediæval Byzantium.

Alexis and Euphrosyne took to ship when Sgurus was defeated, and sailed for Ætolia and Epirus (on the eastern coast of the Adriatic), where a certain Michael, a natural son of the Emperor's uncle Constantine, had set up a sovereignty over the rude mountaineers and few towns of that isolated region. On the voyage the ship was captured by Lombard pirates, but Alexis and Euphrosyne were ransomed by their nephew, and at length reached Arta, the chief town of his dominion. The Byzantine world was at the time full of small rulers, and would-be rulers. The leading Crusaders had received their various slices of the dismembered Empire, and here and there some fugitive Byzantine noble, especially if he were connected with the imperial house, had set up a small throne and defended it against the Latins. In this way Michael, the illegitimate son of Constantine Angelus, had fled from the captured city to Epirus, married a native lady of wealth, and constituted himself "despot" of the whole region. In his chief town, Arta, Euphrosyne tranquilly passed her last year or two of life. Her restless husband still thirsted for power, and, when he found that his nephew was not at all disposed to put on his head once more the crown which he demanded, he took to ship again and sailed for the lands of the Turk in Asia Minor. Euphrosyne did not accompany him. She died at Arta, either just before or soon after his departure. Ten years' experience of imperial life had sated her ambition.

The ex-Empress Maria, now Queen of Saloniki, continued for many years to enjoy the restricted power and state which she had won by her marriage, but they were years of anxiety and care. Two years after her settlement in Thessalonica, the Greeks rebelled and, in alliance with the Bulgarians, spread fire and sword over the province, and pinned Maria in the citadel of her capital. In that rebellion the Latin Emperor Baldwin was captured, and his brother and successor, Henry of Flanders, occupied the throne. Some years later Boniface was killed in his struggle against the Bulgarians, and Maria became regent for her infant son, Demetrius. It is the last glance we have in the chronicles of the beautiful Margaret of Hungary, who, as the Empress Maria, had come to spend so extraordinary a youth in the Byzantine capital.

There remained one other imperial daughter of Euphrosyne, Anna, who had married the able and ambitious noble Theodore Lascaris. When Murtzuphlus had abandoned Constantinople, Theodore had a momentary ambition to collect the scattered troops and make a struggle for the throne. He found that the attempt would be futile, and, with his wife and three daughters, joined the throng of noble families at the quays who were flying from the doomed city and the barbarous troops of the West. They reached Nicæa, but the city, concerned about its future, refused to admit him. He persuaded the citizens, however, to receive his wife and daughters, and departed to seek allies among the Persians. In a short time he had an army powerful enough to take Nicæa, and he established himself as governor in the name of Alexis. When, in the year 1206, the Latins were diverted for a moment by the trouble in Greece, Theodore was crowned by the citizens, and Euphrosyne's second daughter, Anna, attained the dignity of Empress.

Disappointed in Epirus, her father, Alexis, had now, as we saw, deserted the little kingdom of his nephew and sailed for Asia Minor. In earlier years he had befriended the Turkish Sultan of Iconium, and he now proposed to ask the hospitality of the Sultan and intrigue for the crown of his son-in-law. The Turk received him with great cordiality, and wrote to inform the Emperor Theodore that his father-in-law, in whose name he was presumed to hold power, had arrived in Asia. We must not too hastily admire the gratitude of the Turk; he had regarded with some concern the establishment of Theodore's empire at Nicæa, and welcomed a pretext to dispute it. But in the war which followed, the Sultan was defeated, and the active career of Alexis came to a close. He was treated with respect, but his son-in-law prudently confined him in a monastery under his own eyes at Nicæa, and the arch-intriguer ended his days in the monotonous chant of psalms and prayers. His daughter Anna died soon afterwards, the last of the group of imperial women who had struggled for power and wealth while the great Empire tottered to its fall. We shall find that that terrible catastrophe made no deep impression on the men and women who filled the less opulent Court at Nicæa, or on those who, half-a-century later, returned to the lamentable ruin from which they at length dislodged the Western knights.

CHAPTER XV

THE NEW CONSTANTINOPLE

For fifty-seven years the metropolis of the East remained in the power of the Western knights, but our Empresses have already come so frequently from the West that we shall not be tempted to expect a new or higher type of woman on the throne at Constantinople during the Latin occupation. That half-century may, indeed, be dismissed in a few lines as far as the purpose of this work is concerned. We saw that Baldwin, Count of Flanders, was selected by the Venetians and Crusaders to fill the throne. The Blachernæ and Bucoleon palaces were placed at his disposal, and one-fourth of the old Empire was assigned for his immediate rule. But Baldwin's wife, Mary, daughter of the Count of Champagne, did not live to adorn herself with such remnants of the imperial finery as were still to be found in the palaces. Baldwin had left her in Flanders, and, when she at length attempted to join her high-minded husband in his new dignity, she died at Acre, on the journey.

Baldwin himself was captured a few years later by the Bulgarians, and died in prison. His brother Henry, who succeeded him, married the daughter of Boniface, the King of Saloniki, whose adventures we have described. Agnes was, of course, not the daughter of the ex-Empress Maria, but of an earlier wife. She was summoned from Lombardy, married to Henry on 4th February 1207 in St Sophia, and the marriage day ended with a great banquet in the Bucoleon palace, in the older Byzantine fashion. But that is all we know of the Empress Agnes. Henry died in 1216, and his sister Yolande became Empress. Even of Yolande, however, the very scanty chronicles furnish a very poor portrait. Her husband, Peter of Courtenay, was, after being crowned at Rome by the Pope, arrested in Epirus, through which he had foolishly endeavoured to cut his way, and died in prison. As regent for her children Yolande remains almost imperceptible, and an anecdote of the reign of her son Robert is all that need be given to illustrate the character of the new dynasty. Robert, who had a light idea of chivalry, brought into his palace, as mistress, the daughter of one of the Crusaders, and her mother. She had been betrothed to a Burgundian knight, and the embittered lover, supported by a few friends, forced his way into the palace, cut off the nose and lips of the faithless lady, and bore off her mother to be drowned in the Sea of Marmora.

As Robert's brother was a mere boy, the King of Jerusalem, a worthy old man of eighty, was summoned to fill the throne for nine years, and then Baldwin II. entered upon his long and inglorious reign; of which we need only say that, in spite of his extreme liberality in selling, especially to St Louis of France, the valuable relics (the crown of thorns, the rod of Moses, etc.) which had accumulated in Constantinople, and in spite of all the efforts of the Pope to maintain the worthless monarch on his throne, and that throne subservient to the Vatican, the feeble and incompetent rule of the Latins sank lower and lower, until, in 1261, a regiment of Greeks put an end to it.

This slight account of the Latin rule at Constantinople will suffice to enable us to follow intelligently the fortunes of the descendants of the Byzantine monarchs who had set up a throne at Nicæa. Theodore Lascaris had married Alexis's daughter Anna, who died early in the reign of her husband, and her two successors in his affection are even less known to us than she. The first was Philippa, daughter of the

King of Armenia; but, after giving birth to a boy, Philippa was, for some unstated but imaginable reason, sent back to the ruder Court of her father, and Maria, daughter of Yolande of Constantinople, occupied her place. Maria died, childless, after a few years, and, when Theodore himself departed in 1222, his only son (the child of Philippa) was a boy of eight years. The Empire was, therefore, wisely entrusted to a powerful and distinguished noble, John Ducas Vatatzes, and we at length reach an Empress of distinct and admirable personality.

The Empress Irene, who, in the year 1222, ascended the throne with Vatatzes, was the eldest of the three daughters of Theodore Lascaris and Anna, and therefore a granddaughter of the Emperor Alexis and Euphrosyne. While the Princess Eudocia had inherited the character, or lack of character, of Alexis, her elder sister Anna had, as far as we can judge, shared the comparative sobriety of Euphrosyne, and Irene united in her person all the best features of the family, without its ancestral defects. She was prudent, equable, pious and virtuous. Her first husband, Andronicus Paleologus, died prematurely, and her father then united her to the able commander to whom he designed to confide the Empire.[32] When Irene received her share of the imperial responsibility, she proved to be, says Ephrem, "a new Deborah," and the few anecdotes preserved in regard to her suggest a sober and high-minded woman, associated in perfect harmony with (as long as she lived) a sober and high-minded and valiant husband. Unfortunately, Irene led so well-regulated a life during the twenty years in which she shared the rule of Vatatzes that there is little to record of her, and, however much we may resent it, we are dragged onward by the misguided chroniclers until we reach John's later and less virtuous companions. But the contrast of this later period will be the more piquant, and the more honourable to Irene, if we dwell for a moment on the exemplary years that preceded it.

The greater part of John's days were spent in warfare, but in the intervals of his wars he was attentive to the development of his little Empire, and in this he was finely supported by Irene. It is true that they adulterated the coinage, but that device had become a Byzantine tradition and we must set against it a large number of reforms. John was a just and simple-minded monarch. He developed his estates so industriously, in the periods of peace, that he at length relieved his subjects of the financial burden of royalty, and enabled them to prosper. The character of the Court is, perhaps, best seen, and attracts a lively admiration, in the following anecdote. One day John presented his consort with a modest jewelled coronet, and informed her, with pride, that it had been purchased by the profit on the eggs alone which his poultry farms yielded. He forbade his courtiers to wear Persian, or Syrian, or Italian silks, though they might wear the product of the silkworms of his own dominions, and he one day severely rebuked his son for going out to hunt in a tunic of cloth of gold.

Irene admired and encouraged this care for their subjects. Acropolites, our chief authority for the period, was a student attached to the Court at the time, and he gives high praise to the Empress. One day there was an eclipse of the sun, and Irene turned to the learned young man for an explanation. The work of the earlier Greeks was not yet entirely forgotten, and Acropolites was able to tell the Empress, with due modesty, that the body of the moon had passed before the face of the sun and momentarily cut off its light. But superstition was spreading its unhappy growth over the ruins of Greek culture, and other courtiers, especially the Empress's physician, ridiculed the youth's explanation. Irene laughingly told Acropolites that he was "a young fool"; but she regretted afterwards, in telling the matter to John, that she had used so arrogant an expression. Acropolites almost spoils the story by going on to tell us that, in his own conviction, the eclipse foreboded the death of the Empress, which occurred soon afterwards.

One other story confirms this excellent impression of the life of the Court in the palace at Nicæa, or in the country palaces at Nymphæum and Smyrna. Irene had one child, her son Theodore; an accident, as she rode to hunt and was thrown from her horse, prevented her from enlarging her family. When Theodore reached his twelfth year, the Emperor, who was himself over fifty, decided to marry him, and, as he was allied with the Bulgarians against the Latins, he sought the hand of a Bulgarian princess. The only available daughter of John Asan, the Bulgarian king, was a girl of tender years named Helen, and, though the marriage ceremony was performed, the two children lived together only as children under the watchful eye of Irene. The Bulgarian king at length repented of his alliance, and begged that the little Helen, now ten years old, might return for a visit to her parents. Vatatzes and Irene concluded at once that this was only a preliminary to breaking the alliance, but they scorned to detain the child. We read that she wept bitterly at being separated from Irene. During the journey to her father's capital she was so inconsolable, even when Asan took her on his own saddle, that the monarch lost his temper and slapped her face. Helen did in time return to her spouse, but she will have little interest for us.

After nineteen years of this placid and useful co-operation with the Emperor, Irene passed away, and, after a decent interval of mourning, John Vatatzes, though now advanced in years, sought another Empress. He succeeded, in spite of the opposition of the papacy, in obtaining the hand of Anna, daughter of Frederick II., and sister of Manfred of Sicily. Anna was a pretty maiden of tender years, a mere symbol of alliance with the two powerful and independent monarchs I have named. John may have reflected that, as he had now entered his sixth decade of life, the immaturity of his bride would matter little. In the train of the young Empress, however, was an Italian marchioness[33] whose eyes were, the chronicler says, "unescapable nets," and John soon fell into them. Nicephorus says that the lady employed philtres and her fine Italian eyes in the conquest of the Emperor's heart. We will be content to think that the eyes sufficed.

For the remaining decade of John's reign the favoured marchioness was the most prominent figure at the Court. She did not, apparently, desire to interfere in politics. It was enough that she was permitted to wear purple slippers and other ensigns of royalty, and that courtiers should gather about her rather than attend the young Empress. It is related that she on one occasion went, decked in her imperial robes and accompanied by her glittering suite, to visit the famous chapel attached to one of the chief monasteries of Nicæa. The abbot of this monastery, Nicephorus Blemmydas, was tutor to Irene's son Theodore, and, though we shall find his royal pupil affording little proof of the excellence of his education, the Abbot Nicephorus was a rare type among the degenerate clergy of the time. He shut the doors of the chapel and refused to admit the marchioness. Infuriated at the humiliation, and stimulated by her followers, she begged John to punish the abbot. John refused, and tearfully admitted that his own weakness was the proper occasion of the trouble.

In 1254 the valiant Vatatzes bequeathed the crown to his son, and Anna and the marchioness made way for the Bulgarian princess, Helen. Anna seems to have remained attached to the Court, or in some mansion at Nicæa, and we shall meet her again. But Helen died in a year or two; her husband followed after a short and licentious reign of four years, and the relinquishment of the throne to a boy of tender years, their son John, opened the gates of the palace to a shrewd and unscrupulous adventurer and his wife.

One of the commanders of the troops under Vatatzes and Theodore was Michael Paleologus, a grandson of the Emperor Alexis's daughter Irene. Bold and crafty, passionate, yet ever ready to stoop to lies and oaths to cover his ambition, sensible that he was one of the most capable men to undertake the government and that his grandfather had at one time been destined for the throne, Michael directed his steps toward the palace from early youth. In later years his favourite sister, Eulogia, who reared him, used to tell how, when nothing else would soothe the restless infant, she used to put him to sleep with the strange lullaby: "Hush, Emperor of the city. You will go in at the golden gate, and do such-and-such things." She may have mentioned to him this almost miraculous inspiration when he came to years of discretion. By sobriety of life—apart from love affairs—and liberality to his friends and dependants, he won great popularity and early incurred suspicion. John Vatatzes, in his later years, summoned him to reply to a charge of treason, and said that he must purge himself by the ordeal: one of the enlightened practices which the Crusaders had introduced into the East. Michael glanced at the iron balls glowing in the fire, and protested that, although he was innocent of treason, he feared that so sinful a man as he could hardly hope to carry the red-hot globes with impunity. When a bishop, who stood by, rebuked his lack of faith in Providence, he shrewdly suggested that the bishop, being innocent, might take the balls from the fire with his hands and deliver them to him.

His wit and boldness disturbed the solemn Court, and, instead of losing his head or his eyes, he won the favour of John and married the Empress's great-niece, Theodora. She was a daughter of John Ducas, a nephew of the Emperor, and had been left to his guardianship. Michael was then twenty-seven years old, and we cannot say if the young Theodora accompanied him in his new command of the troops. However that may be, he was again denounced, to the new Emperor Theodore, and compelled to take a particularly sonorous oath of fidelity to Theodore and his infant son. In two or three years he was recalled to Court to repeat his oath. His eldest sister Martha—sometimes also called Maria—had a charming daughter, whom the Emperor ordered to marry one of his servants. The young people had just succeeded in falling in love with each other when Theodore, who was now diseased and capricious, changed his mind, and ordered the girl to marry a noble of her own rank. It was reported to the Emperor after a time that this marriage was not consummated, and could not be, because Martha had vindictively laid on it a form of incantation known as "Venus's knot." Martha was put, naked, in a sack with a number of cats; the cats were pricked with pins in order to make them lacerate her; and the abominable Emperor sat by to interrogate her about her incantations. After this it was thought prudent to compel Michael to repeat his oath, which he did fluently, and the impenetrable geniality of his manner quite disarmed Theodore.

Theodore died soon afterwards, and his boy (variously described as six, eight and nine years old) was left to rule the Empire under the tutorship of the first minister, George Muzalon, and the patriarch. Not only Michael, but all the other commanders and nobles, had sworn heavily to respect this arrangement. But the body of Theodore had scarcely been interred before Michael began secretly to agitate and to bribe his colleagues. Muzalon was an upstart, not a noble by birth, and it was not difficult to cast on him the blame of the brutalities of Theodore's later years. Three days after the burial of the Emperor, Muzalon and his brothers and a large company of nobles and noble ladies gathered in the royal monastery at Sosander, without the city, for a memorial service, when, in the midst of the chanting, the heavy and regular tread of soldiers was heard. A band of officers and men burst into the chapel, and, before the eyes of the shrieking dames and the horrified priests, cut Muzalon and his friends to pieces beside the altars. National catastrophe, it will be seen, had not chastened the Byzantine character.

From Constable of the Empire, Michael was now raised to the dignity of Despot, and became tutor of the young Emperor. Then a convenient coalition of Western powers against the Empire gave Michael's friends the opportunity to suggest that the strong man ought to be associated with the boy in the supreme power. On New Year's Day (1259) he was openly proclaimed Emperor. The patriarch almost alone professed some concern about the terrible oath they had all taken only four months before; Michael met his concern by giving him a written affidavit, sealed with ponderous oaths, that he would restore the full sovereignty to John VI. when he came of age, and would recognize no claim of his own heirs to power. It was therefore agreed that Michael and John should be crowned together. When, however, the hour of coronation arrived, John was not present to respond to the call of the patriarch, and Michael and Theodora alone received crowns. Michael had made a little arrangement with the bishops beforehand, and only one of the lords spiritual protested. The crowd may have murmured when, after the ceremony, they saw the boy, crownless, walking after the new Emperor and Empress, but a liberal shower of gold coin put an end to their scruples.

Such was the initiation to power and dignity of the Empress Theodora. Two other women, who will engage our attention, shared the elevation. These were Michael's two sisters, Martha and Eulogia, who began to have an even more important voice than Theodora in the administration. Both of them were widows, and had, after the death of their husbands, assumed the monastic habit. Probably Martha took the name of Maria when she adopted the black robe, and Eulogia was the monastic name of the younger sister, Irene. Finlay remarks that at least in this decaying period of the Empire the women showed no less ability than the men, and assuredly there was not in the Greek world of that time the least effort to confine women within the gynæceum. During the remaining two centuries the chronicles are full of references to active and ambitious women, and we shall see that Maria and Eulogia were not prevented by their religious vows from taking their share in the political life.

From the first year of his reign Michael gave his thoughts to the recapture of Constantinople, and in 1260 he led his troops against the city, but he had not the rams and catapults necessary to shake its stout walls. He retired to the palace at Nymphæum, to arrange for the strengthening of his forces, and one of his generals, hearing that the bulk of the Latin defenders had sailed on an expedition to the Black Sea, and that the Greeks in the city were prepared to aid him, boldly entered Constantinople during the night, burned out the Venetians from their quarters, and, when the Latin galleys hastily returned, laughed at them from the impregnable ramparts. Their monarch had fled at the first shock, and the whole of the Latins now (in the summer of 1261) returned to the West.

On the day following the entry of the city Michael was awakened by his sister Eulogia. The chronicler praises the prudence with which she broke the good news to her brother. One of her servants had heard it in the early morning, and she entered the bedroom of Michael to tell him. She thoughtfully tickled his feet to awaken him in a natural manner, and stood smiling by the bed until he had full possession of his faculties and she could tell him without risk. Michael at once moved his forces and his family to the Asiatic suburbs in view of Constantinople, where the crown and the royal boots were brought to him. Not until a becoming ceremony could be arranged, however, would Michael enter his capital, and then only with the most conspicuous piety. After spending the night of 14th August in a monastery outside the walls, near the Blachernæ palace, he entered, in the dress of a plain citizen, preceded by the picture of the Virgin which was believed to have come from the brush of St Luke.

The brilliant August sun lit up for them a melancholy spectacle, as the Emperor—John had been left to amuse himself in Asia—and his wife and sisters rode or drove down the Mese to the cathedral. The Blachernæ palace itself was uninhabitable. Its mosaic walls were blackened with the smoke of the fires by which Latin soldiers had roasted their game, and its tessellated floors were in a sordid condition. Filthy, too, were the colonnaded streets and squares that had once been the pride of Constantinople. I will presume that the reader knows something of the indescribable ways of our Latin and Teutonic fathers at that time, and for centuries afterwards. Not a statue or ornament of value remained in the public squares; the vast piles of stone still lay where once had been the graceful mansions of the Byzantine nobility; and great areas of the city were now but scorched skeletons of once gay and populous districts. The Bucoleon palace alone had been preserved with any care, and to it, cleansed for their reception, the royal party proceeded, after a thanksgiving service in St Sophia.

Before long the Court stealthily discussed the fate of the young Emperor who had been left at Nymphæum. Michael was said to have reflected that he had now obtained an Empire of his own, and that the obligation of his oath did not extend to this new dominion. Eulogia, a fanatically religious woman, as we shall see, supported her brother; indeed, it is said that the two nun sisters, whom Michael consulted daily, urged him to depose John and bury him in a monastery. Sinister rumours circulated in Constantinople, especially when Michael proceeded to marry John's sisters to obscure Western nobles, who happened to be in the city, and gave them money enough to take their brides away to their distant countries. But this topic was presently displaced for a time by one of greater interest. It was said that Michael proposed to divorce the plain and quiet Theodora, and marry the Italian widow of John Vatatzes.

Anna had remained in the East after the death of her husband in 1254, and would be about twenty years old, or in the ripest development of her beauty, at the time we have reached. She came to Constantinople with the Court, and, from his slender resources, the Emperor supplied her with a revenue which enabled her to live and dress luxuriously. It was, no doubt, politic for Michael to invite the favour of the Italian monarch by this generous treatment of his sister, but Anna soon learned that the policy was strongly supported by inclination. Directly, or by means of his servants, Michael made violent love to her, and begged a fitting return for his liberality. Anna refused to be his mistress. It is characteristic that the chroniclers do not represent her as spurning his advances on the ground of virtue; she was, they say, too conscious of her superior origin to enter into such a relation with Michael, and, instead of rejecting his gifts and returning to her father's Court, she let Michael know that, though she disdained the position of mistress, she would not refuse that of wife. The kindly and patriotic chronicler would have us believe that this was merely a ruse to protect her dignity, and we may or may not believe this. The immediate effect was that Michael began openly to speak of divorcing Theodora. She was, he gracefully acknowledged, a faithful wife and excellent woman, but considerations of State made it advisable for him to marry Anna. There was a fear that the Latins would make an effort to retake the city, and it was prudent to form an alliance with some of their strongest princes. Theodora, who had given birth to her fourth son since they had reached Constantinople, vehemently protested against the proposal and enlisted the interest of the patriarch, so that Michael was forced to send back Anna, with a splendid escort and equipment, to plead his cause in Italy.

Michael now returned to the problem of John, and, when he remarked to his courtiers that it was absurd to have "two heads under one hat," they knew that the youth was doomed. We have no reason to doubt the statement of the chronicler that Eulogia supported him in this design, but we may at least assume that the manner of executing it was due to Michael alone. He ordered that the harmless and helpless young man should be blinded. A long experience had made the Greeks ingenious in this operation, and, instead of removing the eyes with knives, or using hot irons, they now sometimes blinded a man by an elaborate concentration of intense light on the retina or by the use of boiling vinegar. The more humane method of blinding by an intense light was used in the case of John, and the unfortunate youth was then incarcerated for life in a fortress on the coast of Bithynia. This ghastly operation was performed on the day on which the churches and monasteries of the Byzantine Empire offered their clouds of incense in honour of the birth of Christ. It is at least gratifying to find that it did not pass without protest. A warm-hearted youth attached to the Court lost his nose and lips for speaking too freely about it, and many others had to be punished.

THEODORA, WIFE OF MICHAEL VIII

FROM DU CANGE'S HISTORIA BYZANTINA

Theodora seems to have been a silent, perhaps disgusted, witness of her husband's course, and there is some faint evidence that Michael's elder sister dissented from it. In fact, the patriarch Arsenius himself openly resented this flagrant violation of a thrice-repeated oath, and thus led to a long and fierce ecclesiastical struggle in which the two royal nuns were actively engaged. The patriarch's procedure was not as emphatic and thorough as it ought to have been, but he at least distinguished himself among the crowd of corrupt and servile bishops and abbots by more or less excommunicating Michael. A council of bishops then obliged the Emperor by deposing Arsenius and putting a more courtly prelate in his place, but the hostility and derision of the people soon induced Germanus to retire, and a clerical diplomatist named Joseph occupied the see. As the furious schism of the Arsenians and the Josephites, which followed, will cross the lines of our story for some time to come, it is necessary to introduce this fragment of ecclesiastical history. For the moment it is enough to say that in 1268 the patriarch Joseph absolved from his sin the ostentatiously penitent Emperor, before a crowd of weeping Senators and priests.

The twenty years that followed the return to Constantinople were absorbed in the work of restoring the Empire and adjusting the quarrels of the partisans of the rival patriarchs. Of the restoration it is enough to say that, as in all similar efforts during the last three centuries of the Empire, it consisted in recovering the revenue of the Court and enriching the Emperor's supporters, not in any serious attempt to revive the industries and commerce of the Empire.[34] Nor were Michael's attempts to make foreign alliances much more successful. Foiled in his efforts to secure the interest of Latin rulers, he turned to the Servians and Bulgarians. In 1272 he decided that his second daughter, Anna, should marry the King of Servia. Theodora had some misgiving that the barbaric Servians were unfit to receive her daughter, and she directed the ministers who took Anna to the frontier to send on in advance a party to explore the Servian Court, and to linger sufficiently on the journey to receive their report. It proved a wise precaution. The Servians had gathered round the advance party like—as described in the Byzantine chronicles—a group of savages. Anna's eunuchs excited their intense curiosity, though not their admiration, and the superb equipment of the princess was heatedly criticized. They brought out Anna's prospective mother-in-law, a dirty and coarsely dressed woman, to show the Greeks a model queen. They also stole the imperial horses. So the advance party hastily sent a report to the ministers who lingered on the way with Anna and she was conducted back to her mother.

In the same year Eulogia's daughter Maria was married to the King of Bulgaria, but the marriage brought little profit to the Emperor. Eulogia had now quarrelled with Michael. She took the part of the ex-patriarch Germanus, and she and her daughters and her favourite monks threw themselves so ardently into the religious quarrel, which the Emperor vainly endeavoured to settle, that Michael was very angry with them. Monks now travelled constantly between the young Queen of Bulgaria and the Empress-nun, her mother, and gravely disturbed Michael's work. After a time Maria sent some of the monks to Palestine to induce the Sultan to harass her uncle's territory, and she even persuaded her husband to declare war on him. Michael hated the monks as heartily as Eulogia loved them, and he at length expelled his sister from the capital. When he went on to propose a union of the Latin and Greek Churches, and induced a synod at Constantinople to acknowledge the supremacy of the Pope, Eulogia's love was turned into violent hatred of the Emperor.

Martha seems to have died during the struggle, and Theodora was too weak, or too indifferent to clerical matters, to take any part in it. She must have watched with disdain the last vain efforts of her unscrupulous husband to escape the dangers which threatened him. In the early winter of that year (1282) he set out to crush a rebellious noble of the Ducas family. Theodora tried in vain to dissuade him from leading an expedition to Thrace in such a bad season, and a month later she received the news of his death.

Her son Andronicus now took the purple, and, as Andronicus was orthodox and his royal aunt Eulogia at once returned to the scene, Theodora had a more dreary time than ever. Her brother was damned, Eulogia insisted, and his remains and memory were not to be honoured by the pompous ceremonies of the Greek Church. The young monarch—he was in his twenty-fifth year—bent to her commands, and the body of Michael was buried, almost without a prayer, in the military camp where he had died. Theodora feebly protested, and was assured by the fanatical Eulogia that her own soul was in danger, and her name could not be included in the list of those who were commended to the prayers of the faithful in St Sophia until she had purged herself of her guilt. She was compelled to sign a repudiation of the authority of the Pope, which would cost her little, and to promise that she would not ask the prayers of the Church for her husband.

Into the appalling struggle of the Church factions which followed we need not enter. One of the best historians of the time, who saw the Empire slowly perishing while its whole soul was absorbed in this quarrel, bitterly observes that "for the sake of a single coin both sides were prepared to take oaths so horrible that the pen cannot describe them." One day they appealed to miracle; each side wrote out a statement of its case, and a vast crowd gathered to see the two rolls of parchment cast into the flames and howl for the intervention of God in favour of the just cause. But both documents were burned to ashes, and the ferocious struggle continued for decades, while the Turks spread over the Asiatic provinces, pirates swarmed in all the seas, and the Venetians and Genoese captured all the trade of the Empire. Eulogia disappears in the midst of this struggle, fighting to the last in the cause of the monks, a pathetic example of the way in which the age perverted its ablest and most spirited women.

Theodora lived on for twenty-two years, and saw two new Empresses enter the palace, but the chroniclers of the time are too much occupied with the ecclesiastical controversy to tell us much of the personal life of the Court. George Pachymeres has left us a large volume on the history of his times, but fully one-half of it is taken up with the patriarchal struggle. I will therefore be content to tell the later sufferings of Theodora, and then return to the Empresses whom her son Andronicus put on the throne.

The family of the Emperor Michael had consisted of four sons, three daughters and two illegitimate daughters. The daughters were bestowed upon various nobles or petty monarchs, and of the four sons three survived to intrigue, or suspect each other of intriguing, for the throne. Andronicus was the eldest, and he succeeded his father without opposition. The second son, Constantine, had, however, been the favourite of his parents; he had received great wealth from Michael, and it was known that Michael intended, when death closed his career, to set up Constantine as an independent Emperor in Greek territory. From the first, therefore, Andronicus regarded his younger brother with a jealous eye. Constantine was a good-looking and very popular youth, very liberal with his money and surrounded by friends. Unfortunately he had, like most of the Greeks of the time, little or no self-control, and in 1291 he gave his brother an opportunity to destroy him.

Some short time before 1291 Constantine had married the daughter of Raul, one of the chief officials of the Court. She was a beautiful and somewhat vain young woman, very conscious of her new dignity. On the Feast of the Apostles, one of the many days on which the ladies of Constantinople were wont to pay ceremonious visits to the ruling Empress, Constantine's wife—we do not know her name—repaired in great splendour to the palace of Irene. In the hall sat an aged and noble dame named Strategopulina: in other words, a lady of the distinguished Strategopulos family, and herself a niece of a former Emperor. She had arrived too early for the reception, and sat on a couch without the Empress's chamber. On account of her age and rank Strategopulina did not rise, as she ought to have done, when Constantine's wife passed, and the offended princess returned to her husband in such rage that she fell ill. Most probably the old lady knew that Andronicus and his wife would not be very displeased with her action. But Constantine, egged on by his wife, took the matter in his own hands. Acquainted as we are with the morals of Constantinople, we are hardly surprised to learn that Strategopulina was believed, in spite of her age, to be intimate with one of her servants. Constantine sent some of his servants to flog this man in public, and drag him naked round the Forum.

The scandal, the storm of chatter, and the gross injury to one of his wife's friends, angered Andronicus, and for some time he looked darkly on his brother. Constantine was alarmed, and took pains to conciliate him, but he was displaced from his position at Court and sent on some mission to Nymphæum.

With his sixty thousand gold pieces a year and his pretty wife Constantine would still find life desirable in Asia Minor. Presently, however, Andronicus came to Nymphæum, and took up his residence in the old palace of the Nicene Emperors. To this palace Constantine was summoned one morning in March (1291). He found it full of soldiers, learned that his brother had found him guilty of treason, and was given into custody. His luxurious belongings and his great income were confiscated by Andronicus, and he was destined to spend the remaining fifteen years of his life in a new and particularly ignominious prison. Andronicus was afraid to lodge him in a fixed jail, lest his supporters should free him and start a revolt, and he therefore had a portable prison—a litter converted into a strong-barred cage—made for him.

In this plight Theodora found her handsome son when, a month of two later, Andronicus brought him to Constantinople. The Emperor had now taken a decisive step, and he disregarded his mother's prayers and tears. When she pleaded that her son had been convicted, without trial, on the secret denunciation of a monk, Andronicus merely summoned a council in the palace and compelled his obsequious courtiers to ratify his sentence. Theodora continued to assail him, but she had never had much influence in the administration, and under Andronicus she was completely powerless. Andronicus gave her no opportunity to thwart his policy by intrigue or violence. When he was compelled to go into the provinces, he took Constantine with him in his portable prison, and the miserable young prince, dressed and shaven as a monk, dragged out year after year without the least prospect of escape. The third and youngest brother, Theodore, took warning by Constantine's fate, put off all signs of royal estate, and, living as a private citizen, endeavoured to disarm the jealousy of the Emperor. These misfortunes, and the thick gathering of clouds about the Empire, saddened the last years of Theodora's long life. The regaining of Constantinople had put no new spirit, no healthier blood, into either people or Court. The Byzantine power was doomed, and the last sad glances of the aged Empress fell on a capital fiercely rent with ecclesiastical quarrels, a shrunken Empire trodden under the feet of the Turk, and a sea swept by innumerable pirates. She died in 1304, respected and superbly lamented by the citizens of Constantinople. Without strength of character to make her mark on the life of the Empire during nearly fifty years of imperial authority, she had at least kept her slender record unstained by crime or vice in a criminal and vicious world. At the most we can regret only that she clung so faithfully to Michael Paleologus through all the crimes and deceits of his tortuous career.

CHAPTER XVI

IRENE OF MONTFERRAT

The story of the unfortunate Theodora has led us to make a somewhat premature excursion into the fourteenth century. We have now to return a few decades, in order to begin the story of the Empress Irene, who succeeds her in the gallery of prominent Empresses. Andronicus had in his sixteenth year married Anna of Hungary, a daughter of Stephen V. One of the daughters of Theodore Lascaris, the first Nicene Emperor, had married a King of Hungary, so that the daughter of Stephen V. had Byzantine blood—the blood of the Angeli family—in her veins. Her mother, however, was not of royal, or even noble, birth. Stephen had fallen in love with a pretty Choman captive, and married her, and the beautiful young girl whose hand Michael asked for his son was the issue of their marriage. At her baptism according to the Greek rite her name was changed to Anna, and she, with her husband, received the crown of a junior Empress. Unfortunately she died the year before Andronicus attained supreme power, and we have merely to record that she left two sons, Michael and Constantine, to maintain the valuable dynasty of the Paleologi.

As Andronicus intended that one or other of these sons should inherit the purple, he did not seek his second wife among the more powerful courts of Europe. Two or three years after his accession to the throne he married Irene, daughter of the ruling Marquis of Montferrat. At the time she was a very pretty little maiden of eleven summers, and Andronicus may be excused for overlooking the possibility that, even if there were no powerful Court to espouse or create her interests, there might be a character in the lady herself which would interfere with his designs. For some years nothing occurred to make him regret his choice. In the Blachernæ and Bucoleon palaces, or in the old Nicene mansions, Irene slowly grew up to womanhood, and added three sons and a daughter to the imperial family. The daughter, Simonides, will interest us no less than the sons, and an interesting light may be thrown on the character of the time by telling the origin of her very unusual name.

Andronicus desired to have a daughter, and was in despair when Irene had, in succession, three stillborn female children. A daughter, at Constantinople, meant a useful foreign alliance; though Constantinople never seems to have given any aid to the Courts from which it drew its own Empresses. In the year 1292 Irene again approached childbirth, and the anxious Emperor consulted "a venerable and experienced matron" in regard to his hope. Acting on her advice he set up, in a room of the palace, statues of the Twelve Apostles, with candles of exactly equal weight and size before each. A group of monks were then introduced to pray energetically for the issue, the candles were lighted, and careful watch was made to see which of the candles burned the longest. The apostle Simon won the contest, and it was resolved that the forthcoming little daughter should be put under his protection and named Simonides. The superstition must have gained enormous prestige when a daughter was born, and lived to experience a number of highly interesting, though not very apostolic, adventures.

Another incident of the same year illustrates a different aspect of high life in the Eastern metropolis. Theodore, the younger brother of Andronicus, had now reached a marriageable age, and was, as I said, observing a very discreet behaviour in view of the recent fate of his brother Constantine. He bore the lower dignity of "Despot," and was careful not to aspire to anything more than the slender circle of gold, with few jewels, which marked that dignity. Theodora had earnestly pressed her son to grant Theodore the title of Augustus, as it was customary to do, but he gravely replied that he had made some mysterious vow in earlier years which prevented him from doing so. He now decided to marry Theodore to the daughter of Muzalo, one of his chief ministers. They were betrothed, but before the day of the marriage arrived Muzalo's daughter was found to be in a painful condition, as a result of too great a liking for a cousin of hers. Betrothal was a very solemn ceremony in the eyes of the Greek Church, and it took a special synod of the bishops to determine that in this case the bond was invalid. The affections of Theodore were transferred to the daughter of another official, and, to reward the faithful services of her father, the soiled hand of Muzalo's daughter was bestowed on Constantine, the second son of Andronicus and Anna. Experience had taught Andronicus that, if his eldest son, Michael, was to succeed him, all others must be kept away from the throne.

A third curious incident of the time may be recorded to illustrate the kind of world in which Irene grew to womanhood. The fierce struggle of the Arsenians and the Josephites still enlivened the environs of St

Sophia, but the controversy entered upon a new phase after the imprisonment of Constantine. The young prince had been denounced to his brother by a monk who was a favourite of the patriarch, and, as this became known, the opponents of the patriarch assailed him with a furious tempest of invective. Nearly the whole of his clergy turned against him, and the charges they made against his personal character—charges which were loudly echoed in the public streets—were of the most sordid nature. He was compelled to resign, but he planned an elaborate revenge. He wrote a letter in which he invoked eternal punishment on the Emperor and all who had joined in his humiliation, and, in the characteristic Byzantine vein of ruse and intrigue, concealed the letter in one of the holes on the roof of St Sophia where the pigeons nested. He then retired to a monastery and contemplated with malicious joy the spectacle of the priests and citizens going about their work with this dire and authentic sentence of excommunication suspended over their heads. A year later the vase containing the letter was found by some youths who had sought pigeons' eggs, and a panic seized the Court and city. For twelve months they had all lived, unconscious of their danger, on the very brink of hell. Athanasius was quickly summoned from his monastery and forced to withdraw his censure.

In this atmosphere of intrigue, ambition and hypocritical selfishness Irene of Montferrat developed her character. The Empire was tumbling into ruins, yet the one thought of the vast majority of its citizens, of all orders, was to obtain as much money as possible out of its shrinking treasury and close their eyes to its future. Even the Emperor, who looked as far ahead as the next generation, consulted only the future of his family. His eldest son was, apart from any question of merit or competency, to succeed him in the tarnished splendour of the Bucoleon palace. To ensure this Irene saw him stoop to the crime of barbarously imprisoning his brother, and the spectacle of the young prince, travelling everywhere among the Emperor's baggage like a caged bear, would impress deeply on her young mind the first duty of man, as it was conceived in Constantinople. For her own part she would take care to secure her position and that of her children.

Irene was now a mature and very spirited young woman in her early twenties. She had great force of character, a keen and strong intelligence, and an unchallenged virtue. It was an age of general laxity of morals, as we shall realize, yet Irene is not assailed on that ground. But ambition for her children became her dominant quality, and, as it grew stronger and more imperious in face of obstacles, it warped her character, saddened her life, and made her career inglorious and futile. Had she been the first wife of Andronicus, she might have rendered very valuable service to the Empire; as it was, she became recklessly absorbed in her ambition, and only added to its formidable burdens. When, in 1296, Andronicus married his eldest son to Maria of Armenia, she began that sombre brooding on the inferior position of her own children which was to embitter the latter part of her life. The policy of Andronicus would be to make poor matches for her children; her policy was to prevent it.

We shall be glad to think that Irene had no voice in the first matrimonial settlement of one of her children—the marriage of Simonides to the King of Servia—for it was a sordid and abominable transaction, but she seems at least to have played her part in the ceremony without resentment. We had, in the last chapter, a glimpse of the condition of Servia in the thirteenth century. In the year 1298, which we have reached, there was on the throne a particularly objectionable type of "kral," as the Servians called their ruler. He had first married the daughter of a neighbouring king, but he had led astray his brother's wife, who was a sister of Anna of Hungary, and, when a third sister came on a visit to his Court, he conceived so violent a passion for her that he sent his wife home to her father. This lady was a nun, yet the Kral persuaded her to discard her black robe and go through a form of marriage with him. He then tired of the royal nun in turn, and married the daughter of King Terter of Bulgaria. By the year 1298 he was ready for a third change. None of his three queens had given him an heir to the throne, and he was therefore disposed to listen to the expostulations of his clergy and the advances of Andronicus.

At this time the Emperor's sister Eudocia returned, a young and attractive widow, to the Court at Constantinople. She had married, and recently lost, the Emperor of Trebizond, and came home to enjoy her fortune in her native city. Andronicus pressed her to marry the Kral of Servia, whose army would be useful to him. When Eudocia indignantly refused, there was no lady of the imperial house to offer to the Kral except the little Simonides, who had not yet reached her seventh birthday. The only serious obstacle which Andronicus saw to the alliance was the fact that the Kral's first wife still lived, and both the Servian and Byzantine clergy would regard the marriage as invalid. But this obstacle was opportunely, perhaps artificially, removed by the death of that lady, and the child of six summers was taken by Andronicus and Irene to the Servian capital—we notice the caged Constantine still among the Emperor's luggage—and married to the middle-aged and hot-blooded barbarian.

Since we shall find Irene in the following year making a most violent and effective protest against the marriage of her eldest son, and do not find her making any protest at all in regard to the marriage of Simonides, we must conclude that she consented to this abominable procedure. The patriarch of Constantinople, who had been deceived by them, felt so strong a repugnance to the marriage that he followed the Emperor to Servia and vainly endeavoured to secure an audience. Irene seems to have given him no assistance. The husband proposed for her child was a king: the wife proposed for her son in the following year was not of royal birth. We see her ambition already corrupting her nature. She was content to stipulate that Simonides should be treated as a sister until she reached the condition of puberty, and entrusted her to the "honour" of the fiercely sensual and unscrupulous Kral; though we shall find in the course of time that Irene herself became largely responsible for the Kral's breach of his engagement to respect the age of her daughter. Irene and Andronicus returned to Constantinople, bringing with them the Bulgarian princess whom Simonides had replaced. This lady, it is interesting to note, was married soon afterwards to the Emperor's brother-in-law, Michael Cutrules, who had wedded, and recently lost, Andronicus's youngest sister. But her career ended in prison before many years, as Michael was convicted of treason and placed for life, with his wife, in one of the palace dungeons.

In the following year, 1299, Andronicus proposed to marry Irene's eldest son, John, and the struggle of her life began. The wife chosen for him was a daughter of one of the chief ministers, Nicephorus Chumnus, and Irene now fought her husband with such vigour that he was compelled to desist. Andronicus wished to remove her children from any possible rivalry with his son Michael; Irene was determined that they should make royal matches and wear diadems. She had probably by this time conceived the ambitious idea which wrecked her life, and trusted to induce Andronicus to detach fragments of his Empire in which her sons might set up independent Courts. In this she was, no doubt, mainly inspired by ambition for her children, but the later course of the quarrel will show that she had secret personal grievances against her husband, and she may have contemplated retiring to the Court of one of her sons. For five years Irene resisted the design of her husband and, with tears at one time and threats at another, urged her own scheme upon him. Andronicus became weary and irritated. The ecclesiastical quarrel still distracted his capital, the Turk ravaged his provinces, the pirate swept his seas, and a new burden was added to his cares. An army of Spaniards, who had been set free by the termination of the Twenty Years' War in Italy, came eastward in search of adventure, and, being employed by Andronicus to fight the Turk, soon proved a very fertile source of anxiety and trouble.

In the midst of these harassing cares Andronicus impatiently resented the importunity of his wife, and their life became one of incessant quarrel. Irene threatened that she would not share his bed unless he either associated her sons in power with Michael or secured them independent kingdoms at his death; Andronicus retorted by locking his door against her, and Irene was further embittered. In 1304 her son John married Irene, the daughter of Chumnus, and the Empress went at once to live at Thessalonica. The chroniclers relate that Andronicus had at length persuaded his wife to consent to this marriage, but that seems to be a half-truth put forward by the Emperor. He gave John the government of Thessaly, and Irene accompanied him and the younger Irene to Thessalonica, where, as we saw, there had been a palace since the days of Boniface.

In the capital of the Greek province Irene now entered upon an activity that gave her husband more anxiety than ever. He presently learned that she was openly telling to the monks and matrons of her Court certain indelicate details of their conjugal life which "the most brazen courtesan would blush to tell," says the chronicler. Through her daughter these details were forwarded to the Kral of Servia, but such matters were not of a nature to induce that monarch to declare war on his erring father-in-law. The Duke of Athens was then assailed by the ambitious Empress; he was urged to marry his daughter to her second son, Theodore, and then wrest the province of Thessaly from Andronicus. Irene's plan was now clear. The most westerly part of the Empire was to be detached and converted into a kingdom for her and her children. The Duke of Athens declined to pit his small force against the Byzantine mercenaries, and Theodore was sent to Lombardy to wed the daughter of the Marquis Spinola, who held a small territory in the north of Italy. The marriage was spiteful, as Andronicus was not consulted, but it did not bring to Irene an alliance of any material value; and, as John died, childless, about the same time (1307), she turned again to the Kral of Servia.

Andronicus was alarmed. He was at the height of his trouble with the Catalans and at war with Bulgaria, so that fresh trouble with Servia would be a serious complication. He made every effort, short of granting her extreme demand, to conciliate Irene, but the passionate woman determined to profit by the Empire's difficulties and carried on the war with a spirit and ability that deserved a better cause. She had taken with her to Thessaly a vast quantity of money and treasure, and she now employed this more persuasive argument on the Kral of Servia. She sent him a superb crown from the Byzantine treasury and some of the richly embroidered robes of the Byzantine Court for himself and her daughter; and she forwarded to him, the chronicler says, money enough "to equip and maintain a hundred triremes for ever." It is unfortunate that we do not know more particulars about her departure from Constantinople and the way in which she became possessed of all this treasure. It looks as if she had been collecting resources for some years, and had left with a quite definite intention of fighting her husband. Her present policy was to induce the Kral to make war on Andronicus and take Constantinople. Her ambition had degenerated into a disease and a crime.

There is grave reason to blame Irene for another issue of her ambition which, no doubt, she did not intend. Next to the taking of Constantinople Irene most desired to see her daughter have a son to inherit the new Empire, and it is plain that she impressed this on the Servian monarch. Simonides was now fourteen or fifteen years old, and would be regarded in the East as a possible mother, but, whatever the details may be, the fact is recorded by the chroniclers that her womb was injured in some way and Irene was told that her daughter would never have children. Her next plan was that the Kral should adopt one of her sons as his heir, and, as her treasury was ample, the Kral consented. Demetrius, her youngest son, was sent with a splendid escort and luxurious outfit to the Servian Court, but its rough ways disgusted the spoiled youth and he returned to his mother. As a last resource Irene recalled Theodore from Lombardy and sent him to Servia.

When Theodore also found the ways of the Servians unbearable, and returned to Lombardy, Irene's fiery spirit was quenched. Her four years' struggle for a kingdom had entirely failed, and her health was affected. She confessed her defeat and requested Andronicus to allow her to return to Constantinople. We are scarcely surprised that Andronicus refused permission, politely assuring her that, as the Turks now swarmed in the neighbourhood of Constantinople, she was safer at Thessalonica. Even when, in the following year, the Catalan troops returned to the West, and relieved him of one of his burdens, the Emperor gave her no invitation to return. She lived on for eight years in complete obscurity at Thessalonica, and died of fever at Drama, in Thessaly, where she had a country palace, in 1317, leaving, in spite of her great expenditure, a considerable fortune. The dead body of his fiery spouse was not feared by Andronicus. He permitted Simonides to bring it to the metropolis and inter it with imperial ceremonies among the royal graves.

The further career of Simonides herself is not without interest, though we have no very definite portrait of the daughter of Irene and protégée of the Apostle Simon. Once in Constantinople, she declared that she would not return to the less luxurious Court and the rough manners of her husband. Andronicus did not interfere until, after a time, the Kral sent word that he would attack Constantinople if his wife did not return. She was forced by the Emperor to join the Servian envoys, and set out with them for Belgrade. But Simonides had not a little of the spirit of her mother. When they had proceeded some two or three days' journey toward Servia, she cut her hair and donned the black robe of a nun. The Kral's servants were stupefied, and, thinking it better to anticipate the order of their monarch, drew their swords. With Simonides, however, was her half-brother Constantine, who saw a more reasonable solution of the difficulty. He stripped her of the monastic robe with his own hands, compelled her to put on her royal garments, and sent her to her Court. The Kral died a few years afterwards, and Simonides returned to live in Constantinople and find more congenial lovers, as we shall see, amongst its more refined nobility.

But the adventures of Irene's daughter continue into the next reign, and it is time to turn back and consider the new Empress who had been crowned in Constantinople in 1296. Once more we shall find a story of a woman of excellent character, though less gifted than Irene, tainted by the Byzantine atmosphere and driven to assist in rending the dying Empire. Nothing but a strong infusion of virile moral feeling could have arrested the decay of the Empire. Unhappily, moral sentiment sinks lower and lower at Constantinople after the death of Irene, while the energetic Turk slowly advances to its destruction.

CHAPTER XVII

MARIA OF ARMENIA

In the year 1295 Michael, the eldest son of Andronicus II. and Anna, received the imperial title, and there ensued a remarkable competition of monarchs, great and little, for the honour of wedding a daughter to him. Charles of Sicily made an early offer of the hand of his daughter, but the legates returned disappointed to their master, and the smaller kings of the East sent in descriptions of the charms of their marriageable daughters. Amongst them was the King of Armenia, and the patriarch Alexis was deputed to go and examine the candidate. Alexis was captured by pirates as he crossed the sea, and, although the prelate made a skilful and vigorous escape, it was thought that Armenia was too remote and inaccessible. Legates were therefore sent to learn the terms of the King of Cyprus, and observe the merits of his daughter. When these also were unsuccessful, a stronger embassy was sent to Armenia, and the troop presently returned with two blushing candidates for the position of Empress.

The King of Armenia had, it seems, two marriageable daughters, and they were so equal in grace and beauty that no courtier could decide which was the more eligible. The Armenians insisted that both Ricta and Theophano should be conveyed to Constantinople, where noble husbands were still plentiful, and a message was sent to the capital to notify their coming. Andronicus gave them a princely welcome at the palace quay, and decided that the elder of the two should marry Michael. Their names were changed to Maria and Theodora, and, when the elder was united to the young Emperor, and received herself the imperial title, the younger was consoled by an alliance with the "Sebastocrator" John and a share of his sonorous title and more slender diadem. We do not know the age of Maria and are, as usual, without a description of her person; in fact, the quiet, unassuming ways of her very mediocre husband leave her in considerable obscurity for the first half of her life. We find her in 1306 setting out with him for the Bulgarian war and showing a fine spirit of patriotism. Andronicus had no money to pay the troops, and Maria, who remained in Adrianople, sold the jewels and melted the plate which had formed part of her dowry, in order to win success for her husband. They then returned to Constantinople to await, in exemplary patience, the natural transfer to them of the supreme power.

In 1318 their eldest son, Andronicus, was married to Irene, daughter of the Duke of Brunswick, and Michael and Maria went to Thessaly and engaged in the peaceful administration of that province. Two years later came a terrible message from Constantinople which put an end to the life of Michael and changed and saddened the whole course of Maria's career. They had had two sons and two daughters. One daughter, Theodora, married the King of Bulgaria; the elder, Anna, married the Prince of Epirus, and, when he was assassinated, married his murderer. Tragedy seemed to dog the footsteps of the descendants of Michael Paleologus and Theodora, and a far more terrible experience was reserved for the sons, Andronicus and Manuel. Their father had consented to leave them at Court under the eye of the old Emperor, and that monarch's idea of training them was unhappily consistent with a great deal of spoiling and pampering. Manuel, the younger brother, seems to have had a more sober and industrious character; the elder, Andronicus, was a vain, handsome and unscrupulous youth, whose light head was soon turned by the flattery of courtiers. His days were spent in hunting, his nights in the pleasures of the table, the dice-board, or the enervating chambers of courtesans. He was the natural heir to the throne, after his father, and already enjoyed the imperial title, so that parasites gathered thick about his person. He outran his ample income, and was forced to borrow large sums of money from the Genoese bankers of the suburb of Galata in order to maintain his luxuries and his mistresses.

The old Emperor did not fail to perceive the debasement of the character of his favourite grandson, and sharply to reprove him, but the young man sank more deeply into debt, and began at length to feel impatient of the long delay that must ensue before the keys of the imperial treasury would come into his hands. He contemplated a series of wild intrigues for the purpose of securing an immediate independence and control of at least a small dominion. At one moment he meditated seizing the throne of Armenia, on the pretext that it was his mother's appanage; at other times he aspired to rule the island of Lesbos, the Peloponnesus, or any other fragment of the Empire from which he could wring the price of his pleasures.

The older Andronicus watched him vigilantly, and his intemperance soon led to a tragedy which definitely turned his grandfather against him. He was informed that a rival secretly visited the house of one of his mistresses, a lady of the Byzantine nobility and of very Byzantine laxness of morals, and he posted a band of archers and swordsmen near the house, with orders to fall upon any man who approached. It happened that on the same evening, about midnight, Manuel had occasion to see his elder brother at once, and expected to find him at the house of his mistress. He was not recognized by the assassins, and was murdered. This was the news which came to Michael and Maria in the autumn of 1320. Michael was in poor health at the time, and the shock ended his life. Maria seems to have taken the veil, as we generally find her named Xene in the chronicles after this date, but we shall find that she neither repudiated her elder son nor retired wholly from the world.

The elder Andronicus now made it clear that his grandson should not inherit the purple, but he unfortunately committed a fresh blunder, which strengthened the hands of the young Emperor. The proper and most worthy—or least unworthy—heir to the throne was now the younger son of Anna of Hungary, Constantine, who had for some years been content with the lower title of "despot" and the government of Thessaly and Macedonia. He had, as we saw, married the daughter of the minister Muzalo. Finding a pretty maid among the common servants of his wife's household, he had made her his mistress, and, as Muzalo's daughter soon died, Cathara was raised to the rank of companion. They had a remarkably beautiful boy, who went by the name of Michael Cathara. After a time the roving eye of Constantine was arrested by the charm of the wife of one of his secretaries, and he proposed to bestow part of his affection on her. She pleaded the claims of her husband and the prescriptions of virtue; her husband promptly disappeared, as so many inconvenient husbands did in the Byzantine Empire; and the "new Hypatia," as the chronicler calls her, shared the crown and the couch of the Despot of Thessaly. Her beauty, wit and culture are said to have placed her before all other women of her age, though there is a taint of sacrilege in the comparison with the virtuous, philosophical and venerable Hypatia of Alexandria. Cathara was dismissed, and Michael Cathara became a page at the Court of the elder Andronicus.

The Emperor, now a gouty and feeble old man of sixty-four, was again seduced by the superficial charm of a handsome boy, and treated Michael with a favour which clearly marked him for the ultimate possession of the throne. He gave the boy the imperial title, and kept him by his side when he received ambassadors. When the elder Michael died, and it was necessary, according to custom, to frame a new oath of allegiance to the Emperors, the name of the younger Andronicus was expressly excluded, and the officers swore only to obey the old Emperor and whomsoever he might associate with himself. This imprudent choice gave some of the discontented nobles a pretext to disregard their oaths, and they entered into secret alliance with the younger Andronicus. In order, however, to follow intelligibly the further fortunes of the imperial women, it will be necessary to give a brief account of this conspiracy and its leaders.

The most prominent figure among the discontented nobles was John Cantacuzenus, a very distinguished and cultivated noble, a later Emperor, and one of the chief historians of the period. The tortuousness of his career and the cloak of hypocrisy in which he foolishly imagines that he has concealed his ambition warn us to read his account of his times with discretion. His history opens with a deliberate concealment of the murder of Manuel and of the flagrant vices of his associate, Andronicus, and it remains mendacious and hypocritical to the last page. Such was the chief character who will mingle in the story of the Empresses for the next twenty years. He frowned on the low birth of Michael Cathara, was indifferent to the vices of Andronicus, and secretly cherished an ambition to occupy the throne. With him were Theodore Synadenus, a noble of equal distinction and more substantial character; Sir Janni (probably Sir John), an unscrupulous Choman adventurer; and Apocaucus, a successful financier, of low birth, who begged to be allowed to share the risk and profits of the speculation. Secret vows of fidelity were exchanged, and the more wealthy members of the group purchased the administration of distant provinces, in which they might raise and arm troops.

The old Emperor detected the conspiracy, and made an effort to check it. In the spring of 1321, on the morning of Passion Sunday, Andronicus was summoned to the palace of his grandfather and was forbidden to communicate with any person until he had seen the Emperor. The message was alarming, but the messenger was probably open to bribery, and the other conspirators were hastily warned. They decided to bring a troop of armed men into the hall of the palace, and, if the old Emperor were heard to speak angrily to his grandson in the inner chamber, rush in and despatch him. It will be noticed that the Byzantine Court was now but the shadow of its former greatness. The thousands of watchful Scholarians and Excubitors had long disappeared, even the stalwart and faithful English and Scandinavian Varangians could be hired no longer in any number, and a group of venal Cretan or Italian guards alone protected the approach to the throne. But the elder Andronicus, who had gathered the bishops in his chamber to hear him charge and convict his grandson, learned that a troop waited in the hall without, and the conference ended in hypocritical embraces and vows of mutual fidelity. The nobles, however, resented this solution. In their respective provinces, to which they were ordered, they raised their troops and concentrated at Adrianople. When Andronicus saw that they had a serious army he fled to join them, and they soon began to march over the provinces toward the capital.

Andronicus the elder was at first content to send a regiments of priests and monks into the streets of Constantinople with Bibles, making every citizen swear not to desert their lawful monarch. The oath was taken with the customary fluency, and the customary reserve; but the insurgents came nearer and nearer over the roads of Thrace, and a fresh peace had to be arranged. The grandson was now to have Thrace for his personal dominion, with Adrianople for capital, and the right of succession to the whole Empire. The young Empress Irene, who seems to have been little more than a spectator of the stormy seas into which her marriage had drawn her, joined her husband at Adrianople, presented him with a baby, and lived for a few months longer to witness his debauchery and infidelity. Before very long her reckless husband attempted to seduce the wife of one of his chief supporters, Sir Janni, and that commander, already jealous of the greater favour shown to Cantacuzenus, deserted to Constantinople and persuaded the elder Andronicus to try the fortune of war once more.

The Empress Maria, or the nun Xene, as she seems to have become, took the part of her son in the quarrel with the older Emperor. There is no evidence that she was a sincerely religious woman; indeed, the fact that she sided with her worthless son prevents us from supposing this. She probably trusted to return to Court in his train. She had remained in Thessalonica since the death of her husband, and she endeavoured to secure interest for her son in that province. The older Emperor, however, sent his son Constantine to Thessalonica, and Xene was arrested and shipped, in a very unceremonious fashion, to Constantinople. Constantine was now in a fair way to attain the Empire, and his "new Hypatia" must have enjoyed visions of a very speedy accession to power. But soon afterwards Constantine was captured by his nephew's troops and committed to prison, from which he would never emerge. The unknown lady of such remarkable beauty and accomplishments, Constantine's wife, now disappeared into the obscurity from which she had come, and Xene returned to hope.

The old Emperor was checked by the disaster of his son and sued for peace. He sent Xene to negotiate with him, and Andronicus and his friends were soon enjoying themselves once more in the capital. Irene had set out with him from Adrianople, but she died on the journey. Her life must have been unhappy, but the widower found consolation, and we find the earlier Irene's daughter, Simonides, included in the list of the noble dames who consoled him. Simonides had entered the world encircled by a halo of miracle, but she was not destined to issue from it in a corresponding odour of sanctity. Few did in mediæval Byzantium. She had, as I said, returned from Servia after the death of the Kral, and was living in the city, a comfortable widow of thirty-three, when her handsome and profligate nephew came back to Court, more wealthy and luxurious than ever. There is no room for doubt that she entered into a liaison with Andronicus, since the old Emperor himself publicly referred to it as a notorious fact.

Xene had remained in Thrace, where, after a second marriage, which we will describe in the next chapter, Andronicus joined her. The town of Didymoteichus (now Demotica), about twenty miles to the south of Adrianople, became at this point the seat of a royal residence and a most important centre of intrigue in Byzantine history. From that town Xene and her son presently sent a most affectionate message to Xene's daughter Theodora, who had married the King of Bulgaria, or two kings of Bulgaria in succession. The ladies of the Paleologi family were almost all remarkable for their adaptability to changes of domestic circumstances. It was twenty-three years since Xene had sent her daughter to Bulgaria, and she had not seen her since; Andronicus had never seen his sister. They now felt a sudden and most pressing desire to meet her, and she and King Michael came to spend a week at Didymoteichus. The real object was, of course, to arrange an alliance with Bulgaria, to counterbalance the older Emperor's alliance, through Simonides, with Servia. Michael, a man of loose life and coarse and repulsive manners, was flattered by the liberal attentions of the imperial nun, and when Andronicus gave him a more substantial proof of their esteem, in the shape of a large promise of money and territory, he went home to mobilize his troops. In a short time the news reached Constantinople that the banners of civil war were to be raised once more. No one was surprised, as the year had opened with unmistakable portents. A muddy pig had scattered a procession of bishops, which accurately foreshadowed trouble in the Church; and there had been two eclipses of the moon in three months, than which there could be no surer foreboding of trouble in the State.

The senior Emperor had recourse at once to his futile diplomacy and his synods of bishops. He drew up a formidable indictment of his grandson, and submitted to the Empire that a man who had seduced his aunt, appropriated imperial funds, and committed many other grave crimes, was unfit to wear the purple. In his history of the time Cantacuzenus laboriously meets this indictment, but his answers are feeble and evasive, and, since he prudently overlooks the charge of a liaison with Simonides, we have little hope of relieving her character of that imputation. It does not seem to have made any difference to Xene's loyalty to her son, and we must conclude that she was bent on returning with him to the Court. However, after some months of mutual incrimination, the troops were set in motion, Constantinople was taken (23rd May 1328), and the long and lively reign of Andronicus II. came to a close. Few tears were shed, or ever will be shed, over the fall of that selfish and incompetent ruler. He was granted a generous income, and he continued to live, in complete privacy, for four years.

Xene remained at Didymoteichus, which had now become an important centre of the shrunken Empire. The success of her son brought her to realize that he was surrounded by men and women who were bitterly hostile to her, and she no doubt felt it more prudent or agreeable to enjoy the tranquillity of the provincial palace. This tranquillity was rudely disturbed two years later, when Andronicus fell seriously ill at Didymoteichus, and the members of the Cantacuzenus family and faction betrayed their ambition.

The picture of the scene which we have in the pages of Cantacuzenus himself is just as affecting, and just as mendacious, as Anna Comnena's picture of the scene at her father's death. The dying Andronicus—it was, at all events, believed by all that he was dying—summoned his wife and friends to his couch, and, putting the right hand of the Empress in the right hand of his faithful Cantacuzenus, entrusts to him her safety and that of the Empire. When the mother of Cantacuzenus (a quaint type of nun whose acquaintance we shall make presently) asks him his wishes in regard to his mother, he feebly murmurs that "there cannot be two rulers." Cantacuzenus weeps so copiously that he must retire to wash his face, in order to hide his grief from his beloved friend. Courtiers press him to seize the purple, and he refuses. They urge him to put to death, or put out the eyes of, the despot Constantine, Andronicus's uncle, who still lingers in his prison. Again Cantacuzenus shrinks from the suggestion, and, in order to protect Constantine from their murderous designs, he hides him in an underground chamber.

One feels that the whole story is a masterpiece of lying, and it is not difficult to learn the truth. Round the bed of the unconscious Andronicus Cantacuzenus and his mother and friends pursued a desperate intrigue for power. Anna was young and helpless, and might be used for furthering their plan. Xene, however, watched their intrigue with furious anger and fear, and pitted her hatred against that of the mother of Cantacuzenus. Constantine was thrust in a loathsome and secret dungeon by Cantacuzenus, lest any faction should remember that he was the real heir to the throne. Even the old ex-Emperor at Constantinople was approached, and was offered the alternative of death, exile or the monk's tonsure. With many tears he embraced the least painful of the three proposals and adopted the name of Antony. The triumph of Cantacuzenus seemed to be assured when, to their astonishment and mortification, Andronicus emerged from his stupor and returned to health.

Xene at once appealed to her son to punish the intriguers, but he was either deceived by the hypocritical professions of Cantacuzenus or not strong enough to face his hostility. Xene now felt that she had incurred their mortal vindictiveness and retired to Thessalonica. There she induced the citizens to swear that they would protect her, and she even adopted as her son the wily and accommodating Sir Janni, who governed the province. Sir Janni had not long to wait for his reward—the fortune of his "mother." She died four years later (1334), and was buried at Thessalonica, having run a strange course since she had nervously quitted her Armenian home thirty-eight years before.

The older Andronicus had died two years before, at the age of seventy-two. Nicephorus Gregoras, our best authority for the time, tells us how he spent a night in pleasant conversation with the old man in February 1332. Andronicus, or Antony, died the next day, and was buried in his monkish robe. The same passage of Gregoras gives us our penultimate reference to the interesting Simonides. She was present at the conversation, and we seem to be justified in inferring that she "kept house" for her father. The last glimpse we have of her is a fitting crown to her strange career. We faintly discern her, some years later, as a royal nun in the Court of her nephew and former lover.

CHAPTER XVIII

The first wife of Andronicus III., Irene of Brunswick, had died prematurely five years after her marriage. Andronicus had quickly recovered from his grief, and plunged again into his customary pleasures, but his grandfather insisted that the throne of the Empress must not remain vacant. Whatever substitute for an "Almanach de Gotha" the times afforded was scanned once more, and it was discovered that the young Count of Savoy had an eligible sister named Jeanne. The little principality, which was destined to have so important an influence on the fortunes of Europe, had only recently been carved out of the German Empire, and the name of the ruling house was in high esteem. It was still, however, a mere patch of the hills and valleys of Switzerland, and, when legates came from the Byzantine Court for the hand of Jeanne, she was readily yielded to them.

Whether Anna, as the Greeks promptly christened her, would find Constantinople equal to the reputation of its splendour that still lingered in Europe may be doubted. The majority of the gorgeous palaces in which our earlier Empresses had moved were now heaps of ruins. From the roofs of the public and imperial buildings the copper had been torn to make coin, and the marble from their facades and halls had gone to deck the palaces of Venice and Genoa. Great stretches of desolate, ruin-encumbered spaces existed within the crumbling walls, and the streets no longer glittered with a proud display of domestic treasure on the balconies as a royal cavalcade passed along. Some gold and silver may still have lingered in the reduced palaces before the disastrous civil war, but the display now made in the imperial households and processions was largely a display of imitation diamonds and gilded furniture. For the first time, in fact, we find Constantinople itself impressed by its visitors, even from the small Court in Savoy. The Count had sent with his sister a large escort of knights, and, as the marriage was deferred for eight months, they had ample time to exhibit their skill in tournaments. Why the marriage was postponed from February (1326) to October must be left more or less to the imagination. Cantacuzenus observes that Anna was indisposed after her journey, but one may find more enlightenment in his casual remark that Andronicus was ill and, after receiving his betrothed, went for some months into Thrace. It would probably be indelicate and impertinent to attempt a diagnosis. He returned in the autumn, married and crowned Anna, and permitted her train of knights to return to Savoy.

Since Byzantine history is too full of large and tragic matters to recount the small details of domestic life, and since the Empresses would in their early years, if they were fortunate, be confined to these small domestic interests, we pass lightly over the youth of Anna of Savoy. In the spring after their marriage she accompanied Andronicus to Didymoteichus, and would be faintly interested in the conferences of Andronicus and his mother with the King of Bulgaria. In the following year Andronicus dethroned his grandfather, and Anna found herself mistress of the Empire. The scene at Didymoteichus during the illness of her husband two years afterwards would complete her introduction to Byzantine politics, and make her realize the importance of Cantacuzenus and his friends.

Andronicus was, however, still a comparatively young man, and it was probable that he would outlive the older intriguers about him. He was only thirty-four years old at the time of his dangerous illness, and he returned to his boisterous sports and gaieties. In 1332 Anna, who was at Didymoteichus, gave birth to a son, and Andronicus came on the scene in a mood of wild rejoicing. His Olympic games and Western jousts alarmed and scandalized elderly ministers, who shuddered to see the sacred breast of an Emperor expanded boldly to meet a lance. But he laughed at etiquette, told his courtiers to put away the kind of silk-covered mitres that they had hitherto been compelled to wear at Court, and allowed them to have any dress or headgear they pleased. Fun and good-fellowship were his ideals. He kept, to the despair of the imperial treasurer, a vast number of hounds, horses and hawks, and there was no better way to secure a favour than to present him with a good dog or horse.

It is just to add that Andronicus made a sincere attempt to improve the administration of justice in the Empire, but apart from this one sincere and fruitless effort at reconstruction he danced down the road of death like all his frivolous subjects. A little war, the suppression of a rebellion or two, and mighty hunting and jousting filled the thirteen years of his single reign. The Turk drew nearer and nearer, and received no very serious check. The city of Nicæa had now fallen into the hands of the Turks, and the crescent flashed on the shores of the Sea of Marmora. Andronicus could do little more than trust the old Byzantine weapon—intrigue, ruse, diplomacy. His sister Anna, who had married the Prince of Epirus, assassinated her husband and invited her brother to annex the territory. His daughter Irene, who had married the Emperor of Trebizond and found him unfaithful, assassinated her husband, and sent to

Andronicus for a ruler. He was endeavouring to profit by these assassinations when death overtook him. Earlier in his reign the veteran Sir Janni had rebelled. Andronicus, knowing the mettle of his opponent, had fortified and victualled the palace, where he left Anna and her boy, and gone out to the field; but he removed the danger in the end by deception and assassination. At length, in the early summer of 1341, Andronicus became alarmingly ill. He shrewdly put off his stained purple and retired to a monastery, in preparation for death, and he passed away on 15th June, leaving Anna with two boys of nine and four years. Then began the romance of Anna of Savoy.

The chief personæ of the romance, apart from the Empress, are the ambitious intriguers we have previously seen about the sickbed of Andronicus: the courtly and cultivated Cantacuzenus, the meaner though less hypocritical financier, Apocaucus, and the mother of Cantacuzenus. Theodora Paleologina was, as her name implies, herself a member of the Paleologi family. She was a descendant of Martha, the sister and counsellor of Michael Paleologus, the virile lady who had been put in a sack with cats by Theodore Lascaris: a strong and able and ambitious woman, although, since her husband's death, she had worn the robe of a nun. There was a complete understanding between her and her less resolute son. Apocaucus, on the other hand, an active, restless, unscrupulous little man, who slept little at nights, was prepared to ally himself with either Anna or the Cantacuzeni, as seemed most profitable.

We have no reason to doubt the statement of Cantacuzenus that, when Andronicus lay dying, Apocaucus urged him, directly and through his mother, to seize the crown, and that he refused. He was not in the habit of acting so promptly. He went to the palace in which Anna wept with her boys, assured her that he would protect them, and placed five hundred guards about the palace. It may have occurred to Anna that there was no one, except himself, from whom they needed to be protected. Andronicus died on the following day, and she went (as Cantacuzenus would have foreseen) to spend the customary nine days in mourning by the remains of her husband. What Cantacuzenus might have done while she kept her dreary vigil in the monastery we cannot say, for his plans were interrupted. On the fourth day Anna surprised him by breaking the sacred custom and returning to the palace. It argues some strength of character in her that she should take this step, though it was not an original inspiration. Apocaucus had changed sides, and had gone to warn Anna that his rival aimed at the throne and she must return to watch him. But Cantacuzenus was even more surprised and baffled when the patriarch now came forward with the will of the late Emperor, and read from it that he, the patriarch, was to be guardian of the young princes and their Empire.

The maze of intrigue that followed can very well be imagined, and is fairly described in the chronicles. In fact, Gregoras and Cantacuzenus profess to give verbatim reports of the very lengthy speeches which, it seems, took the place of conversation in those days. The three aspirants to power besieged the chamber of Anna in turns, and each spent many hours in assuring her of his loyalty, and of the disloyalty of all the others. Though the strain made the Empress ill, she seems to have acted almost throughout with good judgment. The patriarch was her safest supporter, since each of the other two really aimed at the throne, and to the patriarch she clung, only tempering his advice by a fear of angering the two nobles and driving them to a coalition, which would be fatal to her. The patriarch urged her to crown her elder boy John at once; it would be an effective step, but when Cantacuzenus and Apocaucus protested that it could not be done in a time of mourning, she thought it best to refrain. At last some kind of settlement was reached. Cantacuzenus was to be the Magnus Domesticus (or "major-domo" on an imperial scale), and to lead out the troops to check the advancing Bulgarians and Turks in Thrace.

Apocaucus was dissatisfied, and, as soon as his rival had departed, he made a bold attempt to seize power. He had on the fringe of the city, by the seashore, a strongly fortified house, or castle, in which he could withstand an attack even of troops. It was impregnable, except to a large force, on the land side, and a galley waited always at its private wharf on the other side to convey him by sea in case of need. His plan was to carry off John to this castle and then dictate his terms to the Empress. Anna, however, was warned in time. The young prince was actually in the hands of the schemer, when her servants were sent to the rescue and Apocaucus fled to his fortress and barred the doors. Cantacuzenus returned in haste to the city, and set a troop of soldiers to watch the castle, but the Empress, on the advice of the patriarch, refused to take extreme measures. As long as the two deadly rivals were poised against each other, her position was more secure. We must not, of course, attribute this prudent policy entirely, or mainly, to the inexperienced young Empress. The patriarch was its chief author; and, though the patriarch was by no means disinterested, he could not aspire to the throne. There can be no doubt that, ill and weary as she was, Anna acted with good judgment.

Thwarted and exasperated, Cantacuzenus in his turn now meditated a coup, and it was only the singular irresolution or hypocrisy of his nature and the boldness of the patriarch that prevented it from being successful. One day, while he was discussing the situation with Anna, they heard a tumultuous rush and angry voices in the hall without. Anna asked the cause, and Cantacuzenus, professing that he did not know and going to learn, lightly reported that a crowd of soldiers and young nobles had penetrated the palace and were hectoring the patriarch. They insisted, he said, that Cantacuzenus should be allowed to enter the palace on horseback (an imperial prerogative) when he called, and the patriarch opposed them. He had, he told the Empress, scolded the patriarch for even listening to the young fools, and had driven them from the palace, and he advised the Empress to admonish or punish them. It seems quite clear that in this case a rather weak, but deliberate, plot on the part of Cantacuzenus had been foiled by the patriarch. The Magnus Domesticus then returned to the field, leaving his mother to watch the Empress, and threatening that he would punish any man who gave her anxiety in his absence. Gregoras says that he took with him an enormous sum of money, and we may conclude that he went with a fairly clear intention to raise the provinces.

As soon as he had removed his troops to Thrace his rivals set to work in deadly earnest. Apocaucus was pardoned, at the instance of the patriarch, and promoted to the dignity of Grand Duke and Prefect of Constantinople. So far the policy was sound enough, but it was, no doubt, impossible for the ailing young Empress to maintain the equilibrium any longer in face of their passion and the perfidy of their opponent, and they plunged into civil war. Cantacuzenus was declared to be deposed, and it was even understood in the city that the patriarch promised the open gate of heaven to any man who would assassinate him. His friends and relatives were alarmed and fled to the deserted meadows beyond the walls, where they passed the night; and, as they learned in the morning that their property had been confiscated, they hurried to the camp at Didymoteichus with loud cries of "Cantacuzenus Emperor!" After a becoming parade of real or feigned reluctance, the commander of the troops consented to accept the purple and prepared for civil war. An imperial outfit was hastily made at Didymoteichus—so hastily that, as the vain Cantacuzenus complains, the tunic was far too short, while the mantle hung about him like a sack—and the coronation took place. The ceremony gives us another Empress of a not uninteresting character. Cantacuzenus was married to Irene, daughter of a Court official of the former royal family of Bulgaria; her mother had been Irene Paleologina, daughter of Michael Paleologus and Theodora. She remained, tearful and anxious, at Didymoteichus while her husband led out his troops, but she would afterwards take a vigorous part in the struggle.

Irene's mother-in-law was the first victim of her own and her son's ambition, and of the hatred of his enemies. Cantacuzenus, who always speaks with respect, if not generosity, of Anna, tells us that the Empress was not responsible for the barbarous treatment and death of his mother. She was imprisoned in one of the palace cells as soon as the trouble began, and from her dreary room she could hear the rabble of Constantinople shouting their customary obscene abuse of her and her son, and acclaiming Anna and John V. The young prince had been crowned at once by the patriarch. It was the early winter, and the aged Theodora was treated with studied insult and severity by her jailers. Her health soon broke, and she died in the palace dungeon. Cantacuzenus relates that a royal nun who had assisted and, consoled his mother went to reprove Anna for the brutality to which she had been exposed, but he adds that Anna was ignorant of it and blameless. The close of the career of Theodora Paleologina is one of the many reminders that to the end the Byzantine Empire did not lack strong men and women; what it lacked was sound moral and patriotic feeling. The stock was not "outworn" and "enfeebled," as historical writers are apt to say of decaying civilizations. Its strength was tainted and misdirected. The royal nun, I may add, who had visited Theodora in her cell was Theodora, daughter of Andronicus the elder, and widow of Michael of Bulgaria, who here is seen for the last time.

The course of the long civil war need not be followed here. It opened disastrously for Cantacuzenus. Anna, Cantacuzenus tells us, longed for peace, and proposed that he should hold the chief power in the Empire, though not wear the purple, and that his daughter Helena should marry her son, the Emperor John. It would have been the best settlement, but it did not suit the ambition of Apocaucus and the patriarch. Apocaucus urged the patriarch to live in the palace and bribed Anna's servants to watch her day and night, in order to prevent her from communicating with Cantacuzenus. Later Cantacuzenus visited the famous monks of Mount Athos, and induced them to send a few of their community to plead with Anna to arrest this shedding of Christian blood. But the monks were intercepted by the patriarch, and converted to his view of the situation, before they reached the Empress.

After three years of indecisive warfare Apocaucus was assassinated. He had at the beginning of the war filled the palace dungeons with prisoners, and he augmented their number continually with nobles or officials who ventured to dissent from his plans. In the summer of 1345 he was building a new and formidable prison in the palace grounds, and the prisoners looked with concern on the frowning edifice and readily believed that he was going to inflict all kinds of atrocities on them. One afternoon he went, without his usual company of guards, to see how the work progressed, and imprudently entered the yard where the prisoners were. One of them snatched a heavy piece of wood and felled him, and the others, seizing the axes and tools that lay about, ended his life and exhibited his head to the guards on the other side of the wall. Anna was alarmed and perplexed, and allowed the wife of the dead minister to take a fearful vengeance. The rowers of the fleet were armed and discharged upon the prisoners, and it is said that about two hundred of them were butchered.

Cantacuzenus now sent fresh proposals of peace, which were approved by the patriarch, and Anna made the grave and somewhat obscure blunder of rejecting them. Gregoras says that she was jealous of Irene, but Gregoras, for theological reasons which will appear presently, is not generous to the Empress. It is possible that Cantacuzenus insisted on retaining his crown. However that may be, the war continued for another year, and began to turn in favour of Cantacuzenus, who now detached a large body of Turks from the service of the Empress. Anna's conduct, in fact, now becomes weak and blundering. She quarrelled with the patriarch, and allowed herself to be influenced by the meaner monks and bishops who opposed him. Apocaucus had so completely relieved her of the work of administration that she paid little attention to it after his death, and, as a new heresy now entered Constantinople and won her favour, she became absorbed in a theological quarrel, while her enemy crept nearer to Constantinople.

On 2nd February 1347 Anna convoked a large gathering of bishops and monks at the Blachernæ palace. They met to judge and depose the patriarch John, who opposed the new heresy. Its tenets do not concern us, but, as it will complicate the story of the Empresses throughout the chapter, we may say that Palamism, as it was called, had discovered a plurality of "divinities" (in the sense of divine energies) in God, and its opponents retorted that this was a return to Polytheism. The discovery is said to have been made originally by some of the contemplative monks on Mount Athos, whose quaint device for raising themselves to a state of trance cannot with delicacy be described here. On this second day of February, therefore, Anna listened with delight, in her Blachernæ palace, to the heated discussion of the light which was seen on Mount Thabor and other phases of the controversy. None of the gifted seers were able to tell her that Cantacuzenus and his troops were only a few miles away, and that he had already bribed some of her soldiers to open the Golden Gate to him that very night. The patriarch was deposed, and Anna and her bishops sat down to a festive banquet and the making of "not very modest jokes," says Gregoras, about their late archbishop. They were alarmed for a moment by a messenger who rushed in to say that Cantacuzenus and his army were approaching, but Anna concluded that this was a ruse of the patriarch, and the banquet continued merrily.

She was awakened in the grey dawn the next morning to hear that Cantacuzenus was master of the city. He had marched with a thousand picked men by an unaccustomed route, had been admitted by the Golden Gate at midnight, and was making for the palace. It was at once closed and fortified, and such guards as there were took up a position in its lower approaches. Anna had returned from the light on Mount Thabor to a very vigorous concern about earthly things. Cantacuzenus sent to her a proposal that she should share the imperial title with him; her name would come first in announcements and acclamations, but the real administration should be entrusted to him. She drove out his messengers angrily and abusively, and sent her servants to raise the citizens against him and bring over the Italian soldiers from Galata. There was still a good deal of loyalty to her, though her conduct during the last year had alienated many, but the troops routed her supporters and even began to storm the palace. They were recalled by Cantacuzenus, who then sent the bishops to persuade her to yield. Cantacuzenus behaved with restraint and humanity in his hour of triumph. He was, we may recall, a refined and cultivated noble, though his singular mingling of ambition and moral pretentiousness invests his conduct, and especially his words, with a repellent hypocrisy. Anna refused the mediation of the clergy, but, in the miserable night which followed, she saw the hopelessness of her position, called a council of her supporters, and decided to make peace. The prisoners were set free, and the gates of the palace thrown open. It is said that John, who was now a boy of fifteen, strongly pleaded for peace and weakened the determination of his mother.

When Cantacuzenus entered the palace he found Anna and her sons standing under a picture of the Virgin which adorned the hall. The Empress was sullen and defiant, and probably expected some vindictive action on the part of the victor, but that was never the way of the silken Cantacuzenus. He venerated the sacred picture, kissed the hand of the young Emperor, and swore on the Virgin that he had not, and had never had, any intention of hurting the imperial family. A general amnesty was granted, and the proposal to wed John and Helena was renewed. It was agreed between them that Cantacuzenus should have sole control of the Empire for ten years, and should relinquish it to John on his twenty-fifth birthday. These conditions were singularly moderate, and Cantacuzenus assures us that some of the troops could hardly be persuaded to subscribe to the new oath when it was found to include the name of John. Anna and John, moreover, were left in possession of the best palace, that at Blachernæ, and Cantacuzenus repaired one of the decaying palaces for himself and Irene, who was summoned from Adrianople and graciously received at the gate by Anna.

Thus two royal families settled down once more to an unstable peace on the ruins of the once mighty Empire. The coronation of Cantacuzenus and Irene, which followed on 13th May, served only to exhibit the poverty and decay of Constantinople. St Sophia was partly in ruins from the great earthquake of the previous year, and there was no money to repair it. The ceremony had to be performed in the chapel at Blachernæ, and in the banquet dishes of pewter and earthenware had to serve instead of the opulent gold and silver plate of earlier times. A week later the royal children—John was fifteen years old and Helena thirteen—were married, and a glittering group of two Emperors and three Empresses stood proudly on the balcony of the palace to receive the applause of the dwindling population; but it was commonly known that the stones which flashed from crown and mantle were almost all spurious, and that the apparent golden trappings were merely gilded leather. The treasury was empty; the nobility consisted, not of great lords of the land, but salaried officials; and the Empire that had once spread, under the Roman eagles, to the deserts of Arabia and the waters of the Euphrates was now restricted, on the Asiatic side, to so narrow a strip of the neighbouring coast that you could almost see from the ramparts of Constantinople the victorious crescent gleaming in the sun. On the west there still remained the greater part of what we now know as Turkey and Greece, but they were exhausted by the unceasing ravages of Turk, Servian and Bulgarian, and tens of thousands of Christian slaves passed yearly into the harems and workshops of the East.

In the midst of this desolation Cantacuzenus set up a Court of cheap and showy and incompetent dignitaries. Irene's two brothers, John and Manuel, received the title of Sebastocrator, and were added to the imposing processions and the list of pensionaries. Money was urgently needed, and Cantacuzenus summoned to his palace all the wealthier citizens and eloquently appealed to them to fill his treasury. They refused to make the least donation. Cantacuzenus would have us admire the restraint with which he declined to extort the money from them, but we know that, if he shrewdly avoided violence, he did not scruple to obtain money in other irregular ways. A few years afterwards the Russian Church sent a large sum of money for the repairing of St Sophia, and Gregoras tells us that the Emperor appropriated it for the payment of his Turkish mercenaries. Two years later, again, when another army of Turks had to be paid to defend his throne, he seized a great quantity of the gold and silver vessels and jewels that remained in the churches and monasteries.

We may assume that Anna watched without concern the troubles that now rained upon the head of the impolitic Emperor. In the year after his coronation his son Michael was persuaded to rebel, and set up a sovereignty over part of Thrace. Irene was sent to discuss the matter with him—Gregoras gives us a six-page speech which she is supposed to have made to him—and it ended in the father leaving his son in possession, though without the imperial title. Anna's supporters naturally suggested that there had been collusion between Cantacuzenus and Michael, though that is not at all certain. When Irene returned from her mission, she was pained to learn that the plague had carried off her younger son during her absence. Even greater was her pain, however, the historian says, that her husband favoured the Palamite heresy. Gregoras was one of the chief protagonists of orthodoxy against the heretics, and it will give some idea of the superfluous confusion that was brought upon the affairs of the distracted Empire if I simply observe that some five hundred pages of the remainder of his chronicle are devoted to the controversy.

To this heretical taint Irene tearfully ascribed all the calamities which affected her husband's reign. He had hardly arranged matters in Thrace, and was still detained by illness at Didymoteichus, when he learned that the Genoese of Galata had burned the fleet which he had laboriously collected money to build, and had attacked the capital. The Genoese had for some time farmed the revenues—in plainer terms, pocketed about four-fifths of the revenues—of Constantinople, and the Emperor had endeavoured to lessen their profit. During his absence they made a raid upon the shipping and the city, and Irene is said to have shown great energy in directing the defence. For the next year or two the Bulgarians and Servians ravaged his little Empire, and the Turks, whom he hired to meet them, could be paid only by permission to loot in their turn and carry off his subjects into slavery. In these circumstances Cantacuzenus saw a tide of disaffection rising against him, and the young Emperor John began to dream of independence.

Writing years afterwards in his quiet monastic home, Cantacuzenus says that Irene and he were weary of the unprofitable conflict and were both disposed to abdicate and take the black robe; that only the recurrence of trouble in the West and the danger to the Empire kept them "in the world." This statement is easily refuted by his conduct. He built, not a monastery, but a stout citadel or fortress near the Golden Gate, as if in expectation of the time when John would claim his Empire, and hired a strong guard of Turkish and Spanish soldiers. Then when the Servian outbreak in the west, of which he speaks, took place, he insisted that John should accompany him. Anna vehemently protested. The youth was too young to be left in Thessaly she said, meaning that she distrusted the Emperor. Cantacuzenus smoothly replied that it was necessary for her son's protection; that the sultan, wrongly thinking to oblige him, had sent a eunuch to cut the youth's throat. Anna must have felt that the eunuch, if he existed, would have an easier task in Thessaly than in the Blachernæ palace, but Cantacuzenus refused to yield, and John set out with him. John was now a good-looking and popular, if a somewhat dissolute and entirely worthless, prince of eighteen, and it would be dangerous to leave him in Constantinople. The Genoese across the water were partisans of the Paleologi.

In the course of the following year, 1351, Cantacuzenus returned to attack the Genoese, with the aid of their mortal enemies, the Venetians. As he seems to have intended from the beginning, he left John in Thessalonica, with the young Empress Helena, but he was alarmed and surprised in the following year to hear that the young Emperor was corresponding with the Kral of Servia. Gregoras says that, under pressure from the Kral, John engaged to divorce Helena and marry the Kral's sister. When Cantacuzenus heard this, he went with Anna into the venerable chapel of the Virgin at Blachernæ, and swore that he would resign the crown to John if he would abandon the Kral and bring Helena to Constantinople. The oath was committed to writing, and Anna herself conveyed it to Thessalonica. It says something for the singular character of Cantacuzenus that they implicitly trusted his oath, and the young couple returned to the capital. After a few weeks, however, John distrusted his colleague and returned to Thrace with Helena. Her father seems to have tried to detach her from John, but she protested, Gregoras says, that she would "rather die with John than live with her parents."

In return, apparently, for this fidelity John made a new compact with the Kral and received an army without abandoning his wife. He at once attacked Matthew, the Emperor's son, in Adrianople, and let civil war loose once more upon the surviving province of the Empire; if, indeed, one can call "civil war" a contest in which hardly a single Greek soldier was enlisted. For the sake of rival Byzantine ambitions Turk fought Servian and Bulgarian on land, and Venetian fought Genoese at sea, and the decrepit Empire sank into its last stage.

The Empress Irene once more endeavoured to make peace between the combatants. She went to Thrace and laid before the young Emperor a politic and admirable scheme—admirable, at least, on the supposition that Cantacuzenus is lying when he declares that he and Irene were minded to enter a monastery, which would have been the best solution. On the other hand, John does not command our sympathy and respect. In three years' time he would be twenty-five, and might have laid claim to the throne with perfect right and more success. Irene proposed that John and Matthew should divide the western territory, and that Cantacuzenus should hold the remainder until his death. John refused the terms, Irene returned to Court, and the Turks and Servians flew at each other.

It is only necessary to say that in a comparatively short time John and Helena were flying on ships to the island of Tenedos, and Matthew was declared Emperor. The unceasing pendulum of Byzantine Court life had now thrust the young Empress Helena into obscurity, and brought a young rival into prominence and hope of the succession. John and Helena were declared to have forfeited the imperial title. Matthew and Irene Paleologina (granddaughter of the elder Andronicus) were crowned in 1354. But we have hardly time to glance at the new Empress before the pendulum swings back and Helena returns to the light and the throne. Cantacuzenus was now detested by all in Constantinople. His heresy, his broken oath, his feud with the Genoese, and the consistent record of disaster during his reign, united almost every class against him. Urgent appeals were made to John to come and displace him, and it was not long before a few ships were placed at his disposal and, during an absence of the Emperor, he descended on the capital. But Irene again vigorously defended the cause of her husband, and, after sailing round the walls, firing a few harmless volleys of abuse at the partisans of the Emperor who smiled on the walls, and spending a night with the Italians at Galata, John returned in dejection to his wife and child. Then a quaint type of wealthy adventurer chanced to touch at the port of Tenedos and confer with John, and he returned to power by one of the most singular of adventures.

One stormy night in December (1354), when the Emperor slept peacefully in his palace, the soldiers who lived in the tower which guarded one of the gates by the port were awakened by a heavy crash and loud cries for help. They flung open the gate and descended the stairs, and faintly perceived a few large vessels rolling in the heavy sea. The sailors cried that one of their vessels, which were laden with jars of oil, had been dashed against the walls, and the soldiers went to the water-edge to help them to moor the vessels. Scores of armed men then rushed from the holds, killed the guards, and occupied the tower; and before the citizens could grasp what was happening, the enterprising Genoese had lodged John in the tower, and were marching through the streets at the head of two thousand men, crying "Long live the Emperor John!" The citizens swarmed to the Hippodrome in the faint morning light, repeating the cry, and Cantacuzenus was awakened to hear that his enemy was in the city with an army.

It is worth while giving the explanation of this remarkable change in the fortunes of John and Helena. Their vigorous and resourceful ally was a Genoese noble of some wealth, who, with a small fleet, had sailed east in the hope of securing some fragments of the dismembered Empire. John offered him the island of Lesbos and the hand of his sister Maria if he would help him to gain the throne, and he consented. Two large triremes (galleys with two banks of oars) and sixteen uniremes (with one bank of oars) were not the kind of fleet one needed to carry Constantinople by storm, but Francesco Gattilusio was a strategist. He emptied the oil from the vessels on one of his boats, crept up to the wall in the darkness, and bade the sailors fling the great jars against the wall. This was the noise that awakened the warders of the tower by the quay, and the stratagem succeeded as happily as in a romance. I may add that John afterwards carried out his compact, and Gattilusio became Prince of Lesbos and brother-in-law of the Emperor.

Cantacuzenus did not venture from his palace. He explains that he could easily have scattered the intruders, which is probably more true than he knew at the time, but he conferred with Irene and they decided that the time had come to enter a monastery. Gregoras says that he was afraid to leave the palace, and, as he was isolated from his citadel by the Golden Gate and would hardly know the strength of his opponent, one prefers this explanation. He was by no means anxious to enter a monastery. Drawing up his guards at the entrance to the palace, he entered into negotiations with John and succeeded in getting a promise that the imperial power would be divided. That solution, however, did not please the people, and for several days he was assailed with abuse and threats. He yielded to the "voice of God," abdicated his dignity, and, under the name of Joasaph, retired to the monastic world, to write his flowing and elegant and mendacious chronicle of his times. Irene was now forced to take the veil, and her robust personality was converted into the black-robed figure of the royal nun Eugenia. We do not know when she died, but some years later we find her, in her monastery, guiding the education of her granddaughter, Theodora. Theodora's parents, Matthew and Irene, continued the civil war for two or three years, but Matthew was then captured and was sent, with his ex-Empress, to spend the remainder of their lives in the island to which they had driven John and Helena.

Helena had followed her victorious husband and, with warm and mutual embraces, joined him at the palace. We do not know how long she lived to enjoy her fortune. I find no further reference to her. Anna is not mentioned further in the Byzantine chronicles, but a little more may be gleaned about her from Italian writers. Du Cange quotes the Franciscan historian, Luke Wadding, as saying that she died about the year 1350, and her body was transferred for burial to the shrine of St Francis of Assisi, for whom she had had a great veneration. I do not find this in Wadding—the reference, at least, is wrong—but Wadding does in other pages (at the years 1343 and 1349) refer to Anna. In 1343 she sent a Franciscan monk from the convent at Pera to confer with the Pope in regard to the union of the Latin and Greek Churches. It is clear that she remained Latin at heart, and no doubt she had brought with her from the West a veneration for the gentle saint of Assisi. Then the civil war and the triumph of Cantacuzenus put an end for a time to the project of union, but the correspondence was renewed in 1349. From a reference to her in one of the Pope's letters we may deduce that she still lived in Constantinople in 1349, and it is the last reference. An Italian writer says that she died in that year, but I am unable to find in Wadding's "Annales" the statement that she was buried at Assisi.

CHAPTER XIX

THE LAST BYZANTINE EMPRESSES

A hundred years of life still awaited the Eastern Empire from the time when John IV. returned to the throne, and half-a-dozen Empresses were yet to play their varied parts on the imperial stage. Had any impartial and sagacious observer reflected on the condition of the Empire at the time, as we have described it, he would hardly have promised it a new lease of one hundred years' tenancy of its stricken domain. At Constantinople, of course, no one foresaw the end. It is usually in fairly robust, not in really dying, civilizations that we find an apprehension of impending ruin: as in France and England to-day. But the Byzantine Empire had shrunk to such proportions, the Turks were closing round its capital with such steady advance, and there was so little enlightenment in its mind, or real patriotism in its heart, that it seemed to be very near the end. No miracle was wrought in its favour, but it was saved for a time by one of the accidents of human history. The Tartars or Moguls attained the height of their power under the famous Timour, and the ambition of the Turk was distracted and enfeebled.

There should be a peculiar interest in studying the features of the Empresses who occupy the familiar palaces during this hundred years' grace of the doomed civilization. We are so accustomed to finding the character of a period reflected in the character of the Empresses that the last representatives of the imperial line should afford us an instructive insight into the final life-phase of a civilization. The idea has become somewhat popular that nations grow old, as individuals do, and die of loss of vitality; and that in their last years they pass into singular convulsions or eccentricities. We shall, unfortunately, be impeded in this interesting study by the scantiness of the records. The ample chronicles of Cantacuzenus and his theological rival close, and two or three confused and ill-proportioned writers alone preserve for us a fragmentary record of the last hundred years. As in all such meagre records, the story of the women suffers most. Still, enough is said to give us an adequate idea of the remaining Empresses and their times; and it may be said in a word that we find no convulsions, or eccentricities, or increasing debility of individuals, but the familiar and unfortunate Byzantine character pursuing its selfish ambitions and passions until the great broom of the Turk sweeps the degenerate successors of the Romans for ever out of the East.

John IV., now a young man of twenty-five, occupies the throne for nearly forty years out of the remaining century, but this reign is almost barren of interest for us, and must be treated only as an introduction of his children. Helena had brought with her from Tenedos a young boy named Andronicus, and two brothers, Manuel and Theodore, were added in the course of time to the family. That is all that we find recorded of the Empress Helena. She may have died early in her husband's reign, though the fact that he does not marry again until old age, suggests, in the case of such a man, that she lived to witness his amours and his political ineptitude. The interest passes to her children.

Andronicus, a pretty and spoiled boy, was betrothed in his tenth year to Maria, daughter of Alexander of Trebizond, who was about the same age when she became the Empress-elect. However, the character of Andronicus was to defraud her of the promise of the crown. We do not know in what year they were married, but it must have been before 1369, when John went to Italy, leaving Constantinople in charge of Andronicus. The Turks were again advancing, and John could see no escape except with the assistance of the Latins. He first visited Venice, and received a most flattering welcome, but no material help. Borrowing a sum of money from Venetian bankers, he went on to Rome and opened negotiations with the Vatican. It seemed to the Vatican an excellent opportunity to convince the Greeks that the Holy Ghost did proceed from both the Father and the Son—the chief dogmatical point at issue between the two Churches—and John hurriedly embraced that dogma, and would have embraced any number of dogmas, in the hope of being rewarded with an army. The reward was very meagre, however, and, after trying a few more princes with no more success, he returned to Venice to re-embark for the East. Then the Venetian moneylenders detained his imperial person as a common debtor, and he appealed to Andronicus to seize sufficient Church treasure to pay the debt.

Andronicus was enjoying his short spell of power over the shrunken treasury during his father's absence, and the demand was irksome. He sent word to Venice that the clergy declined to allow him to seize their chalices and reliquaries, and that, to his regret, he saw no way of delivering his father from the debtors' prison. He was a true Paleologus: a selfish voluptuary, eager only to have the sole right to the keys of the treasury. His younger brother Manuel, however, professed indignation, zealously gathered funds to meet the debt, and hastened to Venice to release his father. He may have been prompted by a sincere piety; but the natural effect of his action was that, when John returned dolefully to the city, Manuel began to wear purple boots, and the chances of Andronicus and Maria occupying the throne became slender. It appeared that, the less the Empire became, the fiercer was the struggle for it. The Turks had already reached and taken Adrianople, and Thessalonica was now the only large town in the possession of the Empire besides the capital. A few years later Thessalonica went. Manuel, who governed it, and was a youth of spirit and ambition, made a futile effort to break loose of the Turks. He was pardoned by the Sultan Murad, but he lost Thessalonica.

After the return of John the pressure of the Turks had been evaded by a voluntary subjection, and the Emperor of Constantinople was now a vassal of the Sultan, holding, under his sovereign lord the Turk, the city itself and a few thousand square miles of poverty-stricken territory to the west of the capital. He was compelled to do homage, and to supply a hundred soldiers, captained by one of his sons, whenever the Sultan pleased. There was, however, still a fair revenue from such sources as trade and port duties, and John contrived to excite the envy of his elder son by the luxurious dinners, the choice wines and the pretty dancing-girls, which he could still afford to enjoy. It is enough to say that John IV., in his desolate little Empire, contracted a very severe gout, and Andronicus was not unwilling to run the same risk.

When, therefore, John was summoned to join the Sultan's army in Asia, and Andronicus was once more left in charge, the foolish and egoistical youth made another effort to secure his father's income. Sultan Murad had left his son Saudgi in charge of his European possessions, and the two princes became close friends. In 1376 the news reached the Sultan that they had disowned their fathers and proclaimed themselves independent sovereigns. The unhappy John was at once suspected of collusion, though the Sultan came in time to realize that John was not at all willing to leave the palace to his son until he was compelled to do so. The conspiracy was soon settled. As the Sultan's troops approached, the two youths threw themselves in Didymoteichus, but they were compelled to surrender. Murad put out the eyes of Saudgi, and sent Andronicus to his father with orders to inflict the same punishment on him, under pain of war. John directed that his sight should be destroyed by boiling vinegar, and Andronicus was confined in a tower near the Blachernæ palace. His son, a boy of tender years, was punished in the same way, and Maria sadly joined them in the dreary tower.

For two years Andronicus and Maria lamented their evil fortune in the tower of Anemas. In the course of time it had appeared that the blinding was not complete; Andronicus recovered the use of one eye, and his son was merely afflicted with a squint. The Sultan Murad, moreover, died, and Constantinople was not at all extravagantly devoted to the ruling monarch. Andronicus therefore found a means of communicating with the Genoese at Galata, and, with their aid, the family were stealthily delivered from the tower and taken across the water. During his brief rebellion Andronicus had promised the island of Tenedos to the Genoese in return for their help, and they had, of course, no hope of getting it from John. From Galata Andronicus made his way to the camp of the new Sultan, and promised him several hundred pounds of gold a year if he would lend him an army with which to attack his father. The Turk had, as we may see presently, a large and expensive establishment to maintain, and he accepted the bargain. Of moral or decent feeling there seemed to be a complete absence at the time in all parties. The troops were put under the command of the one-eyed fugitive, and he drew cautiously near the city.

He had the good fortune to find John and Manuel, quite unsuspicious of his approach, in a suburban palace, and the two, together with the younger brother Theodore, were promptly lodged in the tower of Anemas, from which Andronicus had escaped. The more thoroughgoing Sultan urged Andronicus to put them to death, but such conduct did not become a Christian monarch. They were entrusted to the care of a corps of Bulgarian guards, and Andronicus and Maria mounted the gilded thrones. But their tenure did not last more than two or three years, and we may close the series of petty revolutions in a few words.

John and Manuel communicated with the Venetians and offered them the island of Tenedos—one of the few fragments of Empire that a Byzantine ruler might still sell for a tawdry crown—if they would displace Andronicus. The plot was detected in time, and the Venetians were repulsed; though they consoled themselves with taking Tenedos. In the third year of imprisonment, however, the Bulgarian guards were duped by a half-witted servant named Angel, and nicknamed Devil or Devilangel, and John and his sons escaped to Scutari and opened in their turn a deal with the Sultan. They offered him twice the sum offered by Andronicus. He genially sent an officer to learn which monarch the people really did prefer, and would defend, and was informed that Manuel was the favourite. Lest one should be disposed to think Manuel much better than the rest of the family, I may emphasize that Manuel had offered a vast sum of money out of the poor revenue of the city, and had promised to lead out two thousand troops every spring in the service of the Turk, if the crown were conferred on him. It was a sordid squabble for the last coppers of the beggared city, and it ended in a compromise. John was to occupy the throne; Andronicus and his son to be his heirs. A more or less royal residence was found for Andronicus and Maria at Selymbria, and on the revenues of that and a few other towns they contrived to maintain a tolerable state.

As soon as Andronicus had gone John crowned Manuel, in defiance of the treaty, and sought a fitting wife for him; and his search had the effect of bringing one more pathetic young Empress upon the scene. John was now in his sixth decade of life, a prematurely aged and very gouty man, hardly able to stand erect, but his sensuous nature was not extinct. He sent to Trebizond to ask Manuel for the daughter of the Emperor Alexis, and Eudocia Comnena, the young widow of a Turkish noble, proved to be so beautiful that the veteran libertine decided to marry her himself. He was not an old man; Du Cange puts the marriage, with some reason, about the year 1380, when John would be fifty-one years old. But he is described by the indignant chronicler as worn with debauch and tottering with gout, and we must think lightly of the lady who could accept his hand in order to share his crown—the crown of imitation diamonds. We have, however, no direct knowledge of Eudocia. She shared John's imperial poverty for ten years, and disappeared at his death. We are disposed to suspect her influence when we find John, in his old age, beginning to restore the fortifications of the city in order to prepare for the last conflict with the Turk. Sultan Bayezid suddenly called on Manuel to appear at his Court, and then ordered John to destroy the two marble towers he had built beside the Golden Gate, or he would put out the eyes of Manuel. The old Emperor obeyed, and wearily lay down to die (1391).

Andronicus had died before his father, and, by the treaty of 1381, the crown should pass to his son John. But Manuel had been crowned in 1384, and he determined to seize the purple. He was still in the Court of Bayezid when the news of his father's death came. The Turkish monarchs now had their capital at Brusa (originally Prusa), a town about sixty miles from Constantinople across the Sea of Marmora, which had been famed for some centuries as a pleasure and health resort on account of its warm springs. Here the later sultans had gathered all the luxury which would in an earlier age have passed to Constantinople. No imitation stones flashed from the turban or the scimitar of the Sultan and his nobles, for he had great stores of emeralds, rubies and diamonds; a large park sheltered curious beasts and birds from all parts of the known world; and the quiet gardens and gorgeous halls were enlivened by the forced song of the most beautiful boys and women that Greece, Servia, Bulgaria, Hungary, and even more distant Christian countries could supply. On this sybaritic paradise the dreaded Timour was to fall in a few years, but in 1391 the Tartars still lingered in the wilds, and the Turk dreamed of world-dominion. Manuel was one mean vassal among a crowd, the captain of a hundred feudal soldiers, in this glittering Court, and he decided to fly to Constantinople and shut himself behind its still formidable walls. They proved worthy of his trust, and for several years, though to the great suffering of the inhabitants, Manuel defied the Sultan.

During the siege, apparently, Manuel married, so that an Empress shared the straits of the long and terrible siege. She was Irene (or Helene), the daughter of Constantine Dragases, who governed a part of Macedonia. Irene is rarely mentioned in the scrappy and contradictory chronicles of the time, but she is one of the few of whom we have a pictorial representation. The miniature—found in a manuscript of the works of Denis, the so-called Areopagite—is a very quaint, though not very instructive, picture of Irene and Manuel and their two sons, but he would be a bold physiognomist who would venture to make a text of the flat and conventional features of a Byzantine portrait. Her experience of Byzantine life was dreary. During nearly seven or eight years (including the brief respite) the Turks swarmed round the walls of Constantinople, and were only prevented by their lack of powerful rams and slings—to say nothing of that new implement called a cannon, which was just entering European warfare—from penetrating. The great areas of desolation within the walls became more desolate, and the scanty supplies of food sold at appalling prices. With the Sultan outside could be seen John, the son of Andronicus, whom Bayezid affected to consider the lawful Emperor, and, although Manuel was a brave and humane ruler, the weary citizens were ready to acclaim John. But Manuel received the aid of Marshal de Boucicault and two thousand men, as well as a fleet of Venetians and Genoese, and held out stoutly until, at the close of 1399, the appearance of Timour the Tartar in the rear of the Sultan persuaded him to make peace. John was admitted as co-Emperor, and an effort was made to restore the stricken city.[35]

Manuel was the finest of the later Paleologi, and, although we cannot admire many of the steps he took to attain power, he made an excellent effort to use it for the restoration of the Empire. It seemed to him that his hope lay in enlisting the interest of the West against the infidel, and he set out at once with Irene and her two children. He left Irene in Greece, however, with his brother Theodore and Bartholomæa, and thus no Byzantine Empress was ever seen farther west than Greece. Manuel took ship to Italy, where very little was to be obtained, went to Paris, where he found Charles VI. insane, and even crossed the sea to the little island which had once sent so many Varangians to Constantinople. This visit to England induces one of the later Byzantine chroniclers (Chalcocondylas) to tell his readers something of that country, and we are interested to learn that, in the days of Henry IV., Englishmen shared their wives in common when they travelled, and held it their first duty to offer their wives to visitors; but he adds that London is already the greatest city of the West, though the strange island produces no wine and its inhabitants speak a most peculiar language.

Manuel obtained little money and few volunteers, and was returning in dejection when he heard that Timour had routed the Turks. Only a few years before Bayezid had received legates from Timour in his palace at Brusa. He had disdainfully shaved them and sent them back to their barbaric master. Then the Tartars had swept over Asia Minor, scattered all the pretty boys and ladies of the Brusa pleasance, and compelled John of Constantinople to transfer his alliance from Bayezid to himself. Manuel confirmed the vassalage on his return, but he sent John into exile and set about restoring his Empire while the giants wore down each other's strength. But I pass over the next decade, during which the internal troubles of the Turks gave Manuel an opportunity to reform and reconstruct. Our historian, Finlay, speaks somewhat contemptuously of his work, and, able and well-intentioned as Manuel was, it may be admitted that the work was too vast for him. In any case we lose sight of Irene for several decades, after the return of Manuel in 1405, and will pass at once to the next and, as far as we know, last Empress of Constantinople.

The introduction of Maria of Trebizond is preceded by some romantic adventures in the private life of the Court, of which the chroniclers give us a fairly ample account. Irene had six sons, of whom the eldest, John, married the daughter of the Grand Duke of Moscow in the year 1414. He was already twenty-four years old, and of irregular life, but the hands of the princesses and princes of Byzantium were no longer sought in the Courts of the world. Anna was a child of eleven years, and we may assume that John remained with his mistresses until, three years later, Anna was carried off by the plague. Again there seems to have been some difficulty in finding a wife for the heir to the throne, but in or about the year 1420 legates were sent to Italy, and they returned with two eligible young ladies. Cleope, the beautiful and gifted daughter of Count Malatesta of Rimini, was married to Irene's second son, Theodore, and went to spend an unhappy life with that restless prince in Lacedæmonia. For John the legates had brought Sophia, daughter of the Marquis of Montferrat, and she and her husband at once received the imperial title.

The appearance of Sophia of Montferrat on the imperial stage was brief and eventful. She was a tall and very graceful young woman, with golden hair that fell to her feet, a beautiful neck and broad round shoulders, fine arms, and hands and fingers "like crystal," says the chronicler. But nature had spoiled these many perfections by misshaping her nose and giving a very careless finish to her eyes and eyebrows. John disliked her, kept himself coldly aloof from her, and pressed his father to send her back to Montferrat. A more chatty chronicler, however, gives a more serious reason for John's dislike. Sophia had been as virtuous as she was beautiful until she came to Constantinople, but, whether it was the taint in the atmosphere of the Court (most of the Paleologi have natural children) or the example of her husband, she quickly lapsed. There was a natural son of her husband about the Court, and this youth she incited into a most unnatural relation. A maid of the Court caught them in flagrante delicto and told her lover; and the lover informed John. By making a hole in the wall of the bedroom John convinced himself of the truth of the story and was very indignant. It may be stated on behalf of Sophia that, when John spoke of the indignity to one of the Court jesters, he was reminded that he had himself some time before stolen his son's mistress; it is therefore not impossible that the seduction was on the side of the youth and had a vindictive character.

Such was the kind of life witnessed in the last ruins of the Eastern Empire. John insisted that Sophia must go home; Manuel, possibly conscious of the difficulty of finding alliances, was reluctant to send her. Sophia found her position intolerable, however, and decided to run away, with the aid of the Genoese of Galata. They moored a galley at the foot of the imperial gardens, and Sophia, pretending to go for a stroll in the garden with her Italian maids and young courtiers, walked to the quay and was shipped over the water to Pera before her flight became known. It was published in the city the next day, and there was much buckling of arms and preparing of boats to avenge this last outrage of the hated Genoese. Manuel was, however, now overshadowed by his son, and Sophia was permitted to depart quietly for her home. The chronicler adds that she was received with great honour and rejoicing at Montferrat, and ended her days in a nunnery.

The date of Sophia's flight and of John's third marriage is difficult to determine. The plainest reading of the contradictory chronicles is that the trouble occurred in the last year of Manuel's reign and the flight took place a month after his death, but this is inconsistent with the express declaration that the old Emperor intervened in the dispute. Manuel died on 25th July 1425. For some years the ambition of the Turk, who had quickly recovered from the heavy blows dealt by Timour, had fully revived and had given him great anxiety. A young Sultan, Murad II., had succeeded to the throne, and Manuel had imprudently recognized a pretender to the succession. When the young Sultan vigorously took the field, hanged the pretender, and drew up under the walls of Constantinople, Manuel, now a feeble old man of seventy-five, left the direction of affairs to John, and retired to pursue that ardent study of the Scriptures which absorbed him in his later years.

John abjectly apologized, but the angry Sultan ranged his machines against the walls and proceeded to batter them. He was drawn off for a time by the strategy of John, who had the Sultan's brother conveyed to Brusa and set up as Sultan, but Murad returned more angry than ever, and one of the last earthly sounds to catch the ear of the aged Manuel was the roar of the first cannons that seem to have appeared at Constantinople. The diffusion of knowledge at the time may be gathered from the fact that one of the most learned of the chroniclers, in discussing these "bombards," observes that he does not think they are of very ancient origin. Before the end of the siege Manuel was warned by an attack of apoplexy that his death was near. He donned the black robe, became plain Brother Matthew, and died two days—not two years, as Finlay says—afterwards, at the age of seventy-seven. Irene also then retired from the world and became the nun Hypomene, whom we shall later find endeavouring to settle the quarrels of her selfish children. She remained "mistress" (despoine) of the Empire and watched its slow decay with concern.

John was able, after the death of his father, to obtain peace from the Sultan at the price of a heavy annual subsidy, and the Empire entered upon its last quarter of a century of melancholy decay. Long years of effort had taught the sultans that their siege engines were not powerful enough to crack the heavy shell in which earlier Emperors had enclosed the city, and they were content to hold it in vassalage and draw a large tribute from its sinking revenue. The time had gone by for the last serious effort to save the Empire. Its trade had passed to the Italians, and of the provinces from which it had so long extorted its rich supply of gold there now remained only a few towns to the west of Constantinople, a part of the Peloponnesus, and Thessalonica (which would soon be sold to Venice for fifty thousand gold coins). The metropolis, therefore, continued to shrink within its eighteen-mile enclosure, and, as a severe pestilence fell on the inhabitants for the last time in 1431, they were reduced to something like one hundred thousand, instead of the million they had once been.

It was over this dismal little Empire that the last Empress, Maria of Trebizond, was called to preside. Whether the flight of Sophia came before or after the death of Manuel, John V., who succeeded his father, soon found it necessary to seek a bride. He married, in 1427, the daughter of Alexis of Trebizond, a handsome woman of excellent character, and we are fortunate enough to have a short description, from the pen of a French knight, of Maria and her desolate surroundings. Bertrandon de la BrocquiÃ¨re made a pilgrimage to the Holy Land, and returned through Constantinople in the year 1432. The plague had ravaged it in the previous year, and Bertrandon sympathetically refers to the broad spaces of ruin that half filled the enclosure within the walls. He notes that the Greeks are still busy with their processions, religious and imperial, and that they still cherish in their churches such important relics as the pillar at which Christ was scourged, the board on which his body was laid out, the gridiron on which St Lawrence had been martyred, and the stone on which Abraham had offered food to his angel visitors. Apparently the credentials of these relics had not been imposing enough to convince Western purchasers, indulgent as they were.[36]

When the knight heard that the Empress was about to proceed to St Sophia, and on to the Blachernæ palace, he went to the square to see the procession. We know what the spectacle would have been at an earlier date. First would come a corps of Excubitors or Varangians, with shining axes and gold accoutrements, clearing a way through the crowd. Then a regiment of pale-faced eunuchs, their leaders dressed in white silk and glittering with jewels, would precede a large body of maids and dames, from foreign slaves to the greatest ladies of the Empire, more superbly dressed than most of the queens of Europe. And lastly would come the gold-plated, gem-encrusted litter, drawn by four white horses, possibly with one of the highest nobles in Europe at the rein of each, the Empress sitting stiffly in her gold-cloth tunic, over which spread the mantle of purple silk with deep embroidered edges, and, if it were a solemn occasion, a massive domed crown on her head, from which large diamonds and pearls fell in long chains to her shoulders. Very different was the spectacle witnessed by Bertrandon de la Brocquière. Maria's suite consisted of two ladies, three eunuchs, and three aged ministers. With this poor escort she was to drive the several miles of road to the Blachernæ palace. She wore a high hat (probably a silk-covered mitre) with three golden plumes, and she had broad flat rings, set with a few jewels, in her ears. She was young and fair; "I should not," says the pilgrim, "have had a fault to find with her had she not been painted, and assuredly she had not any need of it." The paint seems to have been the one surviving portion of the luxurious inheritance of the Empresses of Constantinople.

Maria was a woman of tame and mediocre, if faultless, character, and, as her husband was weak and incompetent, the miserable Empire lay helplessly awaiting the end. Patriotism was an extinct virtue. "The absence of truth, honour and patriotism," says Finlay, "among the Greek aristocracy during the last century of the Eastern Empire is almost without a parallel in history." The Western Empire had, even in its last years, had its Symmachus, its Prætextatus and its Flavianus. Irene's sons could do no more than quarrel for their selfish interests in the ruins. Andronicus, who had charge of Thessalonica, which was restored to the Greeks for a time, sold it to Venice, and went to enjoy his fortune in the Peloponnesus. In that last fragment of the Empire Theodore and Constantine were on the verge of civil war owing to the clash of their petty ambitions. There seemed to be no resource in the East, and John, leaving the city in charge of his wife and mother, went to make a last appeal to his fellow-Christians of the West to stem the Mohammedan tide. It was now clear that the Greek Church would, as the price of assistance, have to surrender its independence to the papacy, and John took with him the patriarch and his bishops.

It may be read in history how, at the Councils of Ferrara (1438) and Florence (1439), the Greek bishops abandoned the positions they had fiercely maintained for so many centuries against the Western Church and, with one exception, signed the Roman claims. I will add from the Byzantine writers only that, whatever arguments were discussed in open Council, and however pressing the need of the Empire, it was a secret and generous payment of gold to the Byzantine bishops which finally convinced them. They bargained, like Syrian pedlars, for their signature. It may also be read in history how John returned in deep dejection to his mother. Instead of the promised fleet, the Pope had given him only two galleys and three hundred men and a very moderate sum of money. His wife, Maria, had died during his absence; the Sultan was pressing for an explanation of this visit to Italy; and the people and lower clergy of Constantinople were infuriated at the surrender of their spiritual independence, and were now treacherously joined by the corrupt bishops, who had signed the decrees. John wearily sustained the attack, assuring the Sultan that he had visited Italy only in order to discuss certain details of the Christian faith, and secretly pressing the Pope and the Western monarchs to fulfil their promises.

Hypomene, now an aged and venerable lady, sadly watched the struggle of her sons, and endeavoured to curb their selfish tempers. Demetrius, her youngest son, recollected that he, unlike John, had been "born in the Porphyra," and disputed the shaking throne of his brother. He gathered about him a ragged army of Turks and looted whatever was left of the suburbs beyond the walls, until his force melted away on account of the poverty of the plunder, and he consented to be reconciled. Theodore, the second son, complained that he had not enough income to maintain his state in the town of Selymbria, which he governed, and he demanded a share of John's. It was refused, and he in turn was about to lead troops against the capital when John, in his fifty-eighth year, was removed by a greater power (31st October 1448) from the scene of his troubles.

No one even now suspected that the next Emperor would be the last—that in five years the crescent would glitter over the imperial palaces—and the struggle for the throne broke out afresh. Demetrius alone was in the city when John died, and he noisily renewed his claim to the purple, but his character was too well known for him to find serious adherents. His mother united with the citizens in preventing him from succeeding, and they sent legates to ask the Sultan to allow Constantine, the ablest of the brothers, to be crowned. He had lately been opposed to the Sultan, but permission was given, and to his "despotate" at Sparta the legates were sent with the imperial ensigns. Constantinople did not even enjoy a last coronation, as the new Emperor was crowned at Sparta (6th January 1449) and would not have the ceremony repeated. He favoured the union of the Churches. He reached Constantinople in March, and the royal brothers gathered in the presence of Hypomene and such nobles as Constantinople could still boast to swear resonant oaths of peace and loyalty.

Constantine had been twice married and widowed when, in his early forties, he ascended the throne. His first wife, Theodora, daughter of the Count of Tocco, had died in 1429; his second wife, Catharine, daughter of Notaras Paleologus, had died in 1443, two years after her marriage. There were no children of either marriage, and Constantine made it one of his first duties to provide a third wife and an heir to the throne. The historian Phrantzes was entrusted with this delicate mission, and he set out from Constantinople with an escort which, it was thought, would impress the King of Iberia and the Emperor of Trebizond, to whom he was sent. It was, as he describes it, a weird mixture of monks, musicians and medical men; their baggage consisted mainly of musical instruments, instead of the superb robes and plate that an earlier escort might have taken, and Phrantzes says that they did impress and astonish the foreign Courts. But they were unfortunately wrecked on the way to Iberia, a country between the Black Sea and the Caspian, and seem to have been detained for nearly two years by lack of funds; and they then discovered that the King of Iberia expected a gift for his daughter, instead of presenting one with her, and returned unsuccessful to Constantinople.

In the meantime—apparently on 23rd March 1450—Hypomene had brought to a close her long and troubled life. With her death the series of Empresses of Constantinople comes to an end, but their story cannot be intelligibly concluded without a glance at the great catastrophe which, three years later, swept away the tottering thrones and made an end of Christian Byzantium.

The Sultan Murad II., who had so long looked with indulgent eye on the remnant of the Byzantine Empire, died in 1451. His son and successor, Mohammed II., was a young man of twenty-one years: a very able, highly cultivated and extremely ambitious young prince. To him the existence of this Christian island, the city of Constantinople, in the ocean of Mohammedan conquest was an intolerable anomaly. The Turks had long since carried the crescent over what we now call Turkey in Europe, and it was only by sea that Constantinople could communicate directly with the other Christian powers. To put an end to this Christian avenue into the heart of his dominion and make the great city the capital of the Mohammedan world was the early ambition of Mohammed II. Probably every sultan for a hundred years or more had desired this, but their siege machinery had hitherto proved incapable of shattering the stout old walls of that city.

Constantine XI. underrated the young Sultan, and very soon gave him a pretext for an attack. Mohammed had signed a truce with the Hungarians, and gone to settle certain disturbances in his Asiatic dominions, when he received a most insolent and offensive message from Constantinople. He must at once increase the pension of Prince Orkhan (the nephew of Suleiman, then living in retirement at Constantinople), or else the Greeks will consider Orkhan's claim to the Turkish throne. It was the last blunder of the Paleologi. Mohammed courteously heard and dismissed the legates, and proceeded to pacify his Asiatic province. Constantine had grossly failed to appreciate the young Sultan's character. After his coronation at Adrianople his Christian vassals—the Emperors of Trebizond and Constantinople, the Duke of Athens, etc.—had hastened to do homage, and had seen only an accomplished, amiable and, in private life, vicious young man, from whom they had little to fear.

Shortly afterwards the Court at Constantinople was alarmed to hear that a large army of Turkish workmen had arrived at a spot on the Asiatic coast only five miles from the city, and were, with great rapidity, building a powerful fort which would command the entrance to the Black Sea. Constantine sent a protest; Mohammed disdainfully replied that he would do as he liked in his own dominions. In time the Turkish soldiers of the district fell to quarrels with Constantine's subjects, and the Emperor, ordering the gates of the city to be closed, demanded some recompense. Mohammed at once declared war, and went to Adrianople to concentrate his forces and gather a more powerful armament than his predecessors had used. The value of powder was now realized, and, although they were crude objects of only moderate effectiveness, immense cannons, which could throw stone balls weighing more than a hundred pounds, were associated with the old rams and slings and towers.

Constantine quickly realized the gravity of his position, and made every effort to patch the fortifications, enlist troops and provision the town. An urgent appeal was sent to Italy, and hundreds of volunteers and adventurers were attracted; though the Pope was still mainly concerned about the recognition of his supremacy, and sent a cardinal who distracted the doomed city with fierce religious controversy. When the hour came, Constantine found that barely six thousand Greeks could be induced to enlist in the last defence of their city, and these, with other two or three thousand Italians, had to hold fifteen miles of wall, with many gates, against seventy thousand Turks and three hundred vessels.

On 12th December 1452 the church of St Sophia rang with its last great Christian celebration, the solemn union of the Latin and Greek Churches, the price of that secular aid which was destined never to arrive. Four months later the vanguard of the Turks was descried from the walls, and day by day the endless regiments and engines of attack and the monstrous cannons came from the line of the horizon and took up their stations. For a time the spirits of the besieged were maintained by those little successes which so often precede a great catastrophe. Four large Italian ships had fought their way through the Turkish fleet and brought provisions: Mohammed's biggest gun had burst: a general attack of the enemy had been repulsed. But the incessant rain of projectiles made at last a ghastly breach in the stout wall, and on 29th May, before dawn, the dreaded Janissaries flung themselves at the defenders. The last of the Paleologi died like a man. Later in the day the victorious Turks swept over his body and the bodies of some thousands of his people, and the last remnant of the Byzantine Empire was swallowed up in the Mohammedan tide. And the relics of its culture passed westward and, meeting and blending with the humanism of the later Middle Ages, begot the new man and new woman of the Renaissance, the heralds of modern times.

FOOTNOTES

[1] *Readers of Professor Bury's incomplete "History of the Later Roman Empire" may wonder that I continue to use the phrase "Byzantine Empire" after Bury's protest against that phrase. But it seems to me that if "Roman Empire" means an Empire centred in Rome, "Byzantine Empire" is the most congruous name for a dominion that centres in ancient Byzantium and has, during the far greater part of its story, no connexion whatever with Rome. Most historians continue to speak of it as Byzantine.*

[2] *See, especially, J. Ebersolt, "Le Grand Palais de Constantinople." 1910.*

[3] *There was no hereditary right to the throne in the Roman Empire, though a father generally contrived to secure it for his son. "Born in the purple" is, by the way, an inaccurate description of the imperial*

children, though not uncommon. They were "born in the Porphyra," or porphyry-lined palace; but, as the Greek word porphura properly means "purple," it is mistranslated at times. There are those who maintain that the imperial colour was rather red than what we know as purple.

[4] The date of the marriage is much disputed. Chroniclers assign it to various years, and, when the son of Ariadne and Zeno mounts the throne, he is variously described as an infant, a boy of seven, and a youth of seventeen. Professor Bury puts the marriage in 458 or 459. I prefer the estimate of Tillemont, that it took place in 468, the year of the disgrace of Basiliscus.

[5] It is a popular fallacy, as we shall frequently see, that the Romans had abandoned these bloody spectacles in the days of Honorius.

[6] See, especially, the work of Débidour, "L'Impératrice Théodora," and a summary and approval of Débidour's arguments in an article by Mr Mallett in The English Historical Review, January 1887. Mr W.Â G. Holmes's learned work, "The Age of Justinian and Theodora" (2 vols., 1907), is much too meagre in its references to Theodora.

[7] See the Latin translation ("Commentarii de Beatis Orientalibus") by Douwen and Land of this Syriac work (Amsterdam, 1889). John also speaks of her as "a most astute woman," and, although his work teems with the immense services done to his Church by Theodora, he never mentions her with more than stiff and formal respect.

[8] It is necessary to explain to the unfamiliar the "factions" of the Hippodrome. In the chariot contests the rival drivers were distinguished by their colours: white, red, blue and green. The white and red were of little account, but the blue and green divided the populace of Constantinople into bitterly hostile parties or "factions." These parties were almost in the nature of sporting clubs: they were publicly recognized, and had their own premises, chariots, beasts, officers, etc. We shall find the fate of dynasties almost turning at times on the struggle of the "blues" and "greens."

[9] This conversation (preserved in Theophanes) is sometimes described as a free discharge of invectives against Justinian, and surprise is expressed that the character of his wife is not included. The dialogue is not at all a general attack on Justinian. It is, for the most part, a sober and earnest demand of justice, and contains only one insulting line—possibly an isolated cry of some more impetuous member of the party.

[10] I have passed in silence an earlier charge against Theodora in the "Anecdotes." The Gothic queen Amalasuntha had appealed to Justinian, and Theodora is said to have sent an officer to cause her to be assassinated, lest her great beauty should seduce the Emperor. Procopius gives a different version of the murder of Amalasuntha in his "Gothic War," and we have no serious reason to involve Theodora.

[11] Shorthand (notatio) was, of course, familiar to the Romans and daily practised. It may not be superfluous to add that the dignity of Cæsar was a semi-imperial rank conferred usually on sons or possible successors of the Emperor, or King (basileus), as the eastern Romans came to call their monarch.

[12] It should be noted that the organized factions were not nearly so large as these incidents suggest. When Maurice had wished to arm them against the usurper, he found that the blues numbered only nine hundred, and the greens fifteen hundred. The entire population was about a million.

[13] See Pernice's "L'Imperatore Eraclio," 1905, p. 25.

[14] Professor Bury gives his age as twenty-three, and assumes that he was born in 615, but Nicephorus places his birth in the second Persian campaign (623). The first son of Martina had died. His name (or nickname) is spelt either Heraclonas or Heracleonas.

[15] The readers of Gibbon may often notice that words or speeches quoted here differ materially from corresponding quotations in the great historian. The reason is that Gibbon invariably paraphrases such quotations. They are in this work translated literally from the Greek chroniclers.

[16] I have not been able to consult this interesting "Life of St Philaretus," and am quoting Diehl's admirable work, "Figures Byzantines."

[17] A monk of this monastery, Theodore of Studium, has left us a number of letters and works, though they give little satisfaction to the profane historian. One letter, however, is addressed to the ex-Empress Maria, and we learn from it that her daughter, or one of her daughters (Euphrosyne and Irene), pressed her to come and live in her palace. Theodore sternly forbids her to return to that world of sin.

[18] Finlay rejects the story on the ground that Theodora could not possibly have made her husband believe that sacred images were dolls for her children. But that is not the story; Theodora denied that she had any dolls at all.

[19] The mystery of the children of Theophilus is yet unsolved. Michael was born, of Theodora, about 828, and we know that another boy, named Constantine, was born. But the five daughters—Thecla, Anna, Anastasia, Pulcheria and Maria—are a puzzle, to which the wretched Byzantine chroniclers give us no clue. They make Thecla, the eldest, a gay and dissolute woman thirty years afterwards, and they marry Maria, the youngest, about 832; while they speak of the whole of them as young girls, playing with their grandmother's dolls, about the time when the youngest of them marries Alexius. It is frequently suggested that they were the daughters of an earlier wife of Theophilus, but this is hardly consistent with the later gaiety of Thecla (down to 868) or the doll story; nor, although we do not know the exact age of Theophilus, can we easily admit that he had been married for twenty years—which is necessary to make Maria fifteen in 832—before he chose Theodora under the guidance of his stepmother.

[20] "Zwei Griechische Texte über die H. Theophano," edited by E. Kurtz, in the "Mémoires de l'Academie Impériale de St Petersbourg," viii. series, vol 3. Unfortunately, the legendary and partisan character of the essays compels us to use them with discretion. I have also taken much from the Greek life of the patriarch Euthymius, and have been much helped by the notes of its editor, de Boor.

[21] The mixture of palaces and monasteries may cause some perplexity. The explanation is that for a long time it was a pious and very common custom of wealthy Constantinopolitans to ensure prayers for their soul by leaving their palaces to the monks, and even converting them into monasteries before they died, so as to die in the ranks of the monks. We shall find the next Emperor checking this practice, to the great anger of the monks.

[22] G. Schlumherger. "Un Empereur Byzantin au Dixième Siècle." (1890); a very fine and ample study of Byzantine life.

[23] *Basil was a natural son of Romanus I. and a Russian (or else Bulgarian) slave. It is a curious mistake on the part of Gibbon, and even of Schlumberger, to confuse the Basil whom she belaboured with her own son Basil.*

[24] *In point of fact, a writer of the time, Michael Atteliates, says that he had no wife. Flach ("Die Kaiserin Eudokia," 1876) seems to have overlooked this authority.*

[25] *Until recent years Eudocia was, as one reads in Gibbon, reputed to have been the authoress of "Ionia," but later writers have shown that this was an error. She undoubtedly wandered in the fields of letters and philosophy under the guidance of Psellus, and seems to have written a little.*

[26] *Sebastos is the Greek equivalent of the Latin Augustus. It must not be forgotten that, while I continue to use the words "Emperor" and "Empress," they were now more commonly called "King" and "Queen," "Lord" and "Lady," or "Master" and "Mistress."*

[27] *Since the princess, or Cæsaress, has her apologists, if not admirers, this may seem a hasty judgment. It is based simply on her narrative, controlled by the accounts of other chroniclers. The last pages of her history are superb in their mendacity, and she commonly suppresses or perverts the facts. For the difficulties of her father's position, and the great services he rendered to the Empire, which must be put in the scale against his duplicity and fraud, I must send the reader to historians.*

[28] *One or two remarks on the novel may not be without interest. It is far the weakest of Scott's historical romances. Byzantine antiquities were little known in England at the time when it was written, and the great novelist is reduced to a meagreness or inaccuracy of detail which places the story in unfavourable contrast to his Scottish romances, and he is forced to admit countless anachronisms. Anna Comnena was only thirteen years old at the time, and did not begin to write her "Alexiad" until twenty or thirty years later. The golden birds and lions, also, which Scott puts beside the imperial throne, had been melted down by Michael the Drunkard two hundred years before. I mention these features only because Scott is usually so conscientious, even in romance.*

[29] *It may be well to repeat that the neater phrase in Gibbon is an artistic paraphrase, not a translation, of the original Greek.*

[30] *"Typicum, sive Regula, Irenes Augustæ," published by the Benedictines of St Maur in their "Analecta Græca" (1688).*

[31] *The marriage of Alexis is placed by Finlay in 1178, but William of Tyre, who was in Constantinople at the time, says that it took place in the year of the death of Louis VII. and of Manuel. Nicetas also says that Anna was "not quite eleven" when she married Andronicus (in 1183) and "not quite eight" when she married Alexis.*

[32] *Finlay, following Nicephorus Gregoras, wrongly says that Theodore had left "no son" to inherit the purple. George Acropolites, the better authority, says that he left "no mature son." The son of Philippa was eight years old, and seems to have lived under the cloud of his mother's disgrace.*

[33] *This lady is sometimes named Markesina, but the term is merely a Greek attempt to speak of her as "the Marchioness." Her real name is unknown.*

[34] Finlay declines to regard the dominion which was re-established by the Greeks in 1261 as "the Byzantine Empire." But as there had never been any dynastic continuity, and as "Byzantine Empire" merely means an empire which has its seat in Constantinople, or ancient Byzantium (the name still commonly given to the city by its own writers), I see no reason to discard the phrase.

[35] Manuel's younger brother, Theodore, was never crowned and had been crushed by the Sultan, so that his beautiful wife, Bartholomæa, daughter of the Duke of Athens, does not enter our list; and as Bartholomæa had no children (though her husband had several) there was no complication of the new arrangement to be feared from that side.

[36] Bertrandon's interesting narrative may be read in English in T. Wright's "Early Travels in Palestine."